AAT

Business Tax FA 2016

Level 4
Professional Diploma in
Accounting

Course Book

For assessments up to
August 2018

Second edition 2017

ISBN 9781 5097 1497 1
ISBN (for internal use only) 9781 5097 1495 7

British Library Cataloguing-in-Publication Data
A catalogue record for this book is available from the British Library

Published by

BPP Learning Media Ltd
BPP House, Aldine Place
142-144 Uxbridge Road
London W12 8AA

www.bpp.com/learningmedia

Printed in the United Kingdom

Your learning materials, published by BPP Learning Media
Ltd, are printed on paper obtained from traceable
sustainable sources.

BPP
LEARNING MEDIA

Contents

Introduction to the course

Syllabus overview

This unit introduces the student to UK taxation relevant to businesses. It is about the computing of business taxation, preparation of tax returns and how taxation has an impact on the running of a business for sole traders, partnerships and limited companies.

In learning how to prepare tax computations, students will gain skills in the tax treatment of capital expenditure, and the adjustment of accounting profits for tax purposes for sole traders, partnerships and limited companies. In addition, they will be able to allocate profits between partners in a partnership and be able to calculate National Insurance (NI) contributions for the self-employed.

The student will become familiar with the completion of tax returns. They will know when these returns need to be filed with the UK's Revenue and Customs authority (HMRC), and the implications of errors in tax returns, the late filing of returns and the late payment of tax. They will understand how to compute tax on the sale of capital assets and they will have an introduction to some of the tax reliefs available to businesses.

Tax advice is an important part of many accountancy roles. Students will be able to discuss the ethical issues facing business owners and managers in reporting their business tax and the responsibilities that an agent has in giving advice on tax issues to business clients.

Business Tax is an optional unit.

Test specification for this unit assessment

Assessment method	Marking type	Duration of assessment
Computer based assessment	Partially computer / partially human marked	2 hours

Learning outcomes		Approximate weighting
1	Complete tax returns for sole traders and partnerships and prepare supporting tax computations	29%
2	Complete tax returns for limited companies and prepare supporting tax computations	19%
3	Provide advice on the UK's tax regimes and its impact on sole traders, partnerships and limited companies	15%
4	Advise business clients on tax reliefs, and their responsibilities and their agents responsibilities in reporting taxation to HMRC	19%
5	Prepare tax computations for the sale of capital assets	18%
Total		**100%**

Assessment structure

2 hours duration

Competency is 70%

Analysis of the sample paper

The **sample assessment** consisted of 11 tasks as follows:

*Note that this is only a guideline as to what might come up based on the sample paper. The format and content of each task may vary from what we have listed below.

Task	Expected content	Max marks	Chapter ref	Study complete
Task 1	**Adjustment of profits, identification of basis periods, assessable profit and overlap profits for a sole trader.**	10	2,5	
Task 2	**Split of partnership profits for continuing partners** **National insurance**	10	6,7	
Task 3	**Capital allowance computation for a sole traders long period of account**	13	3	
Task 4	**Corporation tax return**	6	4	
Task 5	**Corporation tax long period of account and losses**	9	4,8	
Task 6	**Payments on account for sole trader** **Filing date for limited company**	7	9,10	
Task 7	**Penalties for sole trader and limited company**	8	1,9,10	
Task 8	**Limited company losses**	5	8	
Task 9	**Current tax issues: IR35**	14	10	
Task 10	**Chargeable gains calculations for limited company**	8	11,12	
Task 11	**Disposal of shares by a limited company**	6	13	

Skills bank

Our experience of preparing students for this type of assessment suggests that to obtain competency, you will need to develop a number of key skills.

What do I need to know to do well in the assessment?

This unit is one of the optional Level 4 units.

To be successful in the assessment you need to:

- Calculate business taxation, prepare tax returns and understand how tax has an impact on the running of a business for sole-traders, partnerships and limited companies.

- Apply the tax rules to scenarios given to calculate tax due, be knowledgeable with regard to the administration of tax, the implications of errors, late payment of tax, late filing of returns and also ethical issues facing business owners.

Assumed knowledge

Business Tax is an **optional** unit which requires no assumed knowledge. The Level 4 unit, *Personal Tax*, is associated with this unit, although these units can be taken separately.

Assessment style

In the assessment you will complete tasks by:

1   Entering narrative by selecting from drop down menus of narrative options known as **picklists**

2   Using **drag and drop** menus to enter narrative

3   Typing in numbers, known as **gapfill** entry

4   Entering **ticks**

5   Entering **dates** by selecting from a calendar

6   Writing written explanations in a very basic word processing environment which has limited editing and no spelling or grammar checking functionality

7   Entering detailed calculations in a very basic spreadsheet environment that has limited editing functionality and will not perform calculations for you

You must familiarise yourself with the style of the online questions and the AAT software before taking the assessment. As part of your revision, login to the **AAT website** and attempt their **online practice assessments**.

Answering written questions

In your assessment there will be a written question on ethics. The main verbs used for these type of question requirements are as follows, along with their meaning:

- Identify – analyse and select for presentation
- Explain – set out in detail the meaning of
- Discuss – by argument, discuss the pros and cons

Analysing the scenario

Before answering the question set, you need to carefully review the scenario given in order to consider what questions need to be answered, and what needs to be discussed. A simple framework that could be used to answer the question is as follows:

- Point – make the point
- Evidence – use information from the scenario as evidence
- Explain – explain why the evidence links to the point

For example if an assessment task asked us to explain which three of the fundamental ethical principles are most threatened in the following situation:

You are working on a company's corporation tax return, and notice some errors in the previous year's return which has already been filed. Your manager is concerned about the implications for their own career if the errors are disclosed, and has said that you would be considered for promotion if you agreed to keep quiet about the errors.

We could answer as follows:

1   Point – state which principles are most threatened – objectivity, integrity, professional behaviour

2   Evidence – use information from the scenario – the manager is asking me to keep quiet about an error and offered to consider me for promotion if I keep quiet

3   Explain – explain why the evidence links to the point –the manager is trying to influence my behaviour (objectivity), the manager wants me to act in a way that is not straightforward and honest (integrity), the manager wants me to behave in a way that is not legal and may discredit the profession (professional behaviour)

Introduction to the assessment

The question practice you do will prepare you for the format of tasks you will see in the *Business Tax* assessment. It is also useful to familiarise yourself with the introductory information you **may** be given at the start of the assessment.

You have **2 hours** to complete this sample assessment.

This assessment contains **11 tasks** and you should attempt to complete every task. Each task is independent. You will not need to refer to your answers in previous tasks. Read every task carefully to make sure you understand what is required.

Task 9 requires extended writing as part of your response to the questions. You should make sure you allow adequate time to complete this task.

Where the date is relevant, it is given in the task data.

You may use minus signs or brackets to indicate negative numbers **unless** task instructions say otherwise.

You must use a full stop to indicate a decimal point.

For example, write 100.57 NOT 100,57 or 100 57

You may use a comma to indicate a number in the thousands, but you don't have to.

For example, 10000 and 10,000 are both acceptable.

If rounding is required, normal mathematical rounding rules should be applied **unless** task instructions say otherwise.

---

1   As you revise, use the **BPP Passcards** to consolidate your knowledge. They are a pocket-sized revision tool, perfect for packing in that last-minute revision.

2   Attempt as many tasks as possible in the **Question Bank**. There are plenty of assessment-style tasks which are excellent preparation for the real assessment.

3   Always **check** through your own answers as you will in the real assessment, before looking at the solutions in the back of the Question Bank.

Key to icons

 Key term

A key definition which is important to be aware of for the assessment

Key term

 Formula to learn

A formula you will need to learn as it will not be provided in the assessment

 Formula provided

A formula which is provided within the assessment and generally available as a pop-up on screen

 Activity

An example which allows you to apply your knowledge to the technique covered in the Course Book. The solution is provided at the end of the chapter

 Illustration

A worked example which can be used to review and see how an assessment question could be answered

 Assessment focus point

A high priority point for the assessment

 Open book reference

Where use of an open book will be allowed for the assessment

 Real life examples

A practical real life scenario

AAT qualifications

The material in this book may support the following AAT qualifications:

AAT Professional Diploma in Accounting Level 4, AAT Professional Diploma in Accounting at SCQF Level 8 and Certificate: Accounting (Level 5 AATSA).

Supplements

From time to time we may need to publish supplementary materials to one of our titles. This can be for a variety of reasons, from a small change in the AAT unit guidance to new legislation coming into effect between editions.

You should check our supplements page regularly for anything that may affect your learning materials. All supplements are available free of charge on our supplements page on our website at:

www.bpp.com/learning-media/about/students

Improving material and removing errors

There is a constant need to update and enhance our study materials in line with both regulatory changes and new insights into the assessments.

From our team of authors BPP appoints a subject expert to update and improve these materials for each new edition.

Their updated draft is subsequently technically checked by another author and from time to time non-technically checked by a proof reader.

We are very keen to remove as many numerical errors and narrative typos as we can but given the volume of detailed information being changed in a short space of time we know that a few errors will sometimes get through our net.

We apologise in advance for any inconvenience that an error might cause. We continue to look for new ways to improve these study materials and would welcome your suggestions. Please feel free to contact our AAT Head of Programme at nisarahmed@bpp.com if you have any suggestions for us.

Tax framework

1

Learning outcomes

4.3	Discuss the responsibilities relating to tax for the business and its agents
	• The distinction between tax planning, tax avoidance and tax evasion
	• AAT's ethical standards relating to tax advice and professional conduct in relation to taxation

Assessment context

This chapter provides you with important background to your syllabus and helps you to distinguish between illegal and legal tax measures as well as ethical and unethical behaviour.

You probably will not have to calculate income tax payable in your assessment but you need to know how this works so you can understand other parts of the syllabus (eg loss relief).

Qualification context

You will not see these areas again unless you study the *Personal Tax* unit.

Business context

A tax practitioner needs to know the duties and obligations the taxpayer owes to HMRC.

A tax practitioner needs to know and understand the detailed tax rules.

A tax practitioner needs to adhere to AAT's ethical standards when giving tax advice and dealing with clients.

Chapter overview

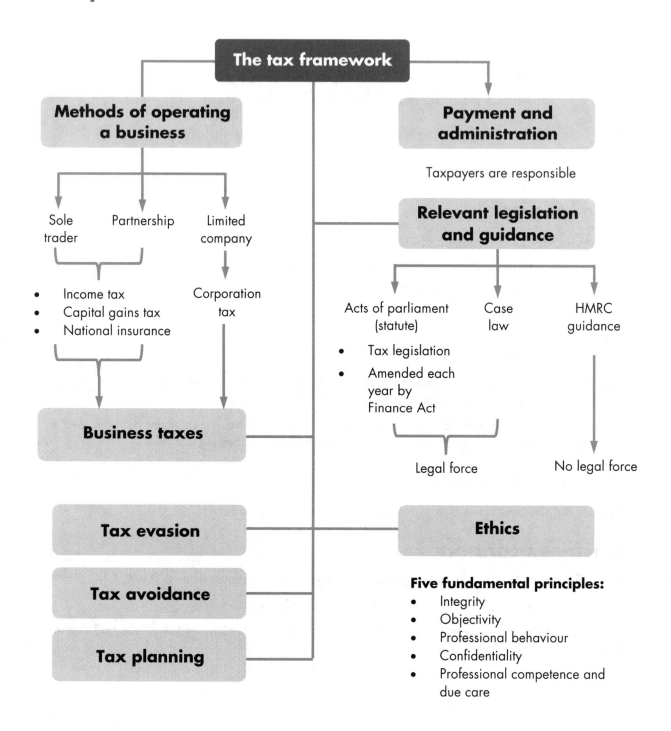

The tax framework

Methods of operating a business

Sole trader   Partnership   Limited company

- Income tax
- Capital gains tax
- National insurance

Corporation tax

Business taxes

Payment and administration

Taxpayers are responsible

Relevant legislation and guidance

Acts of parliament (statute)
- Tax legislation
- Amended each year by Finance Act

Legal force

Case law

HMRC guidance

No legal force

Tax evasion

Tax avoidance

Tax planning

Ethics

Five fundamental principles:
- Integrity
- Objectivity
- Professional behaviour
- Confidentiality
- Professional competence and due care

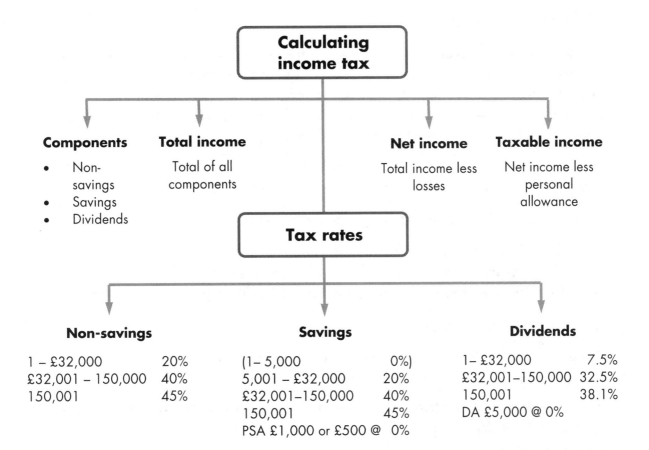

1 Introduction

In this opening chapter we consider the various methods by which a business can operate. The method of operation affects how the business is taxed. We then see that the tax law governing businesses is included in Acts of Parliament and in a body of law known as case law. We will also look at ethics and the fundamental differences between legal and illegal tax planning.

Finally, we briefly consider how to calculate an individual's income tax liability. You may need to be aware of this when dealing with business losses.

2 Method of operating a business

- **Sole trader** – self-employed individual
- **Partnership** – self-employed individuals working together
- **Limited company** – incorporated body legally separate from owners

3 Business taxes

Income is a receipt that is expected to recur (eg trading income) while a **gain** is a one-off profit on the disposal of an asset (eg a factory).

Sole traders and **partnerships are unincorporated businesses**. This means that there is no legal separation between the individual(s) carrying on the business and the business itself.

As a result the individual(s) concerned must pay:

- Income tax on trading income
- Class 2 and Class 4 national insurance contributions (NICs)
- Capital gains tax on disposal of assets

Companies are incorporated businesses. This means they are taxed as separate legal entities independently of their owners.

Companies must pay corporation tax on all profits including gains on disposal of assets.

4 Payment and administration

Taxpayers who are required to perform self-assessment have a legal responsibility to pay their tax on time and submit a tax return before the deadline.

Employees have tax deducted at source by their employer so, for most people other than the self-employed, there is no need to submit a tax return.

5 Relevant legislation and guidance from HMRC

5.1 Statute law

Most of the rules governing income tax, capital gains tax and corporation tax are laid down in **statute law**, which consists of:

- **Acts of Parliament** (the tax legislation), which are created directly by the Government and amended annually by that year's Finance Act. This text includes the provisions of the **Finance Act 2016.** Assessments will test the provisions of the Finance Act 2016 until 31 August 2018.

- **Statutory Instruments**, which are detailed rules created on behalf of the Government by civil servants to amend/alter an act without parliament having to pass a new act.

5.2 HMRC guidance

To help taxpayers, **HM Revenue & Customs (HMRC)**, which administers tax in the UK, publishes a wide range of guidance material on how it interprets the various acts. Much of this information can be found on HMRC's website **www.hmrc.gov.uk.**

None of this guidance material has the force of law.

5.3 Decided tax cases

A taxpayer and HMRC may disagree over the interpretation of the legislation.

Either party may appeal to the tax tribunal. The tax tribunal is independent of the government and will listen to both sides of the argument before making a decision.

A judge will rule in favour of one party.

Cases decided by the courts provide guidance on how legislation should be interpreted, and collectively form a second source of tax law known as **case law**.

You will not be expected to quote the names of decided cases in your assessment but you may need to know the principle decided in a case. Where relevant this will be noted within this Course Book.

6 AAT guidelines on professional ethics

A member shall comply with the following five fundamental principles: (AAT, 2014)

Fundamental principle	What it means
Professional competence and due care	You must maintain professional knowledge and skill (in practice, legislation and techniques) to ensure that a client or employer receives competent professional service.

Fundamental principle	What it means
Integrity	You must be straightforward and honest in all professional and business relationships.
Professional behaviour	You must comply with relevant laws and regulations, and avoid any action that may bring disrepute to the profession.
Confidentiality	You must not disclose confidential professional or business information or use it to your personal advantage, unless you have explicit permission to disclose it, or a legal or professional right or duty to disclose it.
Objectivity	You must not compromise professional or business judgment because of bias, conflict of interest or the undue influence of others.

7 Tax avoidance, tax evasion and tax planning

7.1 Tax evasion

Tax evasion is always illegal. It is when people or businesses deliberately do not declare and account for the taxes that they owe. It includes the hidden economy, where people conceal their presence or taxable sources of income.

Tax evasion can result in fines/imprisonment.

7.2 Tax avoidance

Tax avoidance involves bending the rules of the tax system to gain a tax advantage that Parliament never intended. It often involves contrived, artificial transactions that serve little or no purpose other than to produce this advantage. It involves operating within the letter – but not the spirit – of the law. Most tax avoidance schemes simply do not work, and those who engage in it can find they pay more than the tax they attempted to save once HMRC has successfully challenged them.

7.3 Tax planning

Tax planning involves using tax reliefs for the purpose for which they were intended, for example, claiming tax relief on capital investment, or saving via ISAs or for retirement by making contributions to a pension scheme. However, tax reliefs can be used excessively or aggressively, by others than those intended to benefit from them or in ways that clearly go beyond the intention of Parliament. Where this is the case it is right to take action, because it is important that the tax system is fair and perceived to be so. (HMRC, 2015)

8 Calculating an individual's income tax liability

Illustration 1: Income tax computation for fiscal year (6.4 – 5.4)

	Non-savings income £	Savings income £	Dividend income £
Trading income	22,750		
Less carry forward loss relief	(5,000)		
Employment income	15,200		
Property income	3,400		
Dividends from UK companies			7,000
Building society interest		9,550	
Bank deposit interest		10,450	
Total income	36,350	20,000	7,000
Less current year loss relief	(2,000)		
Net income	34,350	20,000	7,000
Less personal allowance	(11,000)		
Taxable income	23,350	20,000	7,000

8.1 Types of income

An individual may receive different 'components' of income. They may be:

- **Dividend income** – dividends received from UK companies

- **Savings income** – interest income

- **Non-savings income** – any other income, eg income from self-employment, employment or property income

All income is added together to produce **total income**.

Some items, such as loss relief, are deducted from total income to give **net income**.

Often a taxpayer will have no deductions from total income so here the terms total income and net income can be used interchangeably.

A personal allowance is then deducted from net income to give **taxable income**. This represents the amount of income they are allowed to earn tax free.

- Taxpayers are entitled to a personal allowance of £11,000.

- However, individuals with net income in excess of £100,000 will have their personal allowance reduced or removed completely.

Activity 1: Taxable income

An individual has the following gross income in 2016/17.

	£
Trading income	16,000
Building society interest	6,000
Dividends	8,750

Required

His personal allowance is £11,000. His taxable income is:

£	

8.2 Income tax liability

Income is taxed in the following order:

1 Non-savings income
2 Savings income
3 Dividend income

Illustration 2: Calculation of tax liability

Taxable income	Non-saving	Savings	Dividends	
	45%	45%	38.1%	Additional rate
150,000				
	40%	40%	32½%	Higher rate
32,000				
5,000	20%	20%	7.5%	Basic rate
		0%		
0	Starting rate			

This gives us **tax liability** ie the total amount of tax that should be paid on our income.

Non-savings income is taxed in three bands:

1 Basic rate at 20% for income up to £32,000
2 Higher rate at 40% for income over £32,000
3 Additional rate at 45% for income over £150,000

Savings income is taxed in four bands:

1 The first £5,000 of savings income is taxed at 0% and then there is a personal savings allowance of £1,000 for basic rate taxpayers and £500 for higher rate taxpayers, which is taxed at 0%.

> **Note.** Savings income is taxed after non-savings income, so if we have taxable non-savings income in excess of £5,000 then this starting rate band will not be available for savings. In practice few people will get the benefit of this second 0% band.

2 Basic rate at 20% for income between £5,000 (plus the relevant savings allowance) and £32,000

3 Higher rate at 40% for income over £32,000

4 Additional rate at 45% for income over £150,000

Dividend income is taxed in four bands:

1 0% for first £5,000 (dividend allowance available to all taxpayers)
2 7.5% for income up to £32,000
3 32.5% for income over £32,000
4 38.1% for income over £150,000

Illustration 3: Calculating tax liability

Zoë has taxable income (after the deduction of the personal allowance) of £40,000. Of this £21,000 is non-savings income, £10,000 is interest and £9,000 is dividend income.

Zoë's income tax liability for 2016/17 is calculated as follows:

			£
Non-savings income			
	£21,000	× 20%	4,200
Savings income			
	£500*	× 0%	0
	£9,500	× 20%	1,900
Dividend income			
	£5,000	× 0%	0
	£4,000	× 32.5%**	1,300
	£40,000		
Tax liability			7,400

*Savings allowance for higher rate taxpayer

**Higher rate used on dividends as taxable income including the savings and dividend allowances is £36,000, which exceeds £32,000.

Illustration 4: Savings income starting rate

Andreas has taxable income of £12,000. Of this, £2,000 is non-savings income and £10,000 is savings income.

His income tax liability for 2016/17 is calculated as follows:

			£
Non-savings income			
	£2,000	× 20%	400
Savings income			
	£3,000*	× 0%	0
	£1,000**	× 0%	0
	£6,000	× 20%	1,200
	£6,000		
Tax liability			1,600

*Remainder of the £5,000 0% starting rate (£5,000 less NSI £2,000)

**Savings allowance for basic rate taxpayer

Illustration 5: Additional rate taxpayer

Clive has taxable income of £190,000. Of this £140,000 is non-savings income, £30,000 is interest and £20,000 is dividend income.

Clive's income tax liability for 2016/17 is calculated as follows:

			£
Non-savings income			
	£32,000	× 20%	6,400
	£108,000	× 40%	43,200
	£140,000		
Savings income*			
	£10,000	× 40%	4,000
	£20,000	× 45%	9,000
	£30,000		
Dividend income			
	£5,000	× 0%	0
	£15,000	× 38.1%	5,715
Tax liability			68,315

*Additional rate taxpayer so no savings allowance, but still entitled to dividend allowance

Activity 2: Calculation of income tax liability

Arthur has a salary of £17,000. He earned savings income of £10,000 and dividend income of £20,000.

Required

Calculate the income tax liability for 2016/17.

	Non-savings income £	Savings income (excluding dividends) £	Dividend income £

 Assessment focus point

You will not be expected to produce a large income tax computation in your assessment. It is included here for background knowledge and will be useful when you come to study the chapter on Losses.

- A business may be operated by a sole trader, partnership or company.

- Individuals trading as sole traders or in partnerships pay income tax, capital gains tax and NICs.

- Companies pay corporation tax.

- Companies and individuals must submit regular tax returns.

- It is important to be able to distinguish between tax evasion (illegal) and tax planning/avoidance (legal).

- When working in tax one should adhere to the AAT's five fundamental ethical principles of:
  - Confidentiality
  - Integrity
  - Objectivity
  - Professional behaviour
  - Professional competence and due care

- All of an individual's components of income for a tax year are added together to arrive at total income.

- Trading losses are deducted from total income to arrive at net income.

- A personal allowance is deducted from net income to arrive at taxable income.

- Taxable income is taxed at one of seven rates, depending on which rate band it falls into and the type of income it is.

Keywords

- **Confidentiality:** Respecting the confidentiality of client information, and keeping it confidential unless there is a legal or professional obligation to disclose it

- **Integrity:** Being straightforward and honest in all business relationships

- **Net income:** Total income minus, for example, trading losses

- **Objectivity:** Refusing to allow bias, conflicts of interest or undue influence to override professional judgements

- **Professional behaviour:** Compliance with relevant laws and regulations to avoid discrediting the profession

- **Professional competence and due care:** A professional accountant has an obligation to keep their knowledge and skills at a level that enables clients to receive a competent professional service, and to act diligently when providing those services

- **Tax avoidance:** Making use of loopholes in tax legislation in order to reduce tax liabilities. It is currently legal

- **Tax evasion:** To deliberately mislead the tax authorities in order to reduce a tax liability. Tax evasion is illegal

- **Tax planning:** Making use of tax planning opportunities to legally reduce a tax liability

- **Taxable income:** An individual's net income minus the personal allowance

- **Total income:** The total of an individual's components of income for a tax year, from all sources

1 You work in the tax department of a large company. You have prepared the Tax return for the quarter, and submitted it to your Finance Director for her review. On reviewing your draft return, she has asked you to amend it to include some expenditure which was incurred shortly after the start of the next year in order reduce the profit for the year. She mentioned at the end of the conversation that your annual performance appraisal was due.

Which fundamental principle(s) could be breached if you agreed to her request?

Tick THREE boxes.

	✓
Integrity	
Objectivity	
Professional competence and due care	
Confidentiality	
Professional behaviour	

2 Tax avoidance is illegal and can lead to fines/imprisonment.

Show whether this statement is true or false.

Tick ONE box.

	✓
True	
False	

3 A company pays income tax on its total profits.

Show whether this statement is true or false.

Tick ONE box.

	✓
True	
False	

4   **Complete the following statement.**

Each tax year all of an individual's components of income are added together, then a personal allowance is deducted to arrive at:

▼

Picklist:

Net income
Taxable income
Total income

5   Arun (aged 35) has the following gross income in 2016/17:

Non-savings income	£25,000
Savings income	£12,000
Dividend income	£10,000

Calculate Arun's income tax liability for 2016/17. Show your answer in whole pounds.

£	

Computing trading income

2

Learning outcomes

1.1 and 2.1	**Analyse trading profits and losses for tax purposes for sole-traders, partnerships and limited companies**
	• Apply rules relating to deductible and non-deductible expenditure
	• Classify expenditure as either revenue or capital expenditure
	• Adjust accounting profit and losses for tax purposes
1.6	**Complete the individual and partnership tax returns relevant to sole-traders and partnerships**
	• Accurately complete self-employed tax returns
4.3	**Discuss the responsibilities relating to tax for the business and its agent**
	• What are the badges of trade are and how they evolved

Assessment context

Adjustment of profits is highly examinable. In your assessment you could be required to shows these adjustments on a self-employment tax return.

Qualification context

You will not see these areas again in your qualification.

Business context

Adjusting trading profit is one of the core tasks a tax adviser will have to perform for their client.

Chapter overview

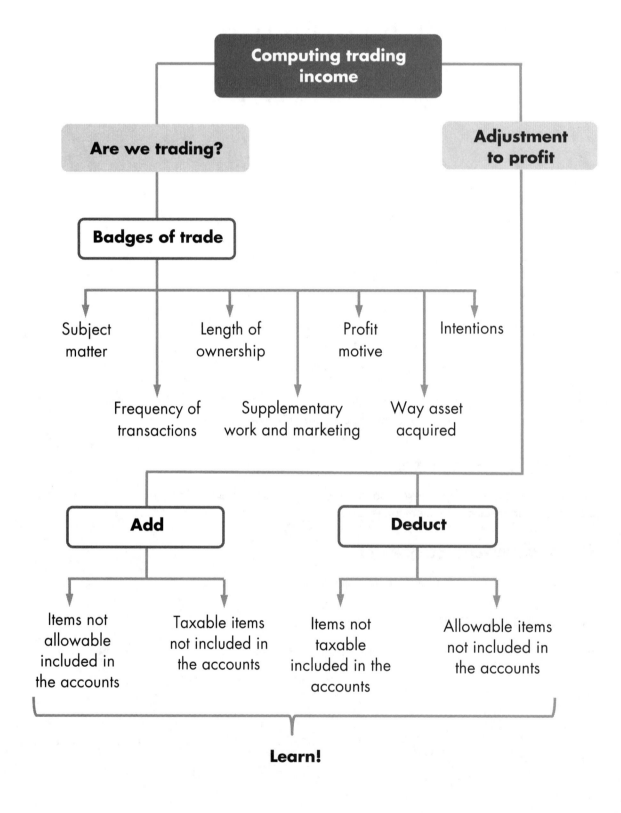

1 Introduction

In this chapter we will look at the differences between earning a profit from trading and making a gain on an investment and how to treat them for tax purposes. We will also look at how to calculate a taxable trading profit figure for the tax return.

2 Is a trade being carried on?

It is important to know whether profits of an individual or company should be assessed as trading income.

For example, a person who buys and sells stamps may be trading as a stamp dealer. Alternatively, stamp collecting may be a hobby of that person. In this case he is probably not trading.

If a trade is not being carried on, any profit arising from selling items could be exempt from tax or chargeable to capital gains tax.

2.1 Badges of trade

The following tests are used by the courts when distinguishing trading from investment or capital transactions and have evolved over the years as a result of the outcome of many court cases arguing trade versus investment:

2.1.1 Subject matter

Some items are commonly held as an **investment**, for example, works of art and antiques. A subsequent disposal may produce a gain of a capital nature rather than a trading profit. However, where the subject matter of a transaction is such that it would not normally be held as an investment (for example, 1,000,000 rolls of toilet paper), it is presumed that any profit on resale is a trading profit.

2.1.2 Frequency of transactions

A series of similar transactions indicates trading. Conversely, a single transaction is unlikely to be considered as a trade.

2.1.3 Length of ownership

The purchase of items followed by sale soon afterwards indicates trading. Conversely, if items are held for a long time before sale there is less likely to be a trade.

2.1.4 Supplementary work and marketing

If work is done to make an asset more marketable, or steps are taken to find purchasers, there is likely to be a trade. For example, when a group of accountants bought, blended and recasked a quantity of brandy they were held to be taxable on a trading profit when the brandy was later sold.

2.1.5 Profit motive

If an item is bought with the intention of selling it at a profit, a trade is likely to exist.

2.1.6 Way in which the asset was acquired

If goods are acquired unintentionally, for example, by gift or inheritance, their later sale is unlikely to constitute trading.

2.1.7 The taxpayer's intentions

Where objective criteria clearly indicate that a trade is being carried on, the taxpayer's intentions are irrelevant. If, however, a transaction (objectively) has a dual purpose, you should consider the taxpayer's intentions. For example, the taxpayer could buy a property, restore it and sell it. You need to consider whether it was purchased purely for resale, which would indicate trade, or did the taxpayer buy it with the intention of making it their home and then changed their mind – not trade.

3 Adjustment of profits

Whether the business is unincorporated (sole trader or partnership) or incorporated (limited company) the tax computation will always start with the **adjustment of profits**. **This is a vital area for all business types**. Many of the rules are the same for unincorporated businesses and for companies, with some differences highlighted in this chapter.

3.1 Taxable trading profits

Taxable trading profits are not the same as accounting profits. The trader arrives at the profit for the year in the accounts by taking income and deducting various trading expenses. However, the trader is unlikely to follow tax rules in arriving at this profit as, for example, there are some costs for which tax legislation does not allow a tax deduction, even though the taxpayer quite legitimately deducts them for accounting purposes.

Profits before tax from the financial statements need adjusting in accordance with tax legislation as follows:

Illustration 1: Adjustment of profit

	£
Net profit before tax per accounts	X
Add back:	
(a) Items charged in the accounts but not deductible for trading profits purposes (eg depreciation)	X
(b) Income taxable as trading profits which has not been included in the accounts (eg goods taken by owner for own use)	X
Deduct:	
(a) Items included in the accounts but not taxable as trading profits (eg profit on disposal of fixed assets)	(X)
(b) Expenditure which is deductible from trading profits but has not been charged in the accounts (eg capital allowances)	(X)
Adjusted profits for AP	X

Activity 1: Adjustment of profits (i)

Pratish trades as a car mechanic. His most recent accounts show a profit of £38,000. In arriving at this figure he deducted entertaining expenses of £2,000 and depreciation of £4,000. These amounts are not allowable for tax purposes. Capital allowances of £3,500 are available for tax purposes.

Required

Using the proforma layout provided, calculate the taxable trading profit.

The starting figure has already been entered for you.

	£
Profit for the year in the accounts	38,000

3.2 General rule for disallowed expenditure

Expenditure incurred not **wholly and exclusively** for business purposes is disallowed.

3.3 Specific disallowed expenses:

3.3.1 Capital expenditure including depreciation

Capital expenditure is one-off expenditure leading to the creation or improvement of an asset (eg a piece of plant).

Revenue expenditure is regular ongoing expenditure required in the day to day running of the business (eg paying the gas bill).

Usually, revenue expenditure is allowable: it can be deducted from income before tax is calculated.

Capital expenditure is not allowable so must be added back if it has been charged in the statement of profit or loss. **Capital allowances** (see later) may sometimes be claimed on capital expenditure.

Repair expenditure can cause problems:

- Maintaining an asset (ie keeping it in its current condition) is allowable.
- Improving an asset is not allowable.

There are special rules where assets are repaired following acquisition:

- If the repairs are to make the asset usable, they are not allowable (eg repairs to an unseaworthy ship).

- If the repairs merely improve the appearance of an asset, they are allowable (eg refurbishing a cinema).

Activity 2: Capital versus revenue

Identify whether the following expenses are revenue or capital in nature by ticking the relevant box.

	Revenue ✓	Capital ✓
Paying employee wages		
Paying rent for premises		
Buying machinery		
Buying a van		
Building an extension to shop		
Paying for repairs to car		

3.3.2 Adjustments to general provisions/general allowances for doubtful debts

Only irrecoverable debts incurred wholly and exclusively for the purposes of the trade are deductible for taxation purposes. Thus loans to employees written off are not deductible unless the business is that of making loans, or it can be shown that the write-off was earnings paid out for the benefit of the trade.

Increases or decreases in a general provision are not allowable and an adjustment is needed.

Illustration 2: Irrecoverable debts account

The account below results in a credit to the statement of profit or loss of £124. What adjustment should be made to the profit for the year when calculating taxable trading profits?

2016	£	£	2016	£	£
			1 January Provisions b/d		
			General	150	
			Specific	381	
					531
Provisions c/d					
General	207				
Specific	200				
		407			
Statement of profit or loss		124			
		531			531
			2017 1 January Provisions b/d		407

The only adjustment you need to consider is the increase in general provision from £150 to £207. Thus £57 is added to the accounts profit to arrive at taxable profit.

3.3.3 Private expenditure of the owner

Strictly, expenditure incurred partly for private purposes and partly for business purposes has a dual purpose and is not deductible. However, HMRC sometimes allows taxpayers to apportion the expenditure between the part that is wholly for business purposes and therefore deductible, and the part that is wholly for private purposes and therefore not deductible.

Goods taken from stock by the proprietor of a business should be treated as if they had been sold for their market value. If correctly accounted for as drawings, this will require an adjustment for the profit, whereas if the cost is still reflected in cost of sales, the full selling price will need to be added back.

Illustration 3: Private use expenditure

A sole trader who runs his business from home incurs £500 on heating and lighting bills. 30% of these bills relate to the business use of his house. £500 has been deducted in arriving at the accounts profit. How much should be added back in the calculation of taxable trading profits?

The 30% relating to business use is allowable. Therefore, 70% × £500 = £350 must be added back to the accounts profit as **disallowable expenditure**.

Assessment focus point

In the CBT you may need to calculate adjusted profits for a sole trader/partnership (unincorporated business) or a company (incorporated business).

The calculation is basically the same; however, there are no private adjustments for a company.

Everybody who works for a company (including a director) is an employee, so any benefit they receive is taxed on them as part of their employment income (rules examinable in *Personal Tax*).

The cost is part of the company's cost of employing the workforce it needs to perform its trade, so the costs are allowable.

3.4 The treatment of various other items

The table below details various types of allowable and disallowable expenditure, with mention of any differences between unincorporated businesses (sole traders and partnerships) and incorporated businesses (companies) where necessary.

Allowable expenditure	Disallowable expenditure	Comments
	Fines and penalties	HMRC usually allows parking fines incurred in parking an employee's car whilst on the employer's business. Fines relating to the owner of the business are, however, never allowed. Similarly, a company would not be able to deduct fines relating to directors
Costs of registering trademarks and patents		This is an exception to the rule of 'capital' related expenditure being disallowable

Allowable expenditure	Disallowable expenditure	Comments
Incidental costs of obtaining loan finance		This deduction does not apply to companies because they get a deduction for the cost of borrowing in a different way. We look at this in Chapter 4 of this Course Book
	Depreciation or amortisation	In specific circumstances a company can deduct these amounts, but this is outside the scope of this assessment
	Any salary or interest paid to a sole trader or partner	
	The private proportion of any expenses incurred by a sole trader or partner	The private proportion of a director's or employee's expenses is, however, deductible
Irrecoverable debts incurred in the course of a business. Specific provisions for irrecoverable debts	General provisions for irrecoverable debts (and other general provisions)	Loans to employees written off despite being specific are not allowable
Patent and copyright royalties		Patent and copyright royalties paid for trade purposes are deductible
Staff entertaining	Non-staff (eg customer) entertaining	

Allowable expenditure	Disallowable expenditure	Comments
Gifts for employees Gifts to customers as long as they: • Cost no more than £50 per donee per year • Carry a conspicuous advertisement for the business • Are not food, drink, tobacco or vouchers exchangeable for such goods Gifts to a small local charity if they benefit the trade	All other gifts including 'qualifying charitable donations'	'Qualifying charitable donations' are charitable gifts by companies on which tax relief is given. These are covered in Chapter 4 of this Course Book. The similar scheme relevant to individuals is not assessable in this *Business Tax* assessment
Subscriptions to a professional or trade association	Political donations	
Legal and professional charges relating directly to the trade	Legal and professional charges relating to capital or non-trading items	Deductible items include: • Charges incurred defending the taxpayer's title to non-current assets • Charges connected with an action for breach of contract
	Accountancy expenses relating to specialist consultancy work	• Expenses for the renewal (not the original grant) of a lease for less than 50 years • Charges for trade debt collection • Normal charges for preparing accounts and assisting with the self-assessment of tax liabilities

Allowable expenditure	Disallowable expenditure	Comments
Interest on loans taken out for trade purposes	Interest on overdue tax	These rules are for unincorporated businesses. Companies have different rules for interest. We look at these in Chapter 4 of this Course Book
Costs of seconding employees to charities or educational establishments		
Expenditure incurred in the seven years prior to the commencement of a trade		Provided expenditure is of a type that would have been allowed had the trade started. Treat as an expense on the first day of trading
Removal expenses (to new business premises)		Only if not an expansionary move
Travelling expenses on the trader's business	Travel from home to the trader's place of business	
Redundancy payments		If the trade ceases, the limit on allowability is 3 × the statutory amount (in addition to the statutory amount)
	15% of leasing costs of car with CO_2 emissions in excess of 130g/km	

Activity 3: Calculation of add back

A sole trader charged the following expenses in computing his accounts profit:

	£
Fine for breach of Factories Act	1,000
Cost of specialist tax consultancy work	2,000
Redundancy payments	10,000
Salary for himself	15,000
Leasing cost of car (CO_2 emissions 150g/km)	3,000

The redundancy payments were made for trade purposes as a result of reorganisation of the business. The trade is continuing.

Required

Calculate how much must be added back in computing taxable trading profits.

Tick ONE box.

Amount to add back	✓
£17,450	
£16,000	
£18,450	
£11,450	

Activity 4: Entertainment and gifts

Decide whether each of the items in the entertainment account below should be added back in computing taxable trading profits.

Expenditure	£	Add back ✓
Staff tennis outing for 30 employees	1,800	
2,000 tee shirts with firm's logo given to race runners	4,500	
Advertising and sponsorship of an athletic event	2,000	
Entertaining customers	7,300	
Staff Christmas party (30 employees)	2,400	

Activity 5: Adjustment of profits (ii)

Hugo Drax, a sole trader, has the following statement of profit or loss for the year ended 31 December:

	£
Sales	100,000
Cost of sales	(50,000)
Gross profit	50,000
Add other income	
Bank interest	4,000
Less expenses	
Depreciation	(5,000)
Entertaining clients	(100)
Office costs	(2,000)
Staff wages and salaries	(15,000)
Hugo's personal council tax bill	(1,000)
Net profit	30,900

Salaries include £5,000 paid to Hugo and £5,000 paid to his wife. His wife's salary is reasonable in respect of the work she performs in the business.

Required

Complete the table below showing the calculation of adjusted trading profits before capital allowances. Complete the narrative by using the items in the picklist below the table.

Solution

Adjustment to profit	£	£
Net profit per the accounts		
Add back		
▼		
▼		
▼		
▼		
Total added back		
Deduct		
▼		
Adjusted profits before capital allowances		

Picklist:

Bank interest
Cost of sales
Council tax
Depreciation
Entertaining
Gross profit
Office costs
Sales
Staff wages

---

4 Self-employment tax return pages

A sole trader needs to provide detailed information about the adjustment of profit in their tax return.

AAT have confirmed that the page shown below is the only page you should expect to see from the self-assessment tax return. You will notice that the boxes on the left side of the return show all a trader's expenses and the boxes on the right-hand side highlight which of those expenses are disallowable for tax purposes. For example, if a trader has a depreciation charge of £500, this will be shown in both box 29 and box 44.

You will be able to practise completing this form in the *Business Tax* Question Bank.

You may need to complete this page of the tax return as part of your CBE.

Illustration 4: Extract from self-employment tax return (using information from Activity 5)

Business expenses

Please read the 'Self-employment (full) notes' before filling in this section.

Total expenses

If your annual turnover was below £83,000, you may just put your total expenses in box 31

Disallowable expenses

Use this column if the figures in boxes 17 to 30 include disallowable amounts

Box	Total expenses	Amount	Box	Disallowable expenses	Amount
17	Cost of goods bought for resale or goods used	£ 5 0 0 0 0 . 0 0	32		£ . 0 0
18	Construction industry – payments to subcontractors	£ . 0 0	33		£ . 0 0
19	Wages, salaries and other staff costs	£ 1 5 0 0 0 . 0 0	34		£ 5 0 0 0 . 0 0
20	Car, van and travel expenses	£ . 0 0	35		£ . 0 0
21	Rent, rates, power and insurance costs	£ 1 0 0 0 . 0 0	36		£ 1 0 0 0 . 0 0
22	Repairs and renewals of property and equipment	£ . 0 0	37		£ . 0 0
23	Phone, fax, stationery and other office costs	£ 2 0 0 0 . 0 0	38		£ . 0 0
24	Advertising and business entertainment costs	£ 1 0 0 . 0 0	39		£ 1 0 0 . 0 0
25	Interest on bank and other loans	£ . 0 0	40		£ . 0 0
26	Bank, credit card and other financial charges	£ . 0 0	41		£ . 0 0
27	Irrecoverable debts written off	£ . 0 0	42		£ . 0 0
28	Accountancy, legal and other professional fees	£ . 0 0	43		£ . 0 0
29	Depreciation and loss/profit on sale of assets	£ 5 0 0 0 . 0 0	44		£ 5 0 0 0 . 0 0
30	Other business expenses	£ . 0 0	45		£ . 0 0
31	Total expenses (total of boxes 17 to 30)	£ 7 3 1 0 0 . 0 0	46	Total disallowable expenses (total of boxes 32 to 45)	£ 1 1 1 0 0 . 0 0

SA103F 2016   Page SEF 2

(Adapted from HMRC, 2016)

Assessment focus point

Please refer to the reference material at the end of this Course Book to see which elements of this chapter will be available to you as a pop-up in the live assessment.

Chapter summary

- The badges of trade give guidance as to whether or not a trade is being carried on.
- Revenue expenses are generally allowable expenses for computing taxable trading profits but capital expenses are not (unless relieved through capital allowances – see next chapter).
- The main disallowable items that you must add back in computing taxable trading profits are:
  - Entertaining (other than staff entertaining)
  - Depreciation charges (deduct capital allowances instead)
  - Increase in general provisions
  - Fines
  - Legal fees relating to capital items
  - Wages or salary paid to a business owner
  - The private proportion of any expenses for a sole trader/partner (not applicable to a company)
- Deduct non-trading income/capital profits included in the accounts from the accounts profit to arrive at taxable trading profits.

- **Adjustment of profits:** The adjustment of the accounting profits to comply with tax legislation

- **Badges of trade:** Indicate whether or not a trade is being carried on

- **Disallowable expenditure:** Expenditure that cannot be deducted in computing taxable trading profit

- **Expenditure wholly and exclusively for trade purposes:** Expenditure that is incidental to the trade and that does not have a dual purpose

Test your learning

1 **Which of the following expenses are allowable when computing taxable trading profits?**

	Allowable ✓
Legal fees incurred on the acquisition of a factory to be used for trade purposes	
Heating for factory	
Legal fees incurred on pursuing trade receivables	
Acquiring a machine to be used in the factory	

2 A sole trader incurs the following expenditure on entertaining and gifts.

	£
Staff entertaining	700
50 Christmas food hampers given to customers	240
Entertaining customers	900
	1,840

How much of the above expenditure is allowable for tax purposes?

£ [ ]

3 **For each of the following expenses, show whether they are allowable or disallowable by ticking the relevant boxes.**

	Allowable ✓	Disallowable ✓
Parking fines incurred by the owner of the business		
Parking fines incurred by an employee while on the employer's business		
Parking fines incurred by the director of a company while on company business		
Legal costs incurred in relation to acquiring a 10-year lease of property for the first time		
Legal costs incurred in relation to the renewal of a lease for 20 years		

	Allowable ✓	Disallowable ✓
Gifts of calendars to customers, costing £4 each and displaying an advertisement for the company		
Gifts of bottles of whisky to customers, costing £12 each		

4 Herbert, a self-employed carpenter, makes various items of garden furniture for sale. He takes a bird table from stock and sets it up in his own garden. The cost of making the bird table amounts to £80, and Herbert would normally expect to achieve a mark-up of 20% on such goods.

Identify the adjustment Herbert needs to make to the accounts for tax purposes, assuming he has reflected in the accounts the deduction for the cost of making the table.

Tick ONE box.

	✓
£80 must be deducted from the accounts profit	
£80 must be added back to the accounts profit	
£96 must be deducted from the accounts profit	
£96 must be added back to the accounts profit	

5 Set out below is the irrecoverable debts account of Kingfisher, a sole trader:

Irrecoverable debts

	£	1.4.16	£
		Provisions b/d	
		General	2,500
		Specific (trade)	1,875
31.3.17			
Provisions c/d			
General	1,800		
Specific (trade)	4,059	Statement of profit or loss	1,484
	5,859		5,859

Insert the amount that needs adjusting and tick whether it should be added to or deducted from Kingfisher's accounts profit to arrive at taxable trading profits.

£ [ ]

Added back ✓	Deducted ✓

6 Trude works from home as a self-employed hairdresser. She incurs £450 on heating and lighting bills and this amount is deducted in her accounts. 20% of this expenditure relates to the business use of her home.

How much of the expenditure is disallowable for tax purposes?

£ [ ]

Capital allowances

3

Learning outcomes

1.3	**Identify and calculate capital allowances for sole-traders and partnerships**
	• Identify the types of capital allowances
	• Calculate capital allowances including adjustments for private use
2.2	**Identify and calculate capital allowances for limited companies**
	• Identify the types of capital allowances
	• Calculate capital allowances

Assessment context

All the rules in this chapter are highly examinable and could be examined in a variety of different combinations. Make sure you can deal with any scenario the assessment throws at you.

Qualification context

You will not see these rules outside of this unit.

Business context

In practice, capital allowances are a significant form of tax relief reducing a taxpayer's tax liability.

The government often uses capital allowances to encourage people to invest in new plant and machinery.

Chapter overview

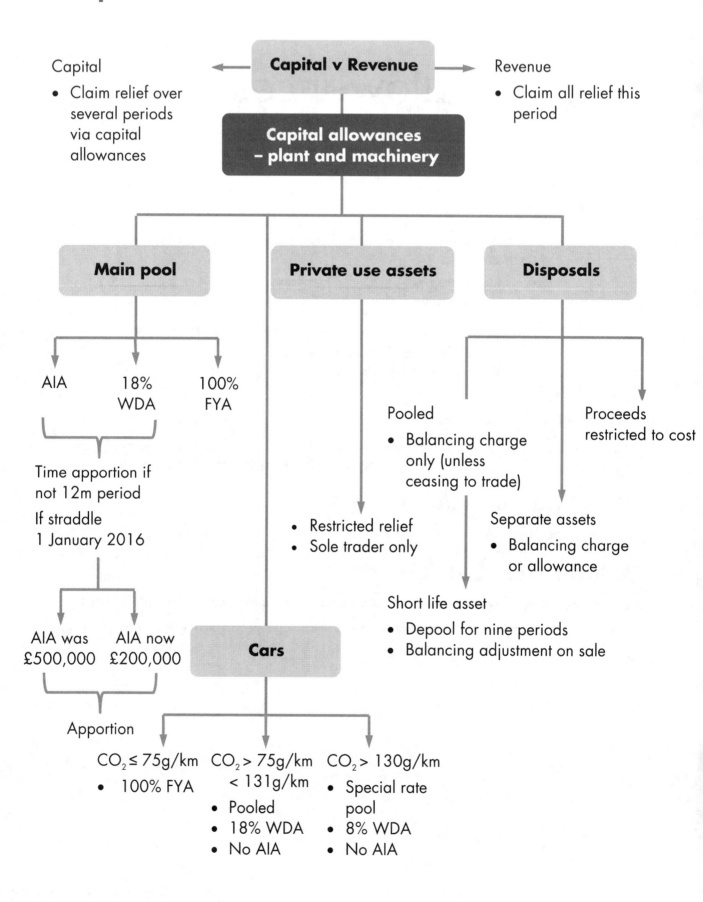

Capital v Revenue

Capital
- Claim relief over several periods via capital allowances

Revenue
- Claim all relief this period

Capital allowances – plant and machinery

Main pool

AIA 18% WDA 100% FYA

Time apportion if not 12m period

If straddle 1 January 2016

AIA was £500,000 AIA now £200,000

Apportion

Private use assets

- Restricted relief
- Sole trader only

Cars

$CO_2 \leq 75g/km$
- 100% FYA

$CO_2 > 75g/km$ < 131g/km
- Pooled
- 18% WDA
- No AIA

$CO_2 > 130g/km$
- Special rate pool
- 8% WDA
- No AIA

Disposals

Pooled
- Balancing charge only (unless ceasing to trade)

Proceeds restricted to cost

Separate assets
- Balancing charge or allowance

Short life asset
- Depool for nine periods
- Balancing adjustment on sale

1 Introduction

This chapter looks at the difference between capital and revenue expenditure and how to get tax relief for the different types of expenditure by either treating them as an expense or plant and machinery for capital allowances.

2 Capital and revenue expenditure

Capital expenditure is one-off expenditure that will bring benefits to the business over a number of years (eg purchase of machinery).

Revenue expenditure is regular ongoing expenditure that only brings benefit in the period in which the expenditure is made (eg payment of electricity bill).

Revenue expenditure, generally, may be deducted against taxable profits before they are taxed (but we saw in the previous chapter that not all revenue expenditure is automatically allowable).

It may be possible to claim **capital allowances** on some capital expenditure. Capital allowances are just the tax version of accounts depreciation. It is calculated to replace the depreciation charged in the accounts.

Both individuals (sole traders and partners) and companies may claim capital allowances.

3 Expenditure qualifying for capital allowances

Plant and machinery is something which has a **function** within the trade as opposed to being part of the **setting** where the business takes place. Essentially, plant and machinery is any capital item used in the business other than buildings. For example, reference books could be plant and machinery.

> **Assessment focus point**
>
> There is much law determining what is allowable as plant and machinery and what is not. The AAT have confirmed that the very detailed rules on this do not form part of your syllabus but, for information, some examples include:
>
> - Moveable office partitions are plant – but fixed partitions are not.
> - Decorative items (eg paintings) in hotels are plant.
>
> The more common items you will see in the assessment are:
>
> - Cars, vans and lorries
> - Furniture
> - Computers

4 Allowances on plant and machinery

4.1 When and how capital allowances are given

Allowances are computed by reference to the period for which accounts are drawn up.

They are deducted from the taxable profits of the period.

They include all additions and disposals occurring in the relevant accounting period. Expenditure must be of a capital nature.

4.2 Main pool for capital allowances

Most expenditure on plant and machinery is put into a 'pool' of assets known as the **main pool**. This includes expenditure on cars with CO_2 emissions of 130g/km or less.

4.3 Annual investment allowance

From 1 January 2016, a business can claim an **annual investment allowance** (AIA), giving 100% tax relief on the first £200,000 of expenditure on plant and machinery in a 12-month **period of account**. The period of account is the period for which the business prepares its accounts. From 6 April 2014 (1 April 2014 for a company), the AIA was £500,000.

The AIA is not available for expenditure on cars.

The amount of the AIA is scaled up/down for short/long periods of account. **Note.** Companies cannot have a corporation tax period that is longer than 12 months.

Activity 1: Annual investment allowance

Delson starts a business on 1 January 2016. In the nine-month period to 30 September 2016 he incurs the following expenditure:

		£
6 April 2016	Computer equipment	120,000
7 May 2016	Office furniture	75,000
13 May 2016	Delivery vans	60,000
20 June 2016	Car	19,000

Required

Delson can claim annual investment allowance of £ _____ .

Workings (on-screen free text area provided in the CBT as part of larger question)

Where an accounting period **straddles 1 January 2016** (for both unincorporated and incorporated businesses) the maximum AIA available for the accounting period is calculated by pro-rating the relevant AIA limits for the number of months in the accounting period that fall either side of 1 January 2016.

For example, if a 12 month accounting period ended on 31 July 2016 five months of that accounting period would be before 1 January 2016 (when the AIA was £500,000) and seven months would be after (when the AIA is £200,000). To calculate the available AIA for that accounting period we multiply the previous AIA by $\frac{5}{12}$ and the current AIA by $\frac{7}{12}$ as follows.

£500,000 × 5/12 + £200,000 × 7/12 = £325,000

Assessment focus point

The rules for calculating the maximum AIA available for periods straddling 1 January 2016 are slightly more complex than we have shown below. However, the AAT have advised us that the full complexity of this will not be needed and tasks in the *Business Tax* assessment will be designed to accommodate this.

Activity 2: Annual investment allowance – accounting period straddles 1 January 2016

Delia starts a business on 1 April 2015 and makes up accounts for the 12 months to 31 March 2016. She incurs the following expenditure:

		£
5 April 2015	Machinery	320,000
8 April 2015	Computers	80,000
5 May 2015	Cars	20,000
10 June 2015	Vans	20,000

Required

Delia can claim annual investment allowance of £ _____ .

Workings (on-screen free text area provided in the CBT as part of larger question)

4.4 First year allowances (FYAs)

These are special allowances given in addition to the AIA.

First year allowances (FYAs) are available at 100% on expenditure incurred on:

- Energy saving or water efficient plant, (the list of approved products is published by the Government. You would be told in the assessment if an asset qualified).

- Low emission cars (ie cars with CO_2 emissions of 75g/km and below)

- Electrically propelled cars.

You must give FYAs at 100% to the assets that are eligible for them. Do not use the AIA against them.

FYAs are **never** time apportioned for short or long accounting periods.

4.5 Writing-down allowances

A **writing-down allowance** (WDA) is given on the main pool at the rate of 18% per year (on a reducing balance basis). The WDA is calculated on the value of pooled plant, after adding current period additions and taking out current period disposals (as explained shortly).

The additions will include:

(a) Expenditure that qualifies for the AIA but is in excess of the maximum AIA available for the period.

(b) Cars with CO_2 emissions of between 76g/km and 130g/km. These are cars that do not qualify for 100% FYA and do not go into the special rate pool (see later).

Illustration 1: Basic proforma for calculating WDAs

	Main pool £	Allowances £
TWDV b/f	X	
Additions (not eligible for AIA/FYA)	X	
Less disposals	(X)	
	X	
WDA @ 18%	(X)	X
TWDV c/f	X	

Note. TWDV = Tax Written-Down Value; this is the value of the pool of assets for tax purposes.

The total allowances for the accounting period can then be deducted in the adjustments to profit working.

WDAs are time apportioned for short/long accounting periods ($n/12 \times 18\%$).

Activity 3: Writing-down allowances in the main pool

Jamie draws up his accounts to 31 December. At 1 January 2016 he has a balance of £10,000 on his main pool.

In his period to 31 December 2016 he has the following transactions:

	£
13 June buys a car (CO$_2$ 125g/km)	8,000
31 August buys a van	9,000
30 October sells plant for	2,000

Required

Jamie can claim annual investment allowance of £ ☐ .

Jamie can claim writing-down allowances of £ ☐ .

Workings (on-screen free text area provided in the CBT as part of larger question)

5 Disposals

When an asset is sold in the year, we deduct the proceeds from the tax written down value of the pool brought forward. However, if an asset is sold for more than its original cost we only deduct the original cost from the pool.

> ### Illustration 2: Disposal proceeds
>
> On 6 April 2016, a sole trader had a balance on his main pool of £47,000. Plant that had cost £7,000 was sold in the year for proceeds of:
>
> (a) £14,000
> (b) £4,000
>
> In (a) proceeds are more than original cost and so only £7,000 would be deducted from the main pool balance of £47,000.
>
> In (b) the actual proceeds are less than original cost and so the proceeds of £4,000 would be deducted from the main pool balance of £47,000.

6 Periods that are not 12 months long

The AIA limit and WDA are adjusted by the fraction: months/12.

The FYA is never adjusted.

A sole trader or partnership may have a period shorter or longer than 12 months. AIA and WDA can therefore be scaled up or down.

A company may have a corporation tax period shorter than 12 months but not longer than 12 months. AIA and WDA could therefore be scaled down but not up.

Activity 4: Short period of account

Edward Ltd has been in business a number of years, drawing up accounts to 31 March.

In 2016 it decided to change its year end to 31 December.

In the period ended 31 December 2016 it had the following additions:

		£
13 April	Car (CO_2 emissions 125g/km)	7,000
15 April	Plant	446,750

It sold a van for £2,000 on 7 July that had cost £3,000.

TWDV b/f at 1 April 2016 was £12,000.

Required

Edward Ltd can claim capital allowances of £ [   ] .

Workings (on-screen free text area provided in the CBT as part of larger question)

7 Cessation of a business

When a business ceases to trade no AIAs, FYAs or WDAs are given in the final period.

Additions in the final period are added to the pool in the normal way. Similarly, any disposal proceeds (limited to cost) of assets sold in the final period are deducted from the balance of qualifying expenditure. If assets are not sold they are deemed to be disposed of on the final day of trading for their market value. For example, a sole trader may keep a car from the business that has just ceased trading and so must deduct the market value from the pool.

If, after the above adjustments, a positive balance of qualifying expenditure remains in the pool then a **balancing allowance** equal to this amount is given. **The balancing allowance is deducted from taxable trading profits**. If, on the other hand, the balance on the pool has become negative, a **balancing charge** equal to the negative amount is given. **The balancing charge increases taxable trading profits.**

Balancing allowances on the main pool and the special rate pool (see below) can only arise on cessation of trade, whereas balancing charges on these pools, although most commonly happening on cessation, can arise whilst trade is still in progress.

Activity 5: Cessation of a business

Baxter normally has a June year end. On 1 July 2016 he has a TWDV in the pool of £12,000. He ceases to trade on 31 January 2017. His additions and disposals in his final period are as follows:

		£
5 September	Buys plant	2,000
12 October	Sells plant	See below

(a) Required

If Baxter sells his plant for £15,500 then he will have a

☐ ▼ of £ ☐ .

Picklist:

balancing allowance
balancing charge

Workings (on-screen free text area provided in the CBT as part of larger question)

(b) Required

If Baxter sells his plant for £11,500 then he will have a

[▼] of £ [ ].

Picklist:

balancing allowance
balancing charge

Workings (on-screen free text area provided in the CBT as part of larger question)

Notes

1 A balancing allowance only arises in the main pool on the cessation of trade.

2 A balancing charge may arise on the main pool at any point in the business's life.

8 Assets that are not included in the main pool

We have seen above how to compute capital allowances on the main pool of plant and machinery. However, some special items are not put into the main pool. A separate record of allowances must be kept for these assets.

These assets are:

- Cars with CO_2 emissions greater than 130g/km

- Assets not wholly used for business purposes in **unincorporated businesses** (such as cars with private use by the proprietor)

- Short life assets

8.1 Cars with CO_2 emissions greater than 130g/km

Cars with CO_2 emissions in excess of 130g/km are put in a pool known as the **special rate pool**. The **WDA rate on the special rate pool is 8% for a 12-month period** calculated on the pool balance (after any additions and disposals) at the end of the chargeable period.

Activity 6: Special rate pool

Myles Ltd prepares accounts to 31 March each year and incurred the following transactions for the year ended 31 March 2017.

1.7.16 Bought car for £17,000, CO_2 emissions of 120g/km

1.10.16 Bought car for £8,000, CO_2 emissions of 180g/km

On 1 April 2016 the TWDV of plant and machinery were as follows:

	£
Main pool	25,000
Special rate pool	10,000

Required

Myles Ltd can claim capital allowances of £ [   ] .

Workings (on-screen free text area provided in the CBT as part of larger question)

		.	

8.2 Assets used partly for private purposes

If a proprietor of a sole trader business or a partner in a partnership uses a business asset for private purposes, the following treatment applies:

- The asset is put in a separate column.

- TWDV is reduced by **full amount** of AIA/FYA/WDA calculated as normal.

- A balancing allowance or charge will arise at the date of disposal.

- Only the business proportion of the allowance/charge is transferred into the allowances column.

An asset with some private use by an employee (not the business owner) suffers no restriction. The employee may be taxed on the private use as a taxable benefit, so the business is entitled to full capital allowances on such assets. This means **there is never any private use restriction in a company's capital allowance computation**, whether the asset is used by an employee or a director.

Assessment focus point

The Chief Assessor has noted that making private use adjustments when they are not required is a common mistake so please ensure you check who you are calculating capital allowances for.

- If it is a soletrader or partnership - make the adjustment.
- If it is a company – **do not** make the adjustment.

Activity 7: Private-use assets

At 1 January 2016 Sweeney has two cars brought forward, a car he uses himself with a TWDV of £20,000 (20% private use, CO_2 emissions 180g/km) and a car used by his employee, Doris, with a TWDV of £16,000 (35% private use, CO_2 emissions 120g/km). He draws up his accounts to 31 December 2016.

Sweeney had no other assets.

(a) Required

Sweeney can claim capital allowances of | £ | | .

Workings (on screen free text area provided in the CBT as part of larger question)

(b) Required

What capital allowances would Sweeney claim if the business instead ceased in this period and both cars were sold for £15,000 each?

£	

Workings (on-screen free text area provided in the CBT as part of larger question)

8.3 Short life assets

A **short life asset** is an asset that a trader expects to dispose of within **eight years** of the end of the period of acquisition.

A trader can make a **depooling election** to keep such an asset in its own individual pool. **The advantage of this is that a balancing allowance can be given when the asset is disposed of**. Such an election would not be made if the asset is entitled to 100% FYA or AIA.

For an unincorporated business, the time limit for electing is the 31 January that is 22 months after the end of the tax year in which the period of account of the expenditure ends (for example, this would be 31 January 2019 for accounting periods ending in 2016/17). For a company, it is two years after the end of the accounting period of the expenditure.

If the asset is disposed of within eight years of the end of the period of account or accounting period in which it was bought, a balancing charge or allowance is made on its disposal. However, if the asset is not disposed of within this period, the tax written-down value is transferred to the main pool at the end of that period. It would not be advisable to depool an asset that will be sold for more than its cost/tax written-down value as this would create a balancing charge. In this instance, the asset would just go into the main pool or special rate pool.

Short life asset treatment cannot be claimed for:

- Motor cars
- Plant used partly for private purposes

The AIA can be used against short life assets but it is more tax efficient to use it against expenditure that would fall into the main pool.

Activity 8: Short life asset election

Pyrocles buys an asset in his year ended 31 December 2016 and makes a depooling election for it. Its written down value at 1 January 2022 is £20,000.

Required

Explain the tax implications if the asset is sold on 1 December 2022 for either £5,000 or £50,000.

Workings (on-screen free text area provided in the CBT as part of larger question)

| |
| |
| |
| |
| |
| |
| |
| |

9 Differences between unincorporated and incorporated businesses

We have seen in this chapter that, broadly, the rules on capital allowances are the same for unincorporated businesses (sole traders and partnerships) and incorporated businesses (companies).

Two important differences in the calculation of capital allowances are as follows:

(a) There is never a **private use asset** column in a company's capital allowance computation.

- The director or employee may suffer a taxable benefit instead and so the company can deduct the allowance in full.

- If a sole trader or partner uses a business asset for private purposes then we restrict the capital allowances claimed on this asset.

(b)   Long **period of account** (accounts that have been made up for more than 12 months).

- If a sole trader/partnership has a period shorter or longer than 12 months we would scale down or scale up the calculation.

- If a company has a long period of account, we perform two capital allowances computations (see Chapter 4).

Activity 9: Calculation of capital allowances

Oscar, a sole trader, makes up accounts for the 18 months to 30 June 2017. The brought forward value on his main pool on 1 July 2016 was £81,000. He bought and sold the following assets:

		£
10 July 2016	Plant	210,000
10 August 2016	Car for salesman	
	(CO$_2$ emissions 70g/km)	11,000
12 September 2016	Plant	550,000
1 June 2017	Disposed of plant (cost £30,000)	32,000

Required

Calculate the capital allowances claim that Oscar can make for the period ended 30 June 2017.

 Assessment focus point

In the live assessment you will be provided with 'taxation data' that can be accessed through pop-up windows. The content of these taxation data tables has been reproduced at the end of this Course Book.

In addition, please refer to the 'reference material' at the end of this Course Book to see which elements of this chapter will be available to you as a pop-up window in the live assessment.

Chapter summary

- Assets that perform a function in the trade are generally plant. Assets that are part of the setting are not plant.

- Most expenditure on plant and machinery goes into the main pool.

- An annual investment allowance (AIA) of £500,000 up until 31 December 2015 (£200,000 from 1 January 2016) is available on expenditure other than cars. The limit is prorated for periods of more or less than 12 months.

- FYAs at 100% are available on low emission cars and energy and water saving plant.

- There is a writing-down allowance (WDA) of 18% on the balance of the main pool in a 12-month period.

- WDAs are time-apportioned in short or long periods.

- FYAs are never time-apportioned for short or long periods.

- Balancing allowances or balancing charges will be given when the trade ceases, and when an asset is disposed of, which is not included in the main pool or special rate pool.

- Private-use of assets by sole traders and partners restricts capital allowances.

- An election can be made to depool short life assets. If a depooled asset is not sold within eight years of the end of the period of acquisition, the value of the short life asset at the end of that period is transferred to the main pool.

- Cars are dealt with according to their CO_2 emissions:
  - Up to 75g/km – FYA at 100%
  - 76g/km to 130g/km – main pool with WDA of 18%
  - Above 130g/km – special rate pool with WDA 8%

Keywords

- **Annual investment allowance (AIA):** Available in a period in which expenditure is incurred on plant and machinery

- **Balancing allowance:** Given when a positive balance remains at cessation or disposal of certain assets

- **Balancing charge:** Given when a negative balance remains at cessation or disposal of certain assets

- **Depooling election:** An election not to put an asset into the main pool of plant and machinery

- **First year allowance (FYA):** Available at 100% on low emission cars and certain energy saving and water efficient plant

- **Period of account:** The period for which a business prepares its accounts

- **Plant:** Apparatus that performs a function in the business. Apparatus that is merely part of the setting is not plant

- **Private-use asset:** Has restricted capital allowances but does not apply to companies

- **Short life asset:** An asset that a trader expects to dispose of within eight years of the end of the period of acquisition

- **Writing-down allowance (WDA):** A capital allowance of 18% per annum, given on the main pool of plant and machinery or 8% per annum on the balance in the special rate pool

1   An item of plant is acquired for £2,000 and sold five years later for £3,200.

The amount that will be deducted from the pool as proceeds when the disposal is made is:

£ [   ]

2   Nitin, who prepares accounts to 30 September each year, had a balance on his main pool of £22,500 on 1 October 2016. In the year to 30 September 2017 he sold one asset and bought one asset as follows:

Addition (eligible for AIA) 1.12.16   £171,250
Disposal proceeds on sale on 1.8.17 (less than cost)   £7,800

The amount of capital allowances available for year ended 30 September 2017 is:

£ [   ]

3   A company starts to trade on 1 July 2016, making up accounts to 31 December, and buys a car with CO_2 emission of 115g/km costing £18,000 on 15 July 2016. The company also buys energy-saving plant costing £5,000 on 1 September 2016.

The capital allowances available in the first period of account to 31 December 2016 are:

£ [   ]

4   Abdul ceased trading on 31 December 2016, drawing up his final accounts for the year to 31 December 2016.

The following facts are relevant:

Main pool balance at 1.1.16   £12,500
Addition – 31.5.16   £20,000
Disposal proceeds
    (in total – proceeds not exceeding cost on any item) – 31.12.16   £18,300

Identify whether the following statement is true or false. Tick ONE box.

There is a balancing charge of £14,200 arising for the year to 31 December 2016.

	✓
True	
False	

5   Raj, a sole trader who makes up accounts to 30 April each year, buys a Volvo estate car, with CO_2 emissions of 180g/km, for £30,000 on 31 March 2017. 60% of his usage of the car is for business purposes.

The capital allowance available to Raj in respect of the car for y/e 30 April 2017 is:

£	

Computing corporation tax

4

Learning outcomes

2.2	Identify and calculate capital allowances
2.3	Calculate taxable total profits and corporation tax payable
	• Calculate the taxable total profits from trading income, property income, investment income and chargeable gains
	• Calculate the total profits and corporation tax payable for accounting periods longer than, shorter than or equal to 12 months
2.4	Complete corporation tax returns
	• Accurately complete a corporation tax return

Assessment context

In the assessment you may be required you to calculate taxable total profits (TTP) and then go on to calculate corporation tax.

You may also be required to complete extracts from the corporation tax return.

Qualification context

You will not see this topic outside of this assessment

Business context

Companies need to know how much corporation tax they need to pay.

Chapter overview

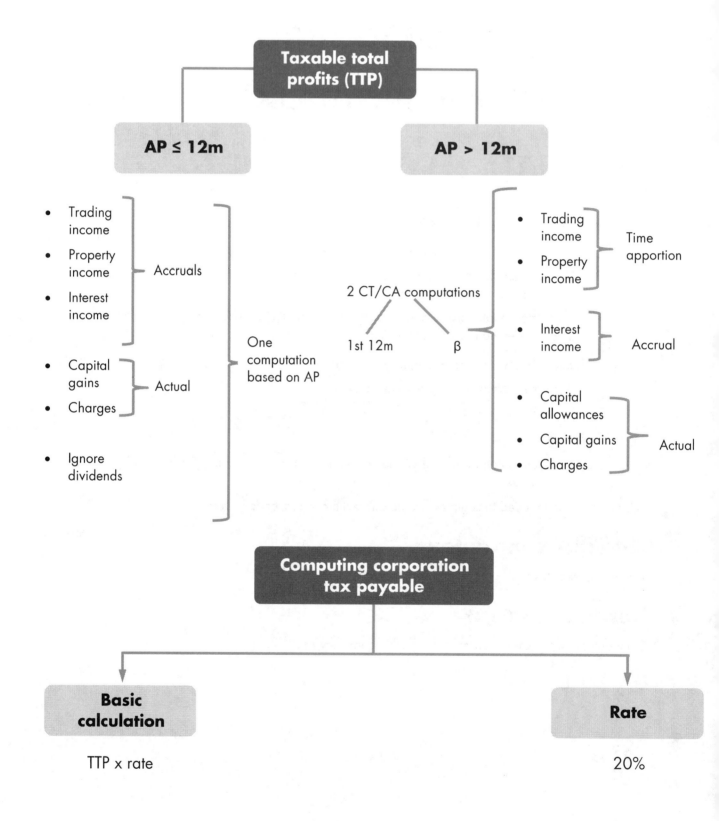

1 Introduction

In this chapter we will look at the different types of income earned by a company, how this income is included on the tax return and how to calculate corporation tax.

2 Taxable total profits (TTP)

Key term

Corporation tax is a tax payable by companies

Taxable total profits (TTP) are the profits on which a company must pay corporation tax

Period of account is the period for which the company prepares its accounts

Set out below is an example of a proforma corporation tax computation:

Illustration 1: Corporation tax computation for the X months to <date>

	£
Trading profits	X
Interest income	X
Other income	X
Property income	X
Net chargeable gains	X
Less qualifying charitable payments	(X)
Taxable total profits (TTP)	X

2.1 Trading profits

The trading profits of a company are, broadly, computed in the same way that the trading profits of a sole trader are computed.

As a reminder, there are two important differences:

(a) There is never any private use adjustments for a company when either adjusting the accounting profit or calculating capital allowances.

(b) Companies deal with a long period of account (accounts that have been made up for more than 12 months) in a different way to individuals or partnerships.

Note. Bad debts may be referred to as impairment losses in the financial statements of a company.

2.2 Interest

Interest received by companies is taxed on the accruals basis.

Interest payable is deductible:

- If the loan is for a **trading purpose** (eg to buy plant and machinery for use in the company's trade), **the interest is deductible when computing the company's trading income.** This means that if it is showing as an expense in the statement of profit or loss, **no** adjustment is needed.

- If the loan is for a **non-trading purpose** (eg to buy investments such as shares or properties to rent out), the interest is **deductible from interest received** (eg from a bank or building society) **to give a net 'interest' figure to be used in computing taxable total profits**. In some cases, there may be a deficit of non-trading interest paid over non-trading interest received, but the treatment of such a deficit is not in your syllabus.

2.3 Property income

A company with property business income must **pool the rents and expenses on all its properties, to give a single profit or loss**. Property business income is taxed on an **accruals basis**.

Assessment focus point

You will not be expected to calculate property business income in your *Business Tax* assessment. However, you may be given a profit figure and be required to include it within the corporation tax computation, as appropriate.

2.4 Chargeable gains

Companies do not pay capital gains tax. Instead their **net chargeable gains** (current period gains less current period and brought forward capital losses) **are brought into the computation of taxable total profits**.

We will look at gains in more detail later.

2.5 Qualifying charitable donations

Qualifying charitable donations are charitable gifts on which tax relief is given; however, they cannot be deducted as a trading expense. If a qualifying charitable donation has been deducted in computing the accounts profit, the amount deducted must be added back in computing taxable **trading** profits (adjustment of profits), but can then be deducted when computing taxable total profits.

2.6 Dividend income

Companies are not taxed on dividends they receive from other companies.

2.7 Dividends paid

Companies may not deduct dividends paid from their taxable total profits.

2.8 Income received/paid net of tax

Companies receive patent royalties from individuals net of 20% income tax. This means that the individual withholds 20% tax and pays it over to HM Revenue & Customs (HMRC) on the company's behalf.

Income received net of tax is included within the corporation tax computation at its gross equivalent. For example, £8,000 of patent royalties received net of tax would need to be grossed up by multiplying by 100/80 to include £10,000 within either trading profits or other income.

Patent royalties and interest, paid by a company to individuals, are paid net of 20% income tax which the company pays over to HMRC. It is the gross amount that is deducted in the corporation tax computation, either from trading profits or from interest or other income as described above.

Payments of royalties and interest by a company to a company are made gross and so there are no income tax implications.

Illustration 2: Adjustment of profits and calculation of TTP

ST Ltd draws up accounts for the year ended 31 March 2016 which show the following results:

	£	£
Gross profit on trading		180,000
Dividends received from other companies		7,900
Bank interest received		222
Profit on sale of investments		20,000
Less: trade expenses (all allowable)	83,400	
bank interest payable (overdraft)	200	
debenture interest payable (gross)	3,200	
qualifying charitable donation	100	
depreciation charge	9,022	(95,922)
Profit before taxation		112,200

Notes

1   The capital allowances for the accounting period total £5,500.

2   The debentures were issued on 1 August 2015 to raise working capital. The £3,200 charged in the accounts represents six months' interest (£2,400) paid and two months accrued.

3   The profit on the sale of investments resulted in a chargeable gain of £13,867.

The calculation of the company's taxable total profits is as follows:

	£	£
Profit for the year per accounts		112,200
Less: dividends received	7,900	
profit on investments	20,000	
interest received	222	
		(28,122)
		84,078
Add: qualifying charitable donation	100	
depreciation charge	9,022	
		9,122
		93,200
Less: capital allowances		(5,500)
Trading profits		87,700
Interest received		222
Chargeable gain		13,867
		101,789
Less: qualifying charitable donation		(100)
Taxable total profits		101,689

Note. The dividends received from other companies are not included within taxable total profits. Interest is deductible on the accruals basis.

Activity 1: Calculating taxable total profits

Abel Ltd, a UK trading company with no associated companies, produced the following results for the year ended 31 December 2016.

Income	£
Adjusted trading profits	2,440,000
Rental income	150,000
Bank deposit interest accrued	40,000
Capital gains: 25 September 2016	350,000
28 December 2016	70,000
(There were capital losses of £80,000 brought forward at 1 January 2016)	
Loan interest accrued	10,000
Qualifying charitable payment	70,000
Dividends received	135,000

Required

Complete the following table calculating taxable total profits for the year ended 31 December 2016.

Solution

Corporation tax computation y/e 31 December 2016

	£
Trading profits	
Rental income	
Interest income	
Capital gains	
Less qualifying charitable payments	
Taxable total profits	

3 Long periods of account

3.1 Accounting periods exceeding 12 months

A **period of account** is the period for which a company prepares its accounts.

An **accounting period** is the period for which corporation tax is charged.

A company's accounting period is usually the same as its period of account. However, **an accounting period cannot be longer than 12 months**. This means that **if a period of account exceeds 12 months, it must be divided into two accounting periods of**:

- The first 12 months
- The remaining balance of months

It is necessary to prepare separate computations of taxable total profits for each accounting period.

Splitting income and expenditure

Income and expenditure is split between the two computations using the following rules:

- Trading income (before deducting capital allowances) is apportioned on a time basis.

- Capital allowances and balancing charges are calculated separately for each accounting period. The annual investment allowance (AIA) and write-down allowance (WDA) will need to be apportioned for the short period.

- Property income is time apportioned.

- Interest income is apportioned on an accruals basis.

- Qualifying charitable donations are allocated to the accounting period in which they are paid.

- Chargeable gains by reference to the date the asset is sold.

Activity 2: Calculating taxable total profits – long period of account

B plc prepared accounts for a 16-month period to 31 December 2016. The results for the period include the following:

	£
Adjusted trading profit before capital allowances	3,600,000
Bank interest receivable (accrued evenly over the period)	32,000
Capital gain	40,000
(sale of asset on 13.10.16)	
Qualifying charitable donation paid (annually on 31.7)	20,000

The tax written-down value of plant and machinery qualifying for capital allowances at 1 September 2015 was £37,500. The only capital transaction during the 16-month period was the purchase of a new van for £6,875 on 15 November 2016.

Required

Complete the following table calculating taxable total profit for the two accounting periods that comprise the long period of account.

Solution

	months to £	months to £
Adjusted trading profits		
Less capital allowances		
Trading profits		
Interest income		
Gain		
Less qualifying charitable payment		
TTP		

4 Computing the corporation tax liability

Corporation tax rates are fixed for financial years. A **financial year** runs from 1 April to the following 31 March and is identified by the calendar year in which it begins.

For example, the year ended 31 March 2017 is the Financial Year 2016 (FY2016) as it begins on 1 April 2016. This should not be confused with a tax year for an individual, that runs from 6 April to the following 5 April.

From 1 April 2015 (FY2015) corporation tax rates became aligned leaving one rate of corporation tax, called the **main rate**.

The main rate, which is 20%, will be used to calculate the corporation tax payable for all companies with accounting periods starting on or after 1 April 2015.

Activity 3: Corporation tax payable

B plc has the following results for the year ended 31 March 2016:

	£
Trading profits	1,500,000
Gain	50,000
Qualifying charitable payments	30,000

Required

How much corporation tax is payable by B plc?

£

Assessment focus point

In the live assessment you will be provided with 'Taxation Data' that can be accessed through pop-up windows. The content of these taxation data tables has been reproduced at the back of this Course Book. Make sure you familiarise yourself with the content and practise referring to it as you work through this Course Book.

5 Company tax return

Assessment focus point

In your assessment you may be asked to complete an extract of the company tax return. A copy of the tax calculation page is available at the end of this chapter. Tasks are expected to cover boxes 145 to 235.

Have a good look at it now to familiarise yourself with the boxes, then you will be able to practise completing this form in the *Business Tax* Question Bank.

Illustration 3

We previously calculated Abel's TTP for the period ended 31 December 2016 as follows:

Corporation tax computation y/e 31 December 2016

	£
Trading profits	2,440,000
Rental income	150,000
Interest income (40,000 + 10,000)	50,000
Capital gains (350,000 + 70,000 − 80,000)	340,000
	2,980,000
Less qualifying charitable payment	(70,000)
TTP	2,910,000

Abel Ltd's tax payable would be as follows:

	£
CT liability	
FY2015 2,910,000 × 3/12 × 20%	145,500
FY2016 2,910,000 × 9/12 × 20%	436,500
Total CT payable	582,000

These details may be shown on the tax return as follows:

Tax calculation
Turnover

145 Total turnover from trade £ [   ] · 0 0

150 Banks, building societies, insurance companies and other financial concerns –
put an 'X' in this box if you do not have a recognised turnover and have not made an entry in box 145 [ ]

Income

155 Trading profits £ [2 , 4 4 0 , 0 0 0] · 0 0

160 Trading losses brought forward claimed against profits £ [   ] · 0 0

165 Net trading profits – *box 155 minus box 160* £ [   ] · 0 0

170 Bank, building society or other interest, and profits from non-trading loan relationships £ [5 0 , 0 0 0] · 0 0

172 Put an 'X' in box 172 if the figure in box 170 is net of carrying back a deficit from a later accounting period [ ]

175 Annual payments not otherwise charged to Corporation Tax and from which Income Tax has not been deducted £ [   ] · 0 0

Income *continued*

180 Non-exempt dividends or distributions from non–UK resident companies £ [   ] · 0 0

185 Income from which Income Tax has been deducted £ [   ] · 0 0

190 Income from a property business £ [1 5 0 , 0 0 0] · 0 0

195 Non-trading gains on intangible fixed assets £ [   ] · 0 0

200 Tonnage Tax profits £ [   ] · 0 0

205 Income not falling under any other heading £ [   ] · 0 0

Chargeable gains

210 Gross chargeable gains £ [4 2 0 , 0 0 0] · 0 0

215 Allowable losses including losses brought forward £ [8 0 , 0 0 0] · 0 0

220 Net chargeable gains – *box 210 minus box 215* £ [3 4 0 , 0 0 0] · 0 0

Profits before deductions and reliefs

225 Losses brought forward against certain investment income £ [   ] · 0 0

230 Non-trade deficits on loan relationships (including interest) and derivative contracts (financial instruments) brought forward £ [   ] · 0 0

235 Profits before other deductions and reliefs – *net sum of boxes 165 to 205 and 220 minus sum of boxes 225 and 230* £ [2 , 9 8 0 , 0 0 0] · 0 0

(Adapted from HMRC, 2015)

Assessment focus point

In the live assessment you will be tested via Gap fills for boxes 145 to 235.

The 2016 version of the tax return was not available at the time of going to print so please ensure you visit gov.uk before your assessment to view the latest version.

Please refer to the tax tables and reference material at the end of this Course Book to see which elements of this chapter will be available to you as pop-up windows in the live assessment.

- Adjustment of profit for companies is similar to that for individuals but there is no private use adjustment.

- To compute taxable total profits, aggregate all sources of income and chargeable gains. Deduct qualifying charitable donations.

- Patent royalties and interest are received/paid to individuals net of 20% tax. Include the gross amounts in the computation of taxable total profits.

- An accounting period cannot exceed 12 months in length.

- A long period of account must be split into two accounting periods: a period of 12 months and then a period covering the balance of the period of account.

- From FY15 all companies will pay corporation tax at the main rate.

Keywords

- **Accounting period:** The period for which corporation tax is charged
- **Financial year:** Runs from 1 April to the following 31 March and is identified by the calendar year in which it begins
- **Period of account:** The period for which a company prepares its accounts
- **Qualifying charitable donations:** Charitable gifts on which tax relief is given
- **Taxable total profits:** The profits on which a company must pay corporation tax

1 **Indicate whether the following statements are true or false.**

	True ✓	False ✓
A company with a nine-month period of account will calculate capital allowances for nine months and deduct them from adjusted trading profits.		
A company with an 18-month period of account will calculate capital allowances for 18 months and deduct them from adjusted trading profits, and then pro-rate the answer between the appropriate accounting periods.		
A company with an 18-month period of account will calculate capital allowances for the first 12 months, then capital allowances for the remaining 6 months, and deduct them from the relevant pro-rated trading profits allocated to each accounting period.		
Dividends are not included in the taxable total profits. They are taxed separately.		

2 A company has accrued interest payable of £4,000 (gross) for the year ended 31 March 2017.

The interest payable was paid on a loan taken out to buy some machinery for use in the company's trade.

Identify how this will be treated in the corporation tax computation. Tick ONE box.

	✓
Added to trading income	
Added to net non-trading interest	
Deducted from trading income	
Deducted from net non-trading interest	

3 On 30 June 2016, Edelweiss Ltd makes a donation to Help the Aged of £385. The donation is a qualifying charitable donation.

The amount of deduction available in respect of the charitable donation when calculating taxable total profits is:

£ [ ]

4 X Ltd had been making up accounts to 31 May for several years. Early in 2016 the directors decided to make accounts to 31 August 2016 (instead of 31 May 2016) and annually thereafter to 31 August.

Tick the box which correctly shows the two chargeable accounting periods for CT purposes for X Ltd.

	✓
1 June 2015 – 31 March 2016 and 1 April 2016 – 31 August 2016	
1 June 2015 – 31 May 2016 and 1 June 2016 – 31 August 2016	
1 June 2015 – 31 December 2015 and 1 January 2016 – 31 August 2016	
1 June 2015 – 31 August 2015 and 1 September 2015 – 31 August 2016	

5 C Ltd prepares accounts for the 16 months to 30 April 2017. The results are as follows:

	£
Trading profits	320,000
Bank interest received (accrued evenly over period)	1,600
Chargeable gain (made 1 January 2017)	20,000
Qualifying charitable donation (paid 31 December 2016)	15,000

Using the proforma layout provided, calculate the taxable total profits for the accounting periods based on the above results. Input 0 if your answer is zero.

	ended	ended
	£	£
Trading profits		
Interest		
Chargeable gain		
Qualifying charitable donation		
Taxable total profits		

6   P Ltd had taxable total profits of £255,000 for its six month accounting period to 31 March 2017.

Its corporation tax liability for the period will be:

£	

7   J Ltd had taxable total profits of £490,000 in the year ended 31 December 2016.

The corporation tax liability for the year is:

£	

8   **Decide whether the following statement is true or false.**

Financial Year 2016 (FY16) begins on 1 April 2016 and ends on 31 March 2017.

Tick ONE box.

	✓
True	
False	

Taxing unincorporated businesses

Learning outcomes

1.2	Identify the correct basis period for each tax year
	• Identify the basis periods using opening year and closing year rules
	• Determine overlap periods and overlap profits
	• Explain the effect on the basis period of a change in accounting date

Assessment context

Basis period rules are highly examinable and need a lot of practice to ensure you are familiar with the different rules that apply in each circumstance.

Qualification context

You will not see these areas again in your studies.

Business context

Taxpayers need to know which fiscal year their profits fall into so they can determine when their tax is due. These rules will often influence when a taxpayer chooses to have his accounting period end.

Chapter overview

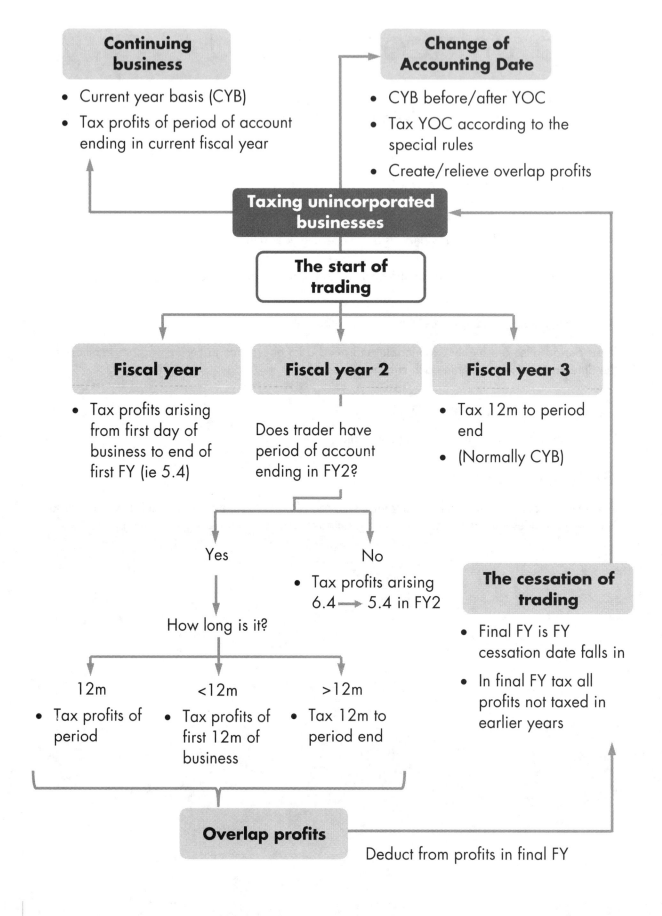

Continuing business

- Current year basis (CYB)
- Tax profits of period of account ending in current fiscal year

Change of Accounting Date

- CYB before/after YOC
- Tax YOC according to the special rules
- Create/relieve overlap profits

Taxing unincorporated businesses

The start of trading

Fiscal year

- Tax profits arising from first day of business to end of first FY (ie 5.4)

Fiscal year 2

Does trader have period of account ending in FY2?

Fiscal year 3

- Tax 12m to period end
- (Normally CYB)

Yes

How long is it?

12m
- Tax profits of period

<12m
- Tax profits of first 12m of business

>12m
- Tax 12m to period end

No
- Tax profits arising 6.4 → 5.4 in FY2

The cessation of trading

- Final FY is FY cessation date falls in
- In final FY tax all profits not taxed in earlier years

Overlap profits

Deduct from profits in final FY

1 Introduction

This chapter will concentrate on computing the figure to insert as **trading profit** in the income tax computation. These rules apply to unincorporated businesses only (ie individuals in business – sole traders and partners, **not** companies).

A sole trader/partnership may make up their accounts for any period they choose. As we have seen in earlier chapters, we use their accounting period as the basis for our adjustment of profit and capital allowances calculations.

However, income tax is calculated with reference to the **fiscal year** (also referred to as the **tax year** or **year of assessment**) (6 April to 5 April).

1.1 Basis periods

A mechanism is needed to link the **taxable trading profits** (as adjusted for tax purposes and after the deduction of capital allowances) to a tax year. This mechanism is known as the **basis of assessment**, and the period whose profits are assessed in a tax year is called the **basis period**.

1.2 Current year basis

The basis of assessment for a **continuing business** is the **12-month period** of account **ending** in a tax year. The profits resulting from those accounts are taxed in that tax year. This is known as the **current year basis of assessment**.

A sole-trader who has been in business for several years and has prepared accounts for the year to 31 May each year will include **all** of the profits in the year ended 31 May 2015 in the tax return for 2015/16 because that is the tax year that the period of account ends in. Likewise all of the profits from the year ended 31 May 2016 will be included in the tax return for 2016/17.

Activity 1: Current year basis (i)

A trader prepares accounts to 31 December each year.

Required

Which year's profits will be assessed in 2016/17?

[▼]

Picklist:

Period 6 April 2016 – 5 April 2017
Year ended 31 December 2015
Year ended 31 December 2016
Year ended 31 December 2017

Activity 2: Current year basis (ii)

Required

(a) Which fiscal year would the profits of year ended 30 June 2016 be taxed in?

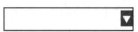

Picklist:

2015/16
2016/17

Required

(b) Which fiscal year would the profits of year ended 31 January 2017 be taxed in?

Picklist:

2015/16
2016/17

2 The start of trading

On commencement of trade, the trader might not make up his first set of accounts for a 12-month period, therefore **special rules are needed to find the basis period in the first three tax years of a new business**. These rules always apply, even if the first set of accounts is for a 12-month period.

2.1 The first fiscal year

The tax year in which an unincorporated business starts is the first tax year in which the profits will be taxed.

The profits are taxed on an actual basis in the first year, ie the profits accruing from the start date until the next 5 April. So if a trader starts to trade on 1 December 2016 and draws up accounts to 30 June 2017 making adjusted profits of £7,000, the first fiscal year is 2016/17 because that is the tax year they start their trade. In 2016/17 the basis period will be the data of commencement to the following 5 April, ie. 1 December 2016 to 5 April 2017. Working to the nearest month the profits made in that basis period is £7,000 × $\frac{4}{7}$ = £4,000.

Activity 3: The first fiscal year

Christian starts trading on 1 January 2015. In the y/e 31 December 2015 he makes profits of £24,000.

Required

What is the first fiscal year of the trade? (XXXX/XX format)

What profits will be assessed in the first fiscal year?

£	

2.2 The second fiscal year

Finding the basis period for the second tax year is tricky, because there are four possibilities:

(a) If the period of account that ends in the second tax year is 12 months, tax the whole 12 months.

(b) If there is a period of account that ends in the second tax year, but it is less than 12 months, the basis period that must be used is the first 12 months of trading (ie increase the period to 12 months).

(c) If there is a period of account that ends in the second tax year, but is longer than 12 months, the basis period that must be used is the 12 months leading up to the end of that period of account (ie reduce the period to 12 months).

(d) If there is no period of account that ends in the second tax year, because the first period of account is a very long one which does not end until a date in the third tax year, the basis period that must be used for the second tax year is the tax year itself (from 6 April to 5 April).

Illustration 1: Opening year rules – second fiscal year

Length of accounting period ending in second tax year	Taxed in second tax year
• 12 months	CYB (ie 12m period ending in fiscal year)
• <12 months	First 12 months of profits
• >12 months	12m to normal accounting year end
• No accounting period	**Actual basis** (ie 6.4 – 5.4)

The following flowchart may help you.

Illustration 2: Opening years – second fiscal year flowchart summary

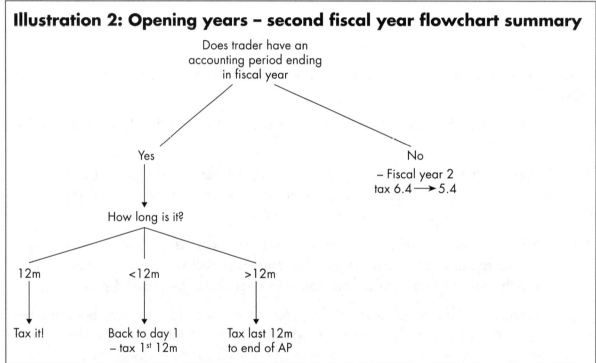

Activity 4: The second fiscal year (trader has 12-month accounting period)

Christian starts trading on 1 January 2015. In the y/e 31 December 2015 he makes profits of £24,000.

Required

What is the second fiscal year of the trade? (XXXX/XX format)

> [   ]

What profits will be assessed in the second fiscal year?

> £ [   ]

2.3 Overlap profits

You may have noticed in the previous example that some profits were taxed twice. This is a side effect of the opening year rules.

These profits are called **overlap profits**.

We will see shortly that overlap profits are deducted from profits in the trader's final fiscal year ensuring that, over the life of the business, all profits are only taxed once.

Overlap profits arise because HM Revenue & Customs (HMRC) would like all traders to have a 5 April year end.

If 5 April is selected as the year end then no overlap profits can arise. This is a clear incentive for taxpayers to follow HMRC's wishes!

Activity 5: Overlap profits

Christian starts trading on 1 January 2015. In the y/e 31 December 2015 he makes profits of £24,000.

In his first fiscal year 2014/15 he is taxed on profits from 1 January 2015 to 5 April 2015 ie £6,000.

In his second fiscal year 2015/16 he is taxed on profits from 1 January 2015 to 31 December 2015 ie £24,000.

Required

His overlap period is (XX/XX/XX) [   ] **to** [   ].

His overlap profits are £ [   ].

2.4 The third fiscal year

Find the accounting period ending in this fiscal year and identify how long it is.

The rules here are:

Period of 12 months:

- Use current year basis (ie 12-month period ending in fiscal year)
- There will be no further overlap

Period > 12 months long:

- Tax profits generated in 12-month period leading to trader's period end
- Additional overlap generated

Activity 6: Opening year rules (short first period)

Linda starts trading on 1 January 2015. She decides on a 30 June year end and her results are:

	£
6m to 30/06/15	18,000
Y/e 30/06/16	48,000

Required

Complete the following table showing the results for the first three fiscal years of the business.

Solution

	Profits taxed			
	Fiscal year (XXXX/XX)	From (XX/XX/XX)	To (XX/XX/XX)	Amount taxed £
First fiscal year				
Second fiscal year				
Third fiscal year				
Overlap periods and profits				
First overlap period				
Second overlap period				
Total overlap				

Activity 7: Opening year rules (long first period ending in second fiscal year)

Peter begins trading on 1 July 2014. He decides on a December year end but draws up his first accounts to 31 December 2015.

He made £18,000 profits in the 18 months to 31 December 2015 and £30,000 in the 12 months to 31 December 2016.

Required

Complete the following table showing the results for the first three fiscal years of the business.

Solution

	Profits taxed			
	Fiscal year (XXXX/XX)	From (XX/XX/XX)	To (XX/XX/XX)	Amount taxed £
First fiscal year				
Second fiscal year				
Third fiscal year				
Overlap period and profits				

Activity 8: Opening year rules (long first period ending in third fiscal year)

Agnetha begins trading on 1 December 2014 and draws up her first accounts to 31 May 2016, her chosen year end. She makes £36,000 of profit in this period.

Required

Complete the following table showing the results for the first three fiscal years of the business.

Solution

	Profits taxed			
	Fiscal year (XXXX/XX)	**From (XX/XX/XX)**	**To (XX/XX/XX)**	**Amount taxed £**
First fiscal year				
Second fiscal year				
Third fiscal year				
Overlap period and profits				

3 The cessation of trading

The final year of assessment is the tax year that the date of cessation falls into. **The basis period for this final tax year normally runs from the end of the basis period for the previous tax year to the date of cessation.**

The previous (penultimate) year is a normal year, so we apply current year basis.

In the final year we tax all the profits arising since those taxed in the penultimate year.

We are allowed to deduct overlap profits from the profits taxed in the final fiscal year. This ensures all profits are only taxed once over the life of the business.

Exceptionally, if a trade starts and ceases in the same tax year, the basis period for that year is the whole lifespan of the trade. If the final year is the second year, the basis period runs from 6 April at the start of the second year to the date of cessation.

Activity 9: Closing year rules (one period ending in final fiscal year)

Albert, who has been trading for some years making up his accounts to 31 December, ceases to trade on 30 April 2016 with profits as follows:

	Adjusted profits after capital allowances £
Year to 31/12/15	22,000
Four months to 30/04/16	12,000

Overlap profits at the start of the business were £4,000.

Required

Complete the following table showing the results for the final two fiscal years of the business.

Solution

	Profits taxed			
	Fiscal year (XXXX/XX)	From (XX/XX/XX)	To (XX/XX/XX)	Amount taxed £
Penultimate fiscal year				
Final fiscal year				

Activity 10: Closing year rules (two periods ending in final fiscal year)

Royce ceases trading on 31 March 2017. His recent results have been as follows:

	£
Y/e 31 December 2015	30,000
Y/e 31 December 2016	25,000
P/e 31 March 2017	4,000

Overlap profits on commencement were £12,000.

Required

Complete the following table showing the results for the final two fiscal years of the business.

Solution

	Profits taxed			
	Fiscal year (XXXX/XX)	From (XX/XX/XX)	To (XX/XX/XX)	Amount taxed £
Penultimate fiscal year				
Final fiscal year				

4 Change of accounting date

4.1 Introduction

A trader may change the date to which they prepare their annual accounts for a variety of reasons. For example, they may wish to move to a calendar year end or to fit in with seasonal variations of their trade. Special rules normally apply for taxing basis periods when a trader changes their accounting date.

On a change of accounting date there may be:

- One set of accounts covering a period of less than 12 months;
- One set of accounts covering a period of more than 12 months;
- No accounts; or
- Two sets of accounts

ending in a tax year. In each case, the basis period for the year relates to the new accounting date.

The **steps** for dealing with a change of accounting date are:

1 Establish year of change (YOC) (ie. first year where CYB is not possible).

2 All years before YOC

   Basis period = 12 months to old year end.

3 All years after YOC

   Basis period = 12 months to new year end.

4   Year of change

Basis period = period missed (gap) between (2) and (3) with the following adjustments:

If 'gap' > 12m, tax the profits of the 'gap' but bring down to 12m by relieving overlap profits from commencement

If 'gap' < 12m, create overlap by taxing 12m period to the end of the gap.

5   Conditions

First accounts to new date must be ≤ 18 months long and HMRC must be notified by 31 January following year of change.

Not permitted if previous change of accounting date in last five years (unless genuine commercial reasons).

4.2 Short accounting period

When a change of accounting date results in one short period of account ending in a tax year, the basis period for that year is always the 12 months to the new accounting date.

Illustration 3: short accounting period

Sue prepares accounts to 31 December each year until she changes her accounting date to 30 June by preparing accounts for the 6 months to 30 June 2016.

There is one short period of account ending during 2016/17. This means the basis period for 2016/17 is the 12 months to 30 June 2016.

Sue's basis period for 2015/16 was the 12 months to 31 December 2015. This means the profits of the 6 months to 31 December 2015 are overlap profits that have been taxed twice. These overlap profits must be added to any overlap profits that arose when the business began. The total is either relieved when the business ceases or it is relieved on a subsequent change of accounting date.

Activity 11: Short accounting period

Harry makes up accounts to 31 August until changing to 31 May. His results are as follows:

	£
Y/e 31.8.15	20,000
9 months to 31.5.16	15,000
Y/e 31.5.17	30,000

Required

What are Harry's assessments for 2015/16, 2016/17, and 2017/18?

Solution

	£

4.3 One long period of account

When a change of accounting date results in one long period of account ending in a tax year, the basis period for that year ends on the new accounting date. It begins immediately after the basis period for the previous year ends. This means the basis period will exceed 12 months.

No overlap profits arise in this situation. However, more than 12 months' worth of profits are taxed in one income tax year and to compensate for this, relief is available for brought forward overlap profits. The overlap relief must reduce the number of months' worth of profits taxed in the year to no more than 12. So, if you have a 14 month basis period you can give relief for up to 2 months' worth of overlap profits.

Illustration 4: long period of account

Zoe started trading on 1 October 2013 and prepared accounts to 30 September until she changed her accounting date by preparing accounts for the 15 months to 31 December 2016. Her results were as follows.

Year to 30 September 2014	£24,000
Year to 30 September 2015	£48,000
Fifteen months to 31 December 2016	£75,000

Profits for the first three tax years of the business are:

2013/14 (1.10.13 – 5.4.14)	
6/12 × £24,000	£12,000
2014/15 (1.10.13 – 30.9.14)	£24,000
2015/16 (1.10.14 – 30.9.15)	£48,000

Overlap profits are £12,000. These arose in the 6 months to 5.4.14.

The change in accounting date results in one long period of account ending during 2016/17 which means the basis period for 2016/17 is the 15 months to 31 December 2016. 3 months' worth of the brought forward overlap profits can be relieved.

2016/17 (1.10.15 – 31.12.16)	75,000
Less overlap profits 3/6 × £12,000	(6,000)
	69,000

The unrelieved overlap profits of £6,000 (£12,000 – £6,000) are carried forward for relief either when the business ceases or on a further change of accounting date.

4.4 No accounting date ending in the year

If a change of accounting date results in there being no period of account ending in a tax year there is a potential problem because basis periods usually end on an accounting date. To get round this problem you must manufacture a basis period by taking the new accounting date and deducting one year. The basis period is then the 12 months to this date.

Illustration 5: No accounting date ending in the year

Anne had always prepared accounts to 31 March. She then changed her accounting date by preparing accounts for the thirteen months to 30 April 2016.

There is no period of account ending during 2015/16 so the basis period for this year is the manufactured basis period of the 12 months to 30 April 2015.

You've probably spotted that this produces an overlap with the previous basis period. The overlap period is the eleven months from 1 May 2014 to 31 March 2015. The overlap profits arising in this period are added to any other unrelieved overlap profits and are carried forward for future relief.

4.5 Two accounting dates ending in the year

When two periods of account end in a tax year, the basis period for the year ends on the new accounting date. It begins immediately following the previous basis period. This means that the basis period will exceed 12 months and overlap relief can be allowed to ensure that only 12 months worth of profits are assessed in the tax year.

Illustration 6 Two accounting dates ending in the year

Elizabeth prepared accounts to 30 September until 2016 when she changed her accounting date by preparing accounts for the six months to 31 March 2017.

The new accounting date is 31 March 2017. This is the end of the basis period for 2016/17. The basis period for 2015/16 ended on 30 September 2015. The 2016/17 basis period is therefore the 18 month period 1 October 2015 to 31 March 2017. Six months' worth of overlap profits can be relieved in this year.

Activity 12: Two accounting periods ending in the year

Zoe makes up accounts to 30 June until changing to 31 December. Her results are as follows:

	£
Y/e 30.6.15	25,000
Y/e 30.6.16	30,000
6 months to 31.12.16	15,000
Y/e 31.12.17	35,000

Zoe has nine months of overlap profits totalling £21,000.

Required

What are Zoe's assessments for 2015/16, 2016/17 and 2017/18?

Solution

	£

Assessment focus point

Please refer to the reference material at the end of this Course Book to see which elements of this chapter will be available to you as a pop-up window in the live assessment.

Chapter summary

- The profits of a 12-month period of account ending in a tax year are normally taxed in that tax year.

- In the first tax year, the basis period runs from the date the business starts to the following 5 April.

- There are three possibilities in the second tax year:

  - If a period of account of 12 months or more ends in the second tax year, the basis period for the second tax year is the 12 months to the end of that period of account.

  - If a period of account of less than 12 months ends in the second tax year, the basis period for the second tax year is the first 12 months from the start of trading.

  - If no period of account ends in the second tax year, the basis period for that year is 6 April to 5 April in the year.

- The basis period for the third tax year is the 12 months to the end of the period of account ending in that year.

- The basis period in the final tax year of a business runs from the end of the previous basis period to the date that the trade stops.

- When trade ceases overlap profits are deducted from the final tax year's taxable profits.

- When a trader changes their accounting date it may result in:

  - One set of accounts covering a period of less than 12 months;
  - One set of accounts covering a period of more than 12 months;
  - No accounts; or
  - Two sets of accounts, ending in the year of change.

- In each case, the basis period for the year relates to the new accounting date.

Keywords

- **Basis period:** The period whose profits are taxed in a tax year

- **Current year basis of assessment:** Taxes the 12-month period of account ending in that tax year

- **Overlap profits:** The profits that are taxed more than once when a business starts

- **Tax year**, **fiscal year** or **year of assessment:** The year from 6 April in one year to 5 April in the next year

1 Oliver starts to trade on 1 May 2016. He makes his first set of accounts up to 31 December 2016 and annually thereafter.

Fill in the following table setting out the basis periods for the first three tax years and the overlap period of profits.

Tax year	Basis period
Overlap profits	

2 **Identify whether the following statement is true or false.**

When the trade ceases, overlap profits are deducted from the final tax year's taxable profits.

	✓
True	
False	

3 Barlow stops trading on 31 December 2016 having been in business since January 2009. Previously he has always made accounts up to 31 May. Overlap profits on commencement were £10,000.

Results for the last few years (as adjusted for tax) are:

Period	Profits £
Period to 31.12.16	15,000
Year ended 31.5.16	25,000
Year ended 31.5.15	32,000
Year ended 31.5.14	18,000

Using the proforma layout provided, compute the taxable profits for the final three tax years of trading.

Tax year	Basis period	Taxable profits £

4   Amarjat started trading on 1 February 2016. He prepared his first accounts to 30 June 2017. Taxable profits for this 17 month period were £34,000.

Show the taxable profits for 2015/16, 2016/17 and 2017/18.

Tax year	Basis period	Taxable profits £

His overlap profits are:

£ _____

5   Susi started to trade on 1 December 2015. Her first accounts were prepared to 30 June 2016. Taxable profits for the first two periods of account were:

Period to 30 June 2016: £70,000

Year to 30 June 2017: £60,000

(a)   **Her taxable profits for 2015/16 are:**

£ _____

(b)   **Her taxable profits for 2016/17 are:**

£ _____

(c)   **Her taxable profits for 2017/18 are:**

£ _____

(d)   **Her overlap profits are:**

£ _____

6   Barbara has been trading for many years with an accounting date of 31 October. She has no overlap from commencement of trade. She recently decided to change her year end to 30 April and made her accounts to 30 April 2016. Her taxable profits were as follows:

Year to 31 October 2015 £80,000

Period ended 30 April 2016 £50,000

Year to 30 April 2017 £120,000

(a)   **Her taxable profits for 2015/16 are:**

£ _____

(b) Her taxable profits for 2016/17 are:

£ [   ]

(c) Her taxable profits for 2017/18 are:

£ [   ]

(d) Her overlap profits are:

£ [   ]

7 Stewart has always made accounts up to 31 July but in 2016 he decided to change his accounting date to 31 October and made up a 15 month set of accounts to 31 October 2016.

Results for the last few years (as adjusted for tax) are:

Period	Profits £
Year ended 31.7.15	15,000
Period to 31.10.16	25,000
Year ended 31.10.17	32,000

Overlap profits on commencement were £8,000 for 8 months.

(a) Using the proforma layout provided, compute the taxable profits for the three tax years from 2015/16 to 2017/18

(b) Overlap to carry forward:

£ [   ]

Partnerships

6

Learning outcomes

1.4	Analyse taxable profits and losses of a partnership between the partners
	• Apportion profits between a maximum of four partners • Determine the basis periods for continuing, new or departing partners • Allocate profits between the partners
1.6	Complete the individual and partnership tax returns relevant to sole-traders and partnerships
	• Accurately complete partnership tax returns

Assessment context

In the assessment you may be required to compute the split of partnership profits for new, continuing and leaving partners as well as the basis periods for the individual partners.

You may also be required to complete extracts from the partnership tax return.

Qualification context

You will have seen partnerships in your accounting studies so the basic treatment will not be a surprise to you. The tax treatment of partnerships is unique to this unit.

Business context

Partners need to know how much tax they owe to the government.

Chapter overview

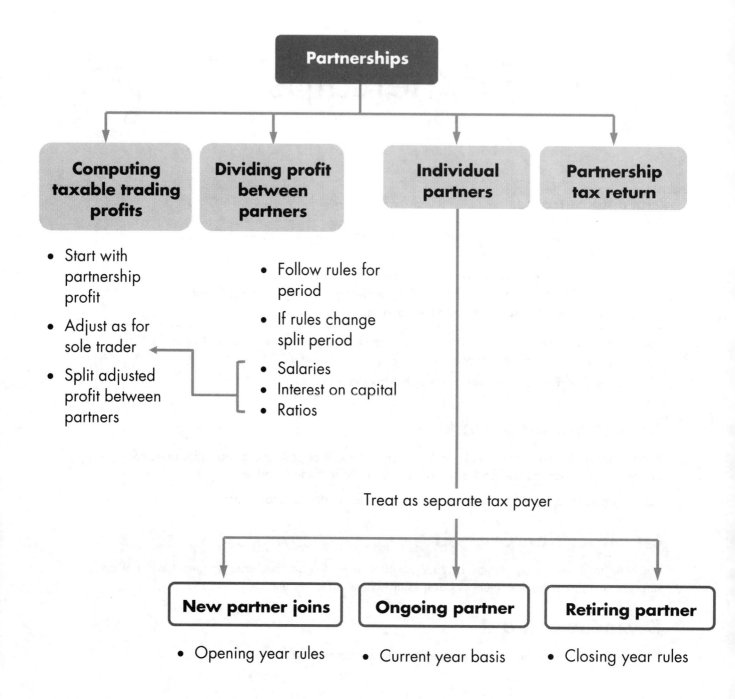

Partnerships

- **Computing taxable trading profits**
- **Dividing profit between partners**
- **Individual partners**
- **Partnership tax return**

Computing taxable trading profits

- Start with partnership profit
- Adjust as for sole trader
- Split adjusted profit between partners

Dividing profit between partners

- Follow rules for period
- If rules change split period
- Salaries
- Interest on capital
- Ratios

Individual partners

Treat as separate tax payer

- **New partner joins**
  - Opening year rules
- **Ongoing partner**
  - Current year basis
- **Retiring partner**
  - Closing year rules

1 Introduction

In this chapter we look at the profits of a partnership, how these profits are shown on the tax return and how these profits are split between the individual partners. We then go on to look at how the individual partners are taxed on their share of the profits.

2 Computing taxable trading profits of partnerships

A **partnership** is a group of self-employed people working together.

The partnership produces a statement of profit or loss for the whole business. Profits will be adjusted for tax purposes, and capital allowances will be calculated, in exactly the same way as for a self-employed sole trader. This means that you must add back disallowable items. You must deduct specifically deductible items that have not been deducted in the accounts (for example capital allowances) and also any income in the accounts that is not part of the taxable trading profit. Finally, add any amounts taxable as trading profits that have not been included in the accounts; for example, the market value of any goods taken for own use.

A particular point worth noting is that any partners' salaries or interest on capital deducted in the accounts must be added back when computing taxable trading profits of the partnership. These items are disallowable expenses because they are a form of drawings. They will be part of each partner's taxable trading profit as described below.

There is an additional stage here, though. The adjusted profits must be split between the partners.

Once profit has been split, each partner is treated as a sole trader and taxed separately.

3 Dividing taxable trading profits between partners

Once you have computed a partnership's taxable trading profit for a period of account, you must divide it between the partners concerned.

The partners may agree to share profits in any way they wish. The agreed division of profits will be set out in the partnership agreement and will always be stated for you in assessment tasks.

Method:

- First, allocate any salaries and interest on capital to the partners
- Second, share the residue of profits between the partners in the agreed ratio

Illustration 1: Dividing profit between the partners

Pearl and Ruby are in partnership. The partnership's taxable trading profits (as adjusted for tax purposes) for the year ended 31 March 2017 were £110,000. The partnership agreement provides for Pearl to be paid a salary of £20,000 per annum and for Ruby to be paid a salary of £30,000 per annum. Any remaining profits are divided between Pearl and Ruby in the ratio 2:1.

First allocate the partners' salaries and then divide the balance of the profit in accordance with the profit-sharing ratio:

	Total £	Pearl £	Ruby £
Salary	50,000	20,000	30,000
Profit (£110,000 – £30,000 – £20,000) 2:1	60,000	40,000	20,000
	110,000	60,000	50,000

Pearl has taxable profits of £60,000 and Ruby has taxable profits of £50,000 for the year ended 31 March 2017. These profits will be taxable in 2016/17.

Activity 1: Partnership profit allocation

Ron and Steve have been in partnership since 1 July 1996 sharing profits and losses as follows.

	Ron	Steve
Salary	5,000	Nil
Balance – profit-share ratio	3	2

During y/e 30 June 2016 the partnership made a trading profit of £60,000.

Required

Complete the table showing how the profits are allocated between the partners.

Solution

	Ron £	Steve £
Profit share		

Workings (not provided in the CBT)

	Ron £	Steve £	Total £

---

4 Change in profit-sharing agreement

Sometimes the profit-sharing agreement may change during a period of account.

Here we apportion the profit before and after the change. We then split the profits before the change using the old rules, and the profits after the change using the new rules.

Do not forget interest and salaries are annual figures so will need time apportioning.

> **Illustration 2: Change in partnership agreement**
>
> Jenny and Chris are in partnership. Taxable trading profits of the partnership for the year ended 31 March 2017 are £60,000. Until 30 September 2016 profits are shared equally. From 1 October 2016 Jenny and Chris agree that the profits should be shared in the ratio 2:1.
>
> Show how the taxable trading profits of the year to 31 March 2017 are divided between Jenny and Chris.
>
> Your first step should be to apportion the profits to the periods before and after the change in the profit-sharing ratio:
>
> 1.4.16 – 30.9.16   6/12 × £60,000 = £30,000
>
> 1.10.16 – 31.3.17   6/12 × £60,000 = £30,000
>
> Next divide these profits between the partners:
>
> | | Total £ | Jenny £ | Chris £ |
> |---|---|---|---|
> | 1.4.16 – 30.9.16 (1:1) | 30,000 | 15,000 | 15,000 |
> | 1.10.16 – 31.3.17 (2:1) | 30,000 | 20,000 | 10,000 |
> | | 60,000 | 35,000 | 25,000 |
>
> For the year to 31 March 2017, Jenny's taxable trading profits are £35,000 and Chris's taxable trading profits are £25,000.

Activity 2: Change in profit-sharing arrangements

During the next year, ended 30 June, the Ron and Steve partnership made profits of £90,000.

On 1 January the partners decided to change their profit-sharing arrangement.

The old arrangement had been:

	Ron	Steve
Salary	5,000	Nil
Balance – profit-share ratio	3	2

After the change both partners receive an equal share of all profits and no one receives a salary.

Required

Complete the table showing how the profits are allocated between the partners.

Solution

	Ron £	Steve £
Profit share		

Workings (not provided in the CBT)

5 The tax positions of individual partners

Once we have allocated profits between partners we treat each partner as an individual sole trader.

We follow normal current year basis, ie we tax each partner's profits in the fiscal year in which their period ends.

Note it is the actual accounting period end that is important when determining the fiscal year in which the profits are taxed. If we have split the period to allocate profit because of a change in profit-sharing arrangements we usually ignore the date of the split when deciding the fiscal year in which the profits will be taxed.

6 Changes in partners

A partnership may continue but individual partners may choose to leave while new partners may join.

If partners have joined or left the partnership they will have their own periods with different starting or finishing dates to ongoing partners.

It is important to identify the periods of each partner. We then apply the relevant tax rules:

- A new partner will be taxed using the opening year rules.
- An ongoing partner will be taxed using the current year basis.
- A retiring partner will be taxed using the closing year rules.

Illustration 3: Partner joining partnership

Francis and Caroline have been in partnership for many years, making up accounts to 31 December each year. Profits were shared equally until 1 June 2014, when Charles joined the partnership. From 1 June 2014 profits were shared in the ratio 2:2:1.

Profits adjusted for tax purposes are as follows.

Period	Taxable profit
	£
1.1.14 – 31.12.14	48,000
1.1.15 – 31.12.15	18,000
1.1.16 – 31.12.16	24,000

Show the taxable profits for each partner for 2014/15 to 2016/17.

We must first share the profits between the partners.

	Total £	Francis £	Caroline £	Charles £
Year ended 31.12.14				
1.1.14 – 31.5.14 (5/12)				
Profits 50:50	20,000	10,000	10,000	
1.6.14 – 31.12.14 (7/12)				
Profits 2:2:1	28,000	11,200	11,200	5,600
Total	48,000	21,200	21,200	5,600
Year ended 31.12.15				
Profits 2:2:1	18,000	7,200	7,200	3,600
Total for y/e 31.12.15	18,000	7,200	7,200	3,600
Year ended 31.12.16				
Profits 2:2:1	24,000	9,600	9,600	4,800
Total for y/e 31.12.16	24,000	9,600	9,600	4,800

The next stage is to work out the basis periods and hence the taxable profits for the partners in each tax year. The most important thing to remember at this stage is to **deal with each of the partners separately**.

Francis and Caroline are taxed on the current year basis of assessment throughout.

Year	Basis period	Francis £	Caroline £
2014/15	1.1.14 – 31.12.14	21,200	21,200
2015/16	1.1.15 – 31.12.15	7,200	7,200
2016/17	1.1.16 – 31.12.16	9,600	9,600

Charles joins the partnership on 1 June 2014, which falls in tax year 2014/15, so the opening year rules apply to him from 2014/15.

Year	Basis period	Working	Taxable profits £
2014/15	1.6.14 – 5.4.15	£5,600 + 3/12 × £3,600	6,500
2015/16	1.1.15 – 31.12.15		3,600
2016/17	1.1.16 – 31.12.16		4,800

Charles has overlap profits of £900 (£3,600 × 3/12) to carry forward and relieve in the tax year in which he leaves the partnership.

Illustration 4: Partner leaving a partnership

Dominic, Sebastian and India have traded in partnership, sharing profits equally for many years. On 1 May 2016 India left the partnership. Profits continue to be shared equally. Accounts have always been prepared to 30 September and recent results have been:

	Profit £
Y/e 30.9.14	36,000
Y/e 30.9.15	81,000
Y/e 30.9.16	60,000

Each of the partners had overlap profits of £10,000 on commencement of the business. Show the taxable trading profits of each partner for 2014/15 to 2016/17.

Firstly allocate the profits of each period of account to the partners.

	Total £	Dominic £	Sebastian £	India £
Y/e 30.9.14	36,000	12,000	12,000	12,000
Y/e 30.9.15	81,000	27,000	27,000	27,000
Y/e 30.9.16				
1.10.15 – 30.4.16 (7/12)	35,000	11,667	11,667	11,666
1.5.16 – 30.9.16 (5/12)	25,000	12,500	12,500	–
	60,000	24,167	24,167	11,666

Dominic and Sebastian are taxed on the current year basis of assessment throughout:

	Dominic £	Sebastian £
2014/15 (y/e 30.9.14)	12,000	12,000
2015/16 (y/e 30.9.15)	27,000	27,000
2016/17 (y/e 30.9.16)	24,167	24,167

India is treated as ceasing to trade in 2016/17.

	£
2014/15 (y/e 30.9.14)	12,000
2015/16 (y/e 30.9.15)	27,000
2016/17 (p/e 30.4.16 less overlap profits)	
(£11,666 – £10,000)	1,666

Activity 3: Change in partnership personnel

M and G began a partnership on 1 June 2004, sharing profits and losses equally. On 1 December 2014 G retired and B joined them, the new arrangement being 2:1. Results have been as follows:

	£
Y/e 31.5.14	33,000
Y/e 31.5.15	51,000
Y/e 31.5.16	72,000

G's overlap profits were £5,000.

Required

Complete the following table showing the assessments on the partners for the tax years 2014/15 to 2016/17. If a partner has no taxable profit, show '0'. Identify B's overlap.

Solution

	M £	G £	B £
2014/15			
2015/16			
2016/17			
Overlap			

7 Partnership tax return

Familiarise yourself with the tax return; you may need to complete it in the CBT.

The following includes Ron's data from Activity 1: Partnership profit allocation

PARTNERSHIP STATEMENT (SHORT) for the year ended 5 April 2017

Please read these instructions before completing the Statement

Use these pages to allocate partnership income if the only income for the relevant return period was trading and professional income or taxed interest and alternative finance receipts from banks and building societies. Otherwise you must download or ask the SA Orderline for the 'Partnership Statement (Full)' pages to record details of the allocation of all the partnership income. Go to www.gov.uk/self-assessment-forms-and-helpsheets

Step 1 Fill in boxes 1 to 29 and boxes A and B as appropriate. Get the figures you need from the relevant boxes in the Partnership Tax Return. Complete a separate Statement for each accounting period covered by this Partnership Tax Return and for each trade or profession carried on by the partnership.

Step 2 Then allocate the amounts in boxes 11 to 29 attributable to each partner using the allocation columns on this page and page 7, read the Partnership Tax Return Guide, go to www.gov.uk/self-assessment-forms-and-helpsheets If the partnership has more than 3 partners, please photocopy page 7.

Step 3 Each partner will need a copy of their allocation of income to fill in their personal tax return.

PARTNERSHIP INFORMATION
If the partnership business includes a trade or profession, enter here the accounting period for which appropriate items in this statement are returned.

Start **1** 1 / 7 / 16

End **2** 30 / 6 / 17

Nature of trade **3**

MIXED PARTNERSHIPS

Tick here if this Statement is drawn up using Corporation Tax rules **4**

Tick here if this Statement is drawn up using tax rules for non-residents **5**

Individual partner details

6 Name of partner Ron

Address

Postcode

Date appointed as a partner (if during 2014–15 or 2015–16)

7 / /

Date ceased to be a partner (if during 2014–15 or 2015–16)

9 / /

Partner's Unique Taxpayer Reference (UTR)

8

Partner's National Insurance number

10

Partnership's profits, losses, income, tax credits, etc

Tick this box if the items entered in the box had foreign tax taken off

Partner's share profits, losses, income, tax credits, etc

Copy figures in boxes 11 to 29 to boxes in the individual's **Partnership (short)** pages as shown below

for an accounting period ended in 2016–17

from box 3.83 Profit from a trade or profession **A**	**11** £ 60,000	Profit **11** £ 38,000	Copy this figure to box 8
from box 3.82 Adjustment on change of basis	**11A** £	**11A** £	Copy this figure to box 10
from box 3.84 Loss from a trade or profession **B**	**12** £	Loss **12** £	Copy this figure to box 8
from box 10.4 Business Premises Renovation Allowance	**12A** £	**12A** £	Copy this figure to box 15

for the period 6 April 2016 to 5 April 2017*

from box 7.9A UK taxed interest and taxed alternative finance receipts	**22** £	**22** £	Copy this figure to box 28
from box 3.97 CIS deductions made by contractors on account of tax	**24** £	**24** £	Copy this figure to box 30
from box 3.98 Other tax taken off trading income	**24A** £	**24A** £	Copy this figure to box 31
from box 7.8A Income Tax taken off	**25** £	**25** £	Copy this figure to box 29
from box 3.117 Partnership charges	**29** £	**29** £	Copy this figure to box 4, 'Other tax reliefs' section on page Ai 2 in your personal tax return

* if you are a 'CT Partnership' see the Partnership Tax Return Guide

SA800 2016   PARTNERSHIP TAX RETURN: PAGE 6

(Adapted from HMRC, 2016)

Assessment focus point

Please refer to the reference material at the end of this Course Book to see which elements of this chapter will be available to you as a pop-up in the live assessment.

Chapter summary

- A partnership is a group of self-employed individuals trading together.

- Calculate tax-adjusted profits for a partnership in the same way as you would calculate the tax-adjusted profits of a sole trader.

- Divide the tax-adjusted profits of a period of account between the partners in accordance with their profit-sharing arrangements during the period of account.

- If profit-sharing arrangements change during a period of account, time apportion profits to the periods before and after the change before allocating them to partners.

- Once you have found a partner's profit for a period of account you can consider which tax year that profit is taxed in. A continuing partner in a continuing business is taxed using the current year basis of assessment.

- The opening year rules apply to a partner joining the partnership. The closing year rules apply to a partner leaving the partnership.

Keywords

- **Partnership:** A group of self-employed individuals trading together

Test your learning

1   **The adjusted profit of a partnership is divided between the partners in accordance with the profit-sharing agreement in existence during what period? Tick ONE box.**

	✓
The calendar year	
The tax year	
The period of account concerned	
The period agreed by the partners	

2   Dave and Joe are in partnership together and make a profit of £18,000 for the year to 31 December 2016. Up to 30 September 2016 they share profits and losses equally but thereafter they share 3:2.

Dave's taxable profits for 2016/17 are:

£

and Joe's taxable profits for 2016/17 are:

£

3   Holly and Jasmine are in partnership sharing profits equally after paying a salary of £5,000 to Holly and a salary of £80,000 to Jasmine. Taxable profits for the year to 31 March 2017 were £200,000.

Using the proforma layout provided, show the taxable profits of each of the partners for the year.

	Total £	Holly £	Jasmine £
Salary			
Division of profits			

4   Barry and Steve have been in partnership for many years. Profits are shared three-quarters to Barry and one-quarter to Steve. For the year ended 31 March 2016, the partnership made a profit of £60,000 and for the year ended 31 March 2017 the profit was £80,000.

The profit taxable on Steve for 2016/17 is:

Tick ONE box.

	✓
£60,000	
£15,000	
£45,000	
£20,000	

5   Abdul and Ghita have been in partnership for many years. On 1 September 2016, Sase joins the partnership and profits are shared between the partners in the ratio 2:2:1 with Sase receiving the smallest profit share. For the year to 31 August 2017, the partnership makes a profit of £120,000.

The profits assessable on Sase in 2016/17 are:

£

The profits assessable on Sase in 2017/18 are:

£

The overlap profits arising for Sase are:

£

6   William, Ann and John have been in partnership for many years sharing profits equally. Accounts have always been prepared to 31 October each year. All partners had overlap profits of £5,000 on commencement. On 31 December 2016 William left the partnership. Profits continued to be shared equally. Recent results were:

	£
Y/e 31 October 2015	21,000
Y/e 31 October 2016	33,000
Y/e 31 October 2017	36,000

(a) Using the proforma layout provided, show how the profits of each period will be divided between the partners.

	Total £	William £	Ann £	John £
Y/e 31.10.14				
Y/e 31.10.15				
Y/e 31.10.16				

(b) Using the proforma layout provided, show the taxable profits for each partner for 2015/16 to 2017/18.

	William £	Ann £	John £

National insurance

Learning outcomes

1.5	Calculate the NI contributions payable by self-employed taxpayers
	• Determine who is liable to pay NI contributions
	• Calculate NI contributions

Assessment context

National insurance calculations are simple and straightforward and should earn you easy marks in the assessment.

Qualification context

You will not see these rules in detail outside of this unit.

Business context

These taxes are a significant extra cost for self-employed people.

Chapter overview

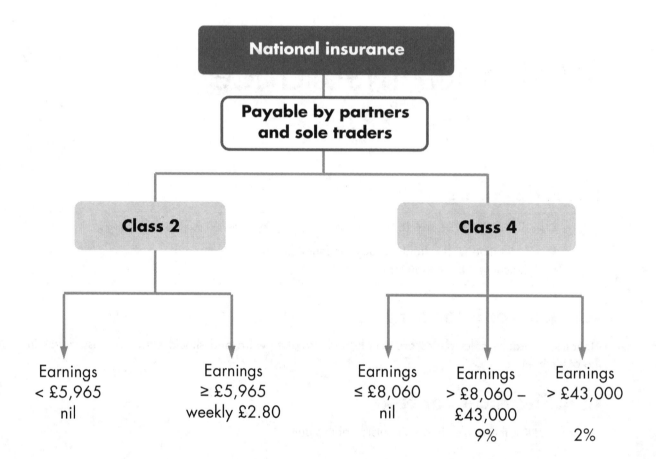

National insurance

Payable by partners and sole traders

Class 2

Earnings
< £5,965
nil

Earnings
≥ £5,965
weekly £2.80

Class 4

Earnings
≤ £8,060
nil

Earnings
> £8,060 –
£43,000
9%

Earnings
> £43,000

2%

1 Introduction

Paying National Insurance Contributions (NICs) builds up an individual's entitlement to certain state benefits, such as pensions.

In the *Business Tax* assessment, you will only need to be aware of the NICs payable by the self-employed.

2 NICs payable by the self-employed

Self-employed people (ie partners and sole traders) must pay two types of NIC:

- **Class 2 contributions**
- **Class 4 contributions**

2.1 Class 2 contribution

Formula provided

This is payable at a flat rate of £2.80 per week.

From 6 April 2015 the amount of Class 2 contributions due are determined at the end of each tax year and are based on the number of weeks of self-employment in that year. This will then be collected through the self-assessment system, along with income tax and Class 4 contributions.

No contributions are due if trading profits for the year are less than the Small Profits Threshold of £5,965.

2.2 Class 4 contribution

Formula provided

This is payable in addition to Class 2.

Class 4 contributions are based on the level of the individual's trading profits after loss relief for a fiscal year.

They are calculated as:

- 9% of 'profits' between the lower earnings limit (LEL) of £8,060 and the upper earnings limit (UEL) of £43,000
- 2% of 'profits' above the UEL of £43,000

Activity 1: National insurance contributions

Note. You should calculate the following to pounds and pence.

(a) Mr Bull, a trader, has trading income of £14,000 for 2016/17.

    Required

    His Class 2 NI contributions for the year are:

    £ [   ]

    His Class 4 NI contributions at 9% are:

    £ [   ]

(b) Mr Seye, a trader, has trading income of £48,000 in 2016/17.

    Required

    His Class 4 NI contributions at 9% are:

    £ [   ]

    His Class 4 NI contributions at 2% are:

    £ [   ]

Assessment focus point

Please refer to the tax tables and reference material at the end of this Course Book to see which elements of this chapter will be available to you as a pop-up window in the live assessment.

Chapter summary

- Self-employed traders pay:
  - Class 2 contributions at a flat rate per week of £2.80 (in 2016/17), and
  - Class 4 contributions based on the level of their profits.
- Main rate Class 4 NICs are 9% of profits between the UEL and LEL.
- Additional Class 4 NICs are 2% of profits above the UEL.

- **Class 2 contributions:** Flat rate contributions payable by the self-employed
- **Class 4 contributions:** Profit-related contributions payable by the self-employed

Test your learning

Compute the following total sole traders' liabilities to NICs for 2016/17.

Note. You should calculate the following to pounds and pence.

1 **Acker**

   Taxable trading profits   £5,050

£		.	

2 **Bailey**

   Taxable trading profits   £50,000

£		.	

3 **Cartwright**

   Taxable trading profits   £10,850

£		.	

Losses 8

4.1	**Appraise the effective use of trading losses**
	• Assess and calculate available loss relief
	• Advise on the best use of a trading loss for sole traders, partnerships and limited companies

Assessment context

Questions could focus on the rules for sole traders, partners or limited companies so ensure you read the question carefully as the rules for companies are different to the rules for sole traders and partners.

Qualification context

You will not see these rules outside of this unit.

Business context

Using loss relief to generate a tax repayment is often a lifeline for struggling businesses.

Chapter overview

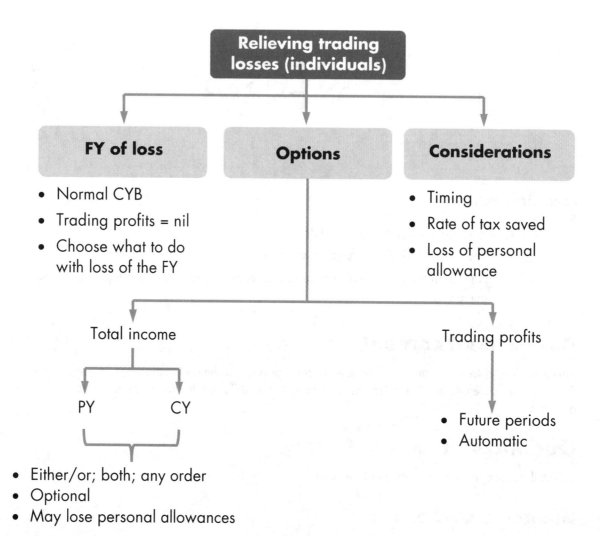

Relieving trading losses (individuals)

FY of loss

- Normal CYB
- Trading profits = nil
- Choose what to do with loss of the FY

Options

Total income

- PY
- CY

- Either/or; both; any order
- Optional
- May lose personal allowances

Trading profits

- Future periods
- Automatic

Considerations

- Timing
- Rate of tax saved
- Loss of personal allowance

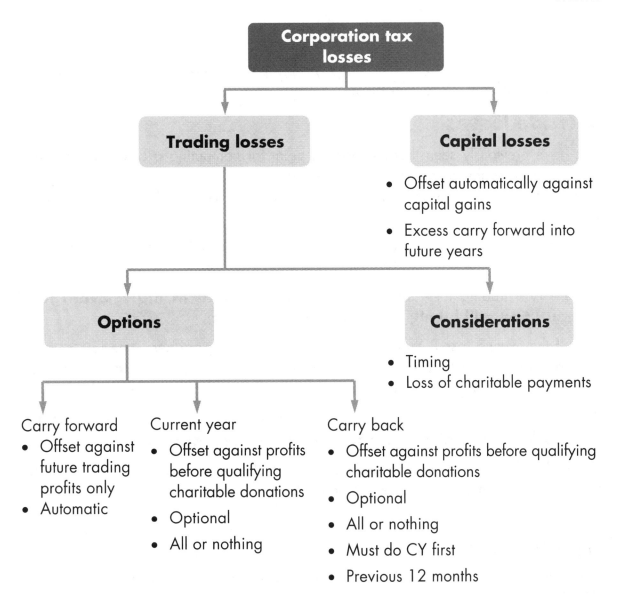

Corporation tax losses

Trading losses

Capital losses
- Offset automatically against capital gains
- Excess carry forward into future years

Options

Considerations
- Timing
- Loss of charitable payments

Carry forward
- Offset against future trading profits only
- Automatic

Current year
- Offset against profits before qualifying charitable donations
- Optional
- All or nothing

Carry back
- Offset against profits before qualifying charitable donations
- Optional
- All or nothing
- Must do CY first
- Previous 12 months

1 Introduction

Not all businesses make profits every year. In this chapter we will see how a business can obtain tax relief for losses.

2 Trade losses

We have previously seen that the starting point for computing a business's trading results is to take the statement of profit or loss and adjust it for tax purposes. If this adjusted figure is negative then there is a **trading loss**, rather than a taxable profit.

Note that the deduction of capital allowances can actually increase an adjusted loss, or even turn an adjusted profit into a trading loss.

If there is a trading loss, the **taxable trading figure in the relevant tax computation will be nil**; it is not the negative amount.

(a)   If the trading loss is that of an individual (including partners), the loss will be allocated to a **tax year** using the basis period rules, and the **trading profit for that tax year will be nil**.

(b)   If the trading loss is incurred by a limited company in an **accounting period**, the **trading profit for that accounting period will be nil**.

Note. Losses in a partnership are allocated to the partners in the same way as profits. Each partner will then decide on the best method of relief for his share of the loss.

> **Illustration 1: How it works**
>
> If a trader makes a loss of £5,000 in the year to 31 December 2016, the **2016/17** taxable profits based on that period will be **£nil**.
>
> There will be a trading loss in **2016/17** of £5,000.
>
> The taxpayer has a choice as to how this loss is relieved, as follows:
>
> - Carry forward of losses against future trading income
> - Losses set against income in the tax year of the loss (current year CY)
> - Losses set against income of the previous tax year (prior year PY)
> - Losses set against capital gains

3 Trading loss relief options for individuals

3.1 Losses set against profits of the same trade

If no claim is made against total income (see below) or some of the loss is left after such a claim, then the balance must be relieved against profits of the same trade.

The loss is relieved against the first available future profits of the same trade.

Set-off is automatic and compulsory.

Any unrelieved loss may be carried forward indefinitely.

3.2 Losses set against total income

The loss is available for set-off against total income of:

- The fiscal year in which the loss-making accounting period ends (**year of the loss**); and/or

- The fiscal year immediately preceding the year of the loss.

A taxpayer does not have to deduct a loss under either method if he does not wish to do so. If he does wish to make either of these deductions he would need to make a claim to do so.

If a claim is made, the maximum possible loss must be set off in that year (ie personal allowances cannot be saved). The taxpayer can choose which year to use the loss first eg current year and then preceding year or vice versa. Any loss left must be carried forward for use against first available profits of the same trade.

Claims to carry the loss forward must be made by 31 January, 22 months following the end of the tax year of the loss.

Illustration 2: Inclusion in the income tax computation

	Non-savings £
Trading income	X
Relief against profits of the same trade	**(X)**
	X
Savings income	X
Rental income	X
Total income	X
Relief against total income	**(X)**
Net income	X
PA	(X)
Taxable income	X

Illustration 3: Loss relief

Ahmed, a sole trader, has the following taxable trading profits/(loss):

	£
Year to 30 September 2015 (and so taxed in 2015/16)	10,000
Year to 30 September 2016 (loss, trading profits = nil in 2016/17)	(49,000)
Year to 30 September 2017 (and so taxed in 2017/18)	20,000

His only other income is rental income of £15,000 a year.

The loss of £49,000 is a loss of **2016/17** and could be deducted from:

- **Total income of £25,000** (trading income of £10,000 + rental income of £15,000) in 2015/16

- **Total income** (rental income) of £15,000 in **2016/17**

If both of these claims are made, the loss remaining unrelieved of £9,000 is automatically deducted from the **taxable trading profits** of £20,000 arising in **2017/18**.

Claiming to relieve the loss against total income of the current year and the prior year is optional. If he chooses not to make a claim to deduct the loss from total income, the loss is carried forward to deduct from taxable trading profits in future years.

The disadvantage of deducting a loss from total income in the year of the loss and/or in the preceding year is that **personal allowances may be wasted**. You will recall that every individual has a personal allowance that he can set against his net income. Income of up to the personal allowance is effectively tax-free income, so there is no benefit if the net income is reduced to an amount lower than the personal allowance.

Activity 1: Income tax trading loss options

Edward runs a gift card shop and his recent actual and budgeted trading results are as follows.

Year ended	£
31.12.14	5,000
31.12.15	(8,000)
31.12.16	20,000

He also receives £12,000 rental income per annum.

Required

Show if the following statements are true or false by ticking the correct box for each.

	True ✓	False ✓
Edward may offset the loss against total income in 2014/15 and then in 2013/14.		
Edward may offset the loss against total income in 2016/17.		
Edward may offset the loss against trading income only in 2014/15.		
Edward may offset the loss against the rental income in 2015/16.		

Activity 2: Utilisation of income tax losses

Pike commenced trading on 1 October 1999, making up his accounts to 30 September 2000 and annually thereafter. His recent actual and budgeted results are as follows:

Year ended	£
30.9.13	2,000
30.9.14	(15,000)
30.9.15	8,000
30.9.16	4,000

He has received rental income as follows:

	£
2013/14	400
2014/15	1,000
2015/16	1,000
2016/17	1,000

(a) Required

Complete the following table showing Pike's total income for 2013/14 to 2016/17 assuming maximum and earliest claims against total income are made. Enter '0' in cells as appropriate.

Solution

	2013/14 £	2014/15 £	2015/16 £	2016/17 £
Trading income				
Loss carried forward				
Property income				
CY loss relief				
PY loss relief				
Net income				

(b) Required

Show if the following statement is true or false by ticking the correct box.

	True ✓	False ✓
Pike has used his loss in the most tax-efficient way possible		

3.3 Relief against capital gains tax

If an individual has used **trading losses** in a tax year (current or prior year) to take their net income down to nil they can then choose to make a further claim to use remaining losses against their capital gains for that year.

The claim is all or nothing so, if possible, the taxpayer must reduce the capital gains to nil.

The claim is deducted before the annual exempt amount (the capital gains tax equivalent of personal allowance), so this may be wasted if the claim is made.

An illustration is shown here for completeness but you should revisit this section after you have studied capital gains tax. .

Illustration 4: Loss relief against capital gains

Guy has the following results for 2016/17:

	2016/17 £
Trading loss	27,000
Total income	19,500
Capital gains less current year capital losses	14,000
Annual exempt amount	11,100

The loss would be relieved against income and gains as follows:

Income tax computation 2016/17	£
Total income	19,500
Less current year loss relief	(19,500)
Net income	0
Personal allowance (wasted)	

Capital gains tax computation 2016/17	£
Current year gains less current year losses	14,000
Less relief for trading loss (27,000 – 19,500)	(7,500)
Chargeable gain	6,500
Annual exempt amount (partly wasted)	(6,500)
Taxable gain	0

4 Corporation tax losses

As we mentioned above, if the trading loss is incurred by a limited company in an **accounting period**, the trading profit for that accounting period will be nil.

You need to be aware of the following three methods by which a company may obtain relief for its trading losses:

(a) Carry forward against future trading profits (automatic)
(b) Set off against current profits (optional)
(c) Carry back against earlier profits (optional)

You will also need to be aware of the impact which losses can have on qualifying charitable donations. This is included within examples and tasks below.

We will look at each of the three methods of obtaining loss relief. These are similar to the rules for individuals but there are some significant differences.

4.1 Relief against future trading income

A trading loss may be carried forward against profits from the same trade in future accounting periods.

This relief is called **carry forward loss relief**. The loss may be carried forward indefinitely.

The relief is automatic and is the default option if no other form of relief is chosen or there are losses left over after other reliefs have been taken.

Illustration 5: Carry forward loss relief

P Ltd has the following results for the three years to 31 March 2017:

	Year ended 31 March		
	2015 £	2016 £	2017 £
Trading profit/(loss)	(8,000)	3,000	6,000
Bank interest	0	4,000	2,000

Carry forward loss relief would be relieved as follows:

	Year ended 31 March		
	2015 £	2016 £	2017 £
Trading profit	0	3,000	6,000
Less carry forward loss relief	–	(3,000) (i)	(5,000) (ii)
Bank interest	–	4,000	2,000
Taxable total profits	0	4,000	3,000

Note. The carried forward loss is set against the trading profits only in future years. It cannot be set against other income such as the bank interest.

Activity 3: Carry forward loss relief

Strontium Lining Ltd has the following actual and budgeted results for the three years to 31 December 2016.

	Year ended 31 December		
	2014 £	2015 £	2016 £
Trading profit/(loss)	(20,000)	5,000	6,000
Property income	–	2,000	2,000

Required

The loss carried forward at 31 December 2016 is:

£ _____

4.2 Relief against total profits

4.2.1 Current year loss relief

The loss may be relieved against total profits (including gains) before qualifying charitable donations in the period in which the loss arose.

The loss relief is 'all or nothing' so any qualifying charitable donations that become unrelieved are lost.

4.2.2 Carry back loss relief

Trading losses can be carried back against total profits (including gains) before qualifying charitable donations of the preceding 12 months.

The carry back claim may only be made **after** a current year claim (note that this is different to the rules for individuals).

This claim is also all or nothing and any qualifying charitable donations which become unrelieved are lost.

Any loss remaining unrelieved after current period and carry back loss relief claims **must be carried forward and set against future profits of the same trade** under carry forward loss relief.

Activity 4: Current year and carry back relief

Kay Ltd has the following actual and budgeted results.

	Year ended 31 December		
	2014 £	2015 £	2016 £
Trading income	20,000	10,000	(100,000)
Capital gains	50,000	50,000	50,000

Required

Show if the following statements are true or false by ticking the correct box for each.

	True ✓	False ✓
Kay Ltd may choose to offset the loss against total profits in 2015 only.		
If Kay Ltd makes the maximum permissible claims it will have £90,000 loss to carry forward at 2016.		
Kay Ltd may offset the loss against total profits in 2015 and then against total profits in 2016.		
Kay Ltd may choose to offset the loss against total profits in 2016 only.		

A company is permitted to carry back the loss for 12 months. If the loss is carried back to an accounting period that partly falls outside the permitted carry back period, then the results of this period must be time apportioned to determine how much of the profits may be relieved.

Activity 5: Comprehensive example

Janet plc has the following actual and budgeted results.

	Y/e 30.6.14 £	P/e 31.12.14 £	Y/e 31.12.15 £	Y/e 31.12.16 £
Trading income	20,000	30,000	(155,000)	15,000
Investment income	10,000	10,000	10,000	10,000
Qualifying charitable payments	(5,000)	(5,000)	(5,000)	(5,000)

Required

Complete the following table assuming the company will make the maximum permissible claims. Use the picklist for narrative entries. Insert '0' as appropriate.

Show all qualifying charitable donations even if the company does not actually claim relief for them.

Solution

	Y/e 30.6.14 £	P/e 31.12.14 £	Y/e 31.12.15 £	Y/e 31.12.16 £
Trading profits	20,000	30,000	0	15,000
▼				
Investment income	10,000	10,000	10,000	10,000
▼				
▼				
▼				
Taxable total profits				

Picklist:

Current year relief
Losses carried forward
Prior year relief
Qualifying charitable donations

5 Individuals and companies – relieving non-trading losses

Capital losses

These can only be set against capital gains. The order of relief here is:

1   First, against current period/fiscal year gains

2   Second, any surplus losses are relieved against gains in future accounting periods/fiscal years

Note. Capital losses cannot be carried back to preceding years.

Companies

We have seen that capital gains form part of a company's taxable total profits (TTP) chargeable to corporation tax.

Any capital losses would be offset automatically against gains before considering how to allocate the trading loss.

Individuals

Capital gains are charged to capital gains tax and income is charged to income tax.

The rules concerning capital losses are therefore independent to the trading loss rules we have just looked at.

We will revisit the rules on capital losses for individuals in a later chapter.

6 Choosing loss relief

6.1 Individuals

As we have seen above, several alternative loss reliefs may be available for an individual, including:

*   Carry forward of losses
*   Losses set against income in the tax year of the loss
*   Losses set against income of the previous tax year
*   Losses set against capital gains

In making a choice, consider:

(a)   **The rate at which relief will be obtained.**

      We saw in Chapter 1 that individuals can pay income tax at the starting rate, the basic rate, the higher rate and the additional rate.

      The most beneficial method is to try to offset losses against any income being taxed at the highest rate.

(b)   **How quickly relief will be obtained.** It is quicker, and therefore could be more beneficial, to obtain loss relief against income of the previous year and current year rather than wait to carry forward loss relief.

(c) **The extent to which personal allowances and the annual exempt amount might be lost.**

6.2 Companies

We have also seen that there are several alternative loss reliefs available for a company, including:

- Carry forward of losses
- Losses set against current profits
- Losses set against profits from earlier years

In making a choice consider:

(a) **How quickly relief will be obtained**; loss relief against total profits is quicker than carry forward loss relief.

(b) **The extent to which relief for qualifying charitable donations might be lost**.

Assessment focus point

Candidates often struggle with loss relief questions so make sure you go over this chapter several times before attempting the questions in the question bank to ensure you are well prepared for the assessment. It is not enough just to read the questions and answers, you need to prepare the computations yourself to fully understand them.

Chapter summary

- For an individual a trading loss can be:
    - Carried forward to be deducted from the first available profits of the same trade
    - Deducted from total income in the tax year of the loss and/or in the preceding tax year
    - Deducted from net gains in the year of the claim against total income
- For a company a trading loss can be:
    - Carried forward and set against future trading profits of the same trade
    - Deducted from total profits in the accounting period of the loss
    - Deducted from total profits in the 12 months preceding the period of the loss
- Current year and carry back relief for a company is given against total profits before deducting qualifying charitable donations.
- An individual can choose the order in which to claim for current year loss relief and prior year loss relief.
- For a company, a claim for current year loss relief must be made before a loss is carried back.
- Capital losses can be set against current year gains or carried forward to gains in the future.
- When selecting a loss relief, consider the rate at which relief is obtained and the timing of relief.

Keywords

- **Carry back loss relief:** Allows a company to set a trading loss against total profits (before deducting qualifying charitable donations) in the 12 months preceding the period of the loss; or an individual to set a trading loss against total income in the tax year prior to the tax year of the loss

- **Carry forward loss relief:** Allows both an individual and a company to set a trading loss against the first available profits from the same trade in the future

- **Current year loss relief:** Allows a company to set a trading loss against total profits before deducting qualifying charitable donations in the loss-making accounting period; and an individual to set a trading loss against total income in the tax year of the loss

- **Trading losses:** These arise when the accounting profit is adjusted for tax purposes, and this adjusted figure is negative

1   Harold (a sole trader), who has been in business for many years, makes a trading
    loss of £20,000 in the year ended 31 January 2017.

    **In which year(s) may the loss be relieved against total income,
    assuming relief is claimed as soon as possible? Tick ONE box.**

	✓
2016/17 only	
2017/18 and/or 2016/17	
2015/16 only	
2016/17 and/or 2015/16	

2   **Identify whether the following statement is true or false.**

    For an individual, trading losses can only be carried forward for deduction in the six
    succeeding tax years.

	✓
True	
False	

3   **Where trade losses are carried forward by an individual, against
    what sort of income may they be relieved? Tick ONE box.**

	✓
Against non-savings income	
Against total income	
Against trading income arising in the same trade	
Against trading income arising in all trades carried on by the taxpayer	

4   Mallory (a sole trader), who has traded for many years, has the following recent
    tax-adjusted results:

Year ended 30 April 2015	Profit	£10,000
Year ended 30 April 2016	Loss	£(40,000)
Year ended 30 April 2017	Profit	£25,000

    Mallory has other income of £9,000 each year.

    Explain how the loss in the year to 30 April 2016 can be relieved.

5

(a) CR Ltd has the following results for the two years to 31 October 2016:

| | Year ended 31 October | |
	2015 £	2016 £
Trading profit (loss)	170,000	(320,000)
Interest	5,000	60,000
Chargeable gain (loss)	(20,000)	12,000
Qualifying charitable donation	5,000	5,000

Calculate the amount of trading loss remaining to be carried forward at 1 November 2016 assuming that all possible loss relief claims against total profits are made.

£ [   ]

(b) Calculate the amount of capital loss remaining to be carried forward at 1 November 2016.

£ [   ]

6   JB Ltd had the following results in the three accounting periods to 30 September 2016:

	Year ended 31 March 2015 £	Six months to 30 September 2015 £	Year ended 30 September 2016 £
Trading profit/(loss)	4,000	6,000	(10,000)
Qualifying charitable donation	1,000	3,000	1,500

Identify the amount, if any, of the trading loss incurred in the year ended 30 September 2016 that may be relieved against total profits in the year ended 31 March 2015. Tick ONE box.

	✓
£Nil	
£2,000	
£4,000	
£3,000	

Self-assessment for individuals

Learning outcomes

3.1	**Demonstrate an understanding of the tax return filing requirements and tax payments due** • Tax return filing deadlines • Payment rules for sole traders and partnerships: amounts and dates
3.2	**Demonstrate an understanding of the penalties and interest payable for non-compliance** • Penalties for late filing of tax returns and failing to notify chargeability • Late payment interest and surcharges • The enquiry window and penalties for incorrect returns
4.3	**Discuss the responsibilities relating to tax for the business and its agent** • What records need to be maintained by a business, for how long and the penalties for not keeping these records

Assessment context

There are a lot of very specific rules, dates and percentages in this chapter that could be tested in the assessment. Make sure you learn the detail.

Qualification context

You will not see the information in this chapter outside of this unit unless you are also studying *Personal Tax*.

Business context

It is vital for a tax adviser to ensure that their client's tax affairs are dealt with in a timely fashion and all information is properly submitted to HMRC. Serious financial penalties will arise if these deadlines are missed.

Chapter overview

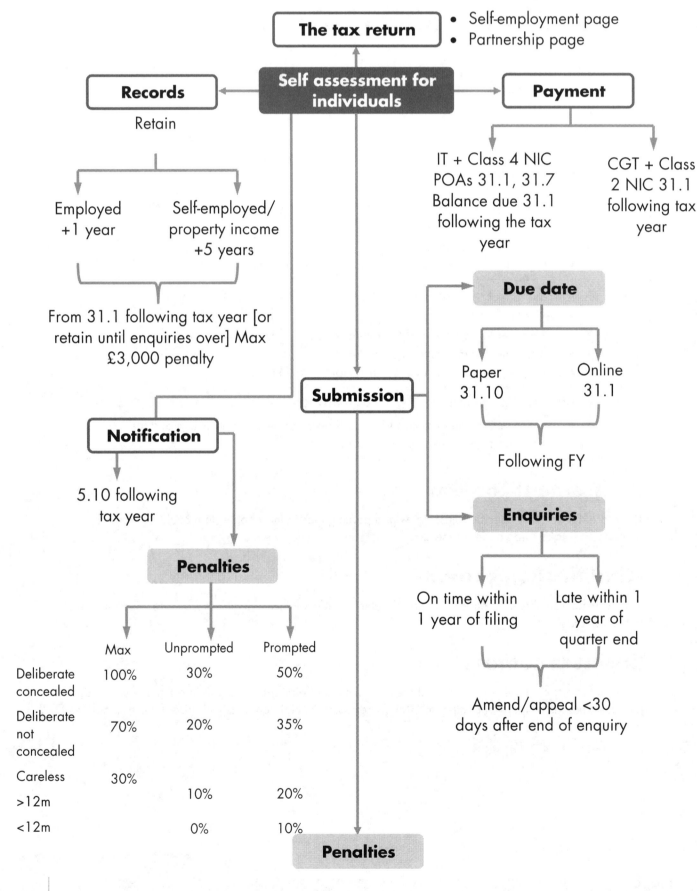

The tax return
- Self-employment page
- Partnership page

Self assessment for individuals

Records

Retain

Employed +1 year

Self-employed/ property income +5 years

From 31.1 following tax year [or retain until enquiries over] Max £3,000 penalty

Notification

5.10 following tax year

Penalties

	Max	Unprompted	Prompted
Deliberate concealed	100%	30%	50%
Deliberate not concealed	70%	20%	35%
Careless	30%		
>12m		10%	20%
<12m		0%	10%

Payment

IT + Class 4 NIC POAs 31.1, 31.7 Balance due 31.1 following the tax year

CGT + Class 2 NIC 31.1 following tax year

Submission

Due date

Paper 31.10

Online 31.1

Following FY

Enquiries

On time within 1 year of filing

Late within 1 year of quarter end

Amend/appeal <30 days after end of enquiry

Penalties

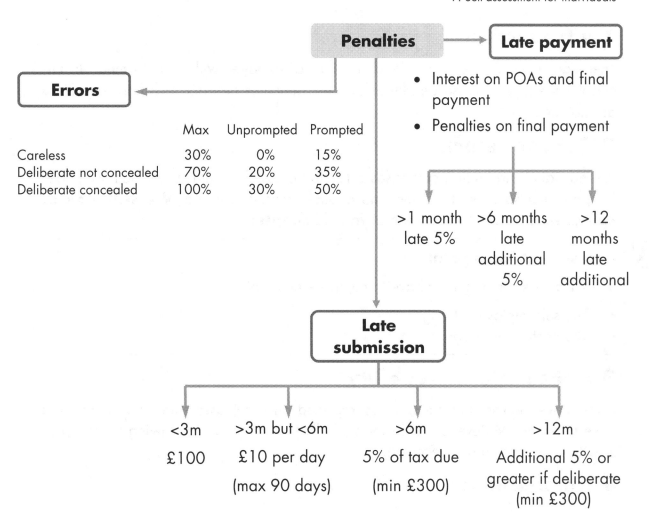

	Max	Unprompted	Prompted
Careless	30%	0%	15%
Deliberate not concealed	70%	20%	35%
Deliberate concealed	100%	30%	50%

Penalties

Late payment

- Interest on POAs and final payment
- Penalties on final payment

>1 month late 5%

>6 months late additional 5%

>12 months late additional

Errors

Late submission

<3m
£100

>3m but <6m
£10 per day
(max 90 days)

>6m
5% of tax due
(min £300)

>12m
Additional 5% or greater if deliberate
(min £300)

1 Introduction

There are a number of strict deadlines that a taxpayer will need to meet. In this chapter we look at those deadlines and the penalties that occur if those deadlines are not met.

2 The tax return

An individual's tax return comprises a tax form, together with supplementary pages for particular sources of income and capital gains if required. **We will look at self-assessment of income tax in this chapter**.

Assessment focus point

In your assessment you may have to complete either of:

- The self-employment page
- The partnership page

---

3 Notice of chargeability

If you have income that needs to be reported on a self-assessment tax return, you have to notify HM Revenue & Customs (HMRC) by 5 October following the tax year in which the income was received.

4 Timetable for 16/17

31/10/2017	31/1/2018
Filing deadline for paper returns	Filing deadline for online returns
HMRC will calculate tax	Automatic electronic calculation of tax

Where a notice to make a return is issued after 31 July following the tax year, a period of three months is allowed for the filing of a paper return.

Where a notice to make a return is issued after 31 October following the tax year, a period of three months is allowed for the online filing of that return.

An individual may ask HMRC to make the tax computation if a paper return is filed. Where an online return is filed, the tax computation is made automatically.

Illustration 1: Filing income tax returns

Advise the following clients of the latest filing date for their personal tax return for 2016/17 if notice to file the return is received on the following dates, and the return is:

(a) Paper
(b) Online

Notice to file tax return issued by HMRC:

Norma   on 6 April 2017
Melanie   on 10 August 2017
Olga   on 12 December 2017

The latest filing dates are:

	Paper	**Online**
Norma	31 October 2017	31 January 2018
Melanie	9 November 2017	31 January 2018
Olga	11 March 2018	11 March 2018

5 Retention of records

All records must be retained until the later of:

- One year following 31 January after the end of the tax year (eg 31 January 2019 for tax year 2016/17)

- Five years following 31 January after the end of the tax year (eg 31 January 2023 for tax year 2016/17) for taxpayers who are self-employed or have property income. **Note**. All records must be retained for this time, not just property and self-employment records.

- Time at which enquiries can no longer be opened

- Time at which enquiries are concluded

The maximum penalty for failure to keep records is £3,000.

6 Penalties for errors

A penalty may be imposed where a taxpayer makes an inaccurate return if he has:

(a) **Been careless** because he has not taken reasonable care in making the return or discovers the error later but does not take reasonable steps to inform HMRC

(b) **Made a deliberate error** but does not make arrangements to conceal it

(c) **Made a deliberate error and has attempted to conceal it**, eg by submitting false evidence in support of an inaccurate figure

If there is more than one error HMRC may charge more than one penalty.

Penalties may be reduced if the errors are brought to HMRC's attention by the taxpayer.

This could be **unprompted**, where the taxpayer admits the error before HMRC has any knowledge of irregularity, or **prompted**, when the taxpayer suspects the error has been or is about to be discovered.

Key term

> **Potential lost revenue (PLR)** is the tax that would have been lost if the error had gone undetected.

Penalties are as follows:

Type of error	Maximum penalty	Minimum penalty with prompted disclosure	Minimum penalty with unprompted disclosure
Simple	No penalty	No penalty	No penalty
Careless	30%	15%	0%
Deliberate but not concealed	70%	35%	20%
Deliberate and concealed	100%	50%	30%

The scale of the reduction will vary depending upon the help the taxpayer has given HMRC in respect of:

- Advising about the error, making full disclosure and explaining how it was made
- Assisting HMRC to enable it to quantify the error
- Allowing access to records

A penalty for a careless error may be suspended by HMRC to allow the taxpayer to take action to ensure that the error does not occur again (eg where the error has arisen from failure to keep proper records).

HMRC will impose conditions which the taxpayer has to satisfy, eg establishing proper record-keeping systems.

The penalty will be cancelled if the conditions imposed by HMRC are complied with by the taxpayer within a period of up to two years.

A taxpayer may appeal against:

- The penalty being charged
- The amount of the penalty
- A decision by HMRC not to suspend a penalty
- Conditions set by HMRC in relation to the suspension of a penalty

Activity 1: Penalties

Kelly deliberately omitted an invoice from her trading income in her 2015/16 tax return, but did not destroy the evidence. She later disclosed this error, before she had reason to believe HMRC might investigate the matter.

Required

Complete the following sentence:

Kelly's penalty can be reduced from [   ] % of the potential lost

revenue (for a deliberate, but not concealed error) to [   ]%, with the unprompted disclosure of her error.

7 Penalties for late notification

A penalty can be charged for failure to notify chargeability to income tax and/or capital gains tax. Penalties are behaviour-related, increasing for more serious failures, and are again based on 'potential lost revenue'. This time the PLR is the income tax or capital gains tax which is unpaid on 31 January following the tax year.

The minimum and maximum penalties as percentages of PLR are as follows:

Behaviour	Maximum penalty	Minimum penalty with prompted disclosure		Minimum penalty with unprompted disclosure	
Deliberate and concealed	100%	50%		30%	
Deliberate but not concealed	70%	35%		20%	
		≥12m	<12m	≥12m	<12m
Careless	30%	20%	10%	10%	0%

Penalty may be reduced to 0% if the failure is rectified within 12 months through unprompted disclosure.

Penalties may be reduced at HMRC's discretion in 'special circumstances'. Inability to pay is not a 'special circumstance'.

If failure is not deliberate there is no penalty if the taxpayer has a 'reasonable excuse'.

8 Penalties for late filing

The **filling due date** for a tax return is 31 October or 31 January in the following tax year depending on whether paper or online returns are made. The penalties for filing a late tax return are:

Return outstanding	Penalty
⟶ 3 months	£100
3 ⟶ 6 months	Daily penalty of £10 per day (max 90 days)
6 ⟶ 12 months*	5% of the tax due (min £300)
⟶ 12 months*	(a) 100% of the tax due where withholding of information is deliberate and concealed
	(b) 70% of the tax due where withholding of information is deliberate but not concealed
	(c) 5% of the tax due in other cases (eg careless)

*These tax based penalties are subject to a minimum of £300

Penalties may be set aside if the taxpayer had a reasonable excuse.

9 Due dates for 2016/17 self-assessed tax

9.1 Income tax

A taxpayer must usually make **three payments of tax**:

Date	Payment
31 January in the tax year	First payment on account
31 July after the tax year	Second payment on account
31 January after the tax year	Final payment to settle any remaining liability

Each **payment on account** (POA) is equal to 50% of the tax payable under self-assessment (ie not deducted at source) for the previous year.

If HMRC is late in requesting a tax return then the final payment date is extended to three months following the 'notice to deliver' date (provided the taxpayer has notified chargeability on time).

POAs may be reduced if the taxpayer expects this year's liability to be lower than last year's. Interest will be charged if POAs are reduced and the final tax is greater than expected.

POAs are not required if the income tax payable for the previous year is less than £1,000 or if more than 80% of last year's liability was deducted at source.

Illustration 2: Payments on account

Jeremy's tax liability for 2015/16 totalled £12,000. None of the tax was deducted at source.

Each payment on account would therefore be £6,000 (50% × £12,000)

9.2 Capital gains tax

Capital gains tax is due on 31 January following the tax year. Capital gains tax is never paid by instalments.

9.3 National insurance

Class 4 national insurance contributions (NICs) are paid along with the income tax. Instalments and balancing payments are calculated in the same way.

Class 2 NICs are paid on 31 January following the tax year.

Activity 2: Payments on account and balancing payments

Vorus's tax for 2015/16 was as follows:

	£
Income tax liability	7,000
PAYE (tax deducted at source from employment income)	4,000
Capital gains tax	5,000

His tax for 2016/17 is as follows:

	£
Income tax liability	8,000
PAYE (tax deducted at source from employment income)	2,500
Capital gains tax	1,000

Required

How is his tax bill for 2016/17 settled?

	£

10 Penalties for late payment

Penalties for late payment of tax will be imposed in respect of balancing payments of income tax.

A penalty is chargeable where tax is paid after the penalty date. **The penalty date is 30 days after the due date for tax.** Therefore no penalty arises if the tax is paid within 30 days of the due date.

Paid	Penalty
⟶ 30 days	0%
30 days – 6 months	5% of unpaid tax
6 months – 12 months	Further 5% of unpaid tax (10%)
12 months ⟶	Further 5% of unpaid tax (15%)

Penalties for late payment of tax **apply to balancing payments** of income tax only. They **do not apply to late payments on account**.

11 Interest

Interest is chargeable on **late payment of payments on account and of balancing payments**. In both cases interest runs from the **due date until the day before the actual date of payment**.

- POAs
    - From 31 January during fiscal year
    - From 31 July following end of fiscal year
- Final payment
    - From 31 January following end of fiscal year

If a taxpayer claims to reduce his payments on account and there is still a final payment to be made, interest is normally charged on the payments on account as if each of those payments had been the lower of:

(a) The reduced amount, plus 50% of the final income tax payable

(b) The amount which would have been payable had no claim for reduction been made

12 Repayment of tax and repayment interest

Overpaid tax is repaid unless a greater payment of tax is due in the following 30 days, in which case it is set off against that payment.

Repayment Interest is paid on overpayments of:

- Payments on account
- Final payments of tax
- Penalties

Interest runs from the later of the due date and the actual date of payment until the day before repayment is made.

13 Agent vs Principal

Where a taxpayer uses an agent, such as an accountant or tax adviser, to complete the tax return, it is the taxpayer's responsibility to ensure that the information disclosed in that return is correct. The taxpayer is referred to as the 'principal'.

The agent responsible for preparing the tax return must ensure confidentiality at all times. Only in limited circumstances may the agent disclose client information to third parties without the client's permission, for example if money laundering is suspected.

14 Compliance checks and enquiries

Usually, under self-assessment, HMRC will accept taxpayers' figures.

However, HMRC has the power to conduct a compliance check.

Some returns are selected for a compliance check at random, others for a particular reason – for example, if HMRC believes that there has been an underpayment of tax due to the taxpayer's failure to comply with tax legislation.

There are two types of compliance check:

- Pre-return check using information powers
- Enquiries into submitted returns

Examples of when a pre-return check may be carried out in practice include:

- To assist with clearances or ruling requests

- Where a previous check has identified poor recordkeeping

- To check that computer systems will produce the information needed to support a return

- To find out about planning or avoidance schemes

- Where fraud is suspected

HMRC must give notice of intention to conduct an enquiry not later than:

- 12 months after filing (if not late); or
- 12 months after quarter end in which return delivered

(Quarters are 31 January, 30 April, 31 July and 31 October if submitted late.)

HMRC has only one opportunity to open a formal enquiry and a tax return cannot be subject to a formal enquiry more than once.

In the course of the enquiries the taxpayer may be required to produce documents, accounts or other information. The taxpayer can appeal to the Tax Tribunal against this.

HMRC must issue a closure notice when the enquiries are complete, state the conclusions and amend the self-assessment accordingly. If the taxpayer is not satisfied with the amendment he may, within 30 days, appeal to the Tax Tribunal.

Assessment focus point

Please refer to the reference material at the end of this Course Book to see which elements of this chapter will be available to you as a pop-up window in the live assessment.

Chapter summary

- A tax return must be filed by 31 January following a tax year provided it is filed online. Paper returns must be filed by 31 October following the tax year.

- Taxpayers must keep records until the later of:

  (a) One year after 31 January following the tax year

  (b) Five years after 31 January following the tax year if in business or with property income

- A penalty may be imposed if the taxpayer makes an error in his tax return based on the potential lost revenue as a result of the error.

- A penalty may be imposed if the taxpayer does not notify HMRC of his liability to pay income tax or capital gains tax. The penalty is based on potential lost revenue.

- A fixed penalty of £100 applies if a return is filed late; followed by a potential daily penalty of £10 if the return is filed between three and six months late.

- A tax-geared penalty will also apply if a return is filed more than 6 months late, with a further penalty if this is over 12 months late.

- Payments on account of income tax are required on 31 January in the tax year and on 31 July following the tax year.

- Balancing payments of income tax are due on 31 January following the tax year.

- Late payment penalties apply to balancing payments of income tax. They do not apply to late payments on account.

- Interest is chargeable on late payment of both payments on account and balancing payments.

- HMRC can enquire into a return, usually within one year of receipt of the return

- An accountant or tax adviser may act as the 'agent' for a client by preparing their tax return, but it remains the responsibility of the client, 'principal', to ensure the accuracy of the information submitted.

Keywords

- **Filing due date:** The date by which a return must be filed

- **Interest:** Charged on late payments on account and on late balancing payments

- **Payment on account:** An amount paid on account of income tax

- **Repayment interest:** Payable by HMRC on overpaid payments on account, balancing payments and penalties

1 **The due filing date for an income tax return for 2016/17 assuming the taxpayer will submit the return online is (insert date as XX/XX/XX):**

    [   ]

2 **Select the correct answers to the four questions from the four picklists provided.**

    The 2017/18 payments on account will be calculated as

    [1   ▼]

    of the income tax payable for

    [2   ▼]

    and will be due on

    [3   ▼]

    and

    [4   ▼].

Picklist 1:	Picklist 2:	Picklist 3:	Picklist 4:
50%	2016/17	1 January 2018	31 July 2018
25%	2015/16	31 January 2017	31 December 2018
100%	2017/18	31 January 2018	31 January 2019

3 A notice requiring a tax return for 2016/17 is issued in April 2017 and the return is filed online in May 2018. All income tax was paid in May 2018. No payments on account were due.

    Explain what charges will be made on the taxpayer.

4 Susie filed her 2016/17 tax return online on 28 January 2018.

    By what date must HMRC give notice that it is going to enquire into the return?

    Tick ONE box.

	✓
31 January 2019	
31 March 2019	
6 April 2019	
28 January 2019	

5   Jamie paid income tax of £12,000 for 2015/16. In 2016/17, his tax payable was £16,000.

Jamie's 2016/17 payments on account will each be

£ [   ]

and will be due on (insert date as XX/XX/XX)

[   ]

and

[   ]

Jamie's balancing payment will be

£ [   ]

and will be due on (insert date as XX/XX/XX)

[   ] .

6   Tim should have made two payments on account of his 2016/17 income tax payable of £5,000 each. He actually made both of these payments on 31 August 2017.

State the amount of any penalties for late payment.

£ [   ]

7   **(a)   By what date must a taxpayer generally submit a tax return for 2016/17 if it is filed as a paper return?**

	✓
30 September 2017	
31 October 2017	
31 December 2017	
31 January 2018	

(b)   On which dates are payment on accounts due for 2016/17?

	✓
31 January 2018 and 31 July 2018	
31 January 2017 and 31 July 2017	
31 October 2017 and 31 January 2018	
31 July 2017 and 31 January 2018	

8   Lola accidentally fails to include an invoice of £17,000 on her 2016/17 tax return. She pays basic rate tax at 20%, and has not yet disclosed this error.

Identify the maximum penalty that could be imposed on her. Tick ONE box.

	✓
£5,100	
£3,400	
£1,020	
£2,380	

Self-assessment for companies

10

Learning outcomes

3.1	**Demonstrate an understanding of the tax return filing requirements and tax payments due**
	• Tax return filing deadlines • Payment rules for limited companies: amounts and dates
3.2	**Demonstrate an understanding of the penalties and interest payable for non-compliance**
	• Penalties for late filing of tax returns and failing to notify chargeability • Late payment interest and surcharges • The enquiry window and penalties for incorrect returns
4.2	**Demonstrate an understanding of the current tax reliefs and other tax issues**
	• Current tax reliefs available to businesses • Current tax issues and their implications for businesses

Assessment context

The assessment may require you to explain various aspects of the taxation rules specifically including payments, penalties, filing dates and payment dates.

You may have to explain the effect of IR35 and the reliefs obtained for research and development expenditure.

Qualification context

You will not see these rules outside of this unit.

Business context

Serious financial consequences will arise if a company pays tax late or fails to file a tax return on time.

Chapter overview

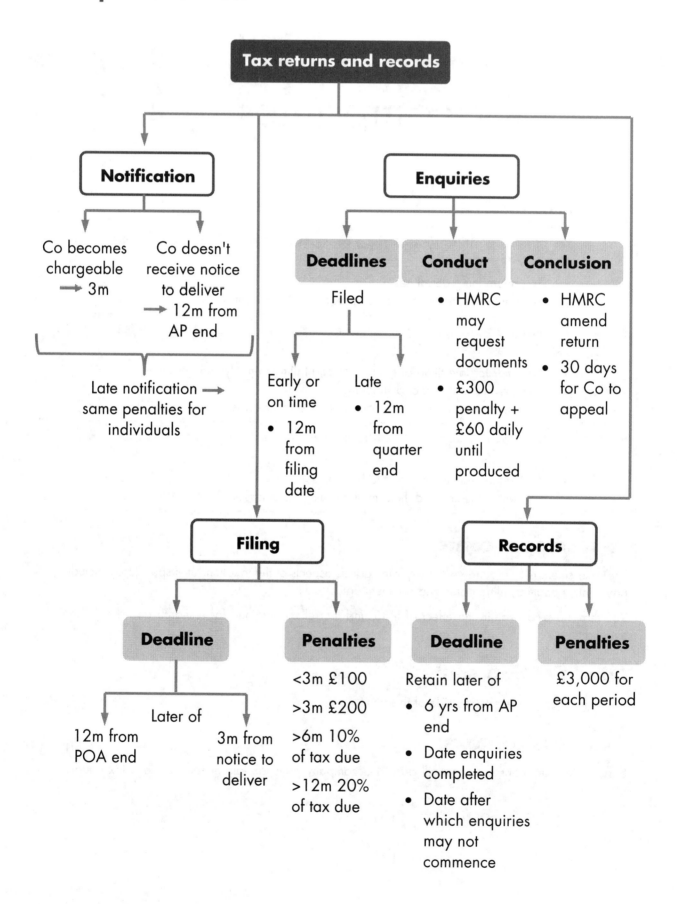

Tax returns and records

Notification

- Co becomes chargeable → 3m
- Co doesn't receive notice to deliver → 12m from AP end

Late notification → same penalties for individuals

Enquiries

Deadlines

Filed

- Early or on time
  - 12m from filing date
- Late
  - 12m from quarter end

Conduct

- HMRC may request documents
- £300 penalty + £60 daily until produced

Conclusion

- HMRC amend return
- 30 days for Co to appeal

Filing

Deadline

Later of

- 12m from POA end
- 3m from notice to deliver

Penalties

<3m £100

>3m £200

>6m 10% of tax due

>12m 20% of tax due

Records

Deadline

Retain later of

- 6 yrs from AP end
- Date enquiries completed
- Date after which enquiries may not commence

Penalties

£3,000 for each period

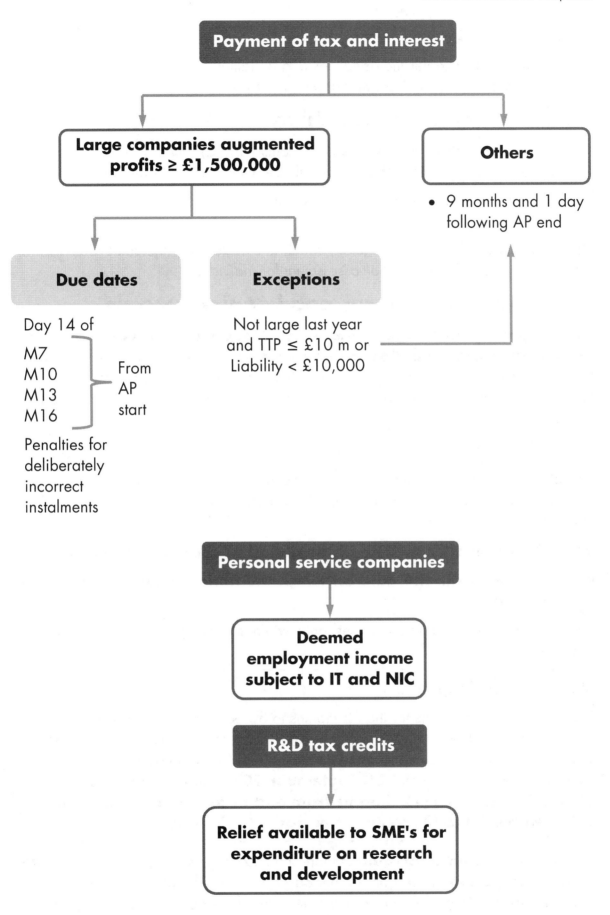

Payment of tax and interest

Large companies augmented profits ≥ £1,500,000

Others

- 9 months and 1 day following AP end

Due dates

Day 14 of

M7
M10
M13
M16
} From AP start

Penalties for deliberately incorrect instalments

Exceptions

Not large last year and TTP ≤ £10 m or Liability < £10,000

Personal service companies

Deemed employment income subject to IT and NIC

R&D tax credits

Relief available to SME's for expenditure on research and development

1 Introduction

We saw in the last chapter the deadlines and penalties that apply to individuals. In this chapter we look at the those that apply to companies.

2 Notification of chargeability

A company must notify HM Revenue & Customs (HMRC) when it first comes within the scope of corporation tax. This will usually be when it starts trading.

The notice must be made within three months of the date when it first became chargeable.

There is a penalty for late notification, which is calculated in the same way as that for individuals (see Chapter 9 *Self-assessment for individuals*).

3 Company tax returns and keeping records

All companies and organisations must submit their Company Tax Return (Form CT600) online, except in exceptional circumstances. Additionally, tax computations and (with very few exceptions) the accounts that form part of the Company Tax Return must be submitted in 'Inline eXtensible Business Reporting Language' (iXBRL) format.

3.1 Filing date

Complete accounts, computations and tax return for each of the company's accounting periods is due on or before the **filing due date**. This is normally the **later of**:

(a) **12 months after the end of the period of account concerned**

(b) **3 months from the date on which the notice requiring the return was made**

An obligation to file a return arises only when the company receives a notice requiring a return.

> **Illustration 1: Filing date**
>
> Size Ltd prepares accounts for the 12 months to 30 September 2015. A notice requiring a CT600 return for the year ended 30 September 2015 was issued on 1 June 2016. The date by which Size Ltd must file its Company Tax Return for the year to 30 September 2015 is **30 September 2016 (being the later of: 30 September 2016 (12 months from end of period of account) and 1 September 2016 (3 months after notice to deliver).**

Note that if a **period of account** is more than 12 months long, there will be **two accounting periods** based on the period of account. The first accounting period is 12 months long; the second is for the remainder of the period of account (PA).

A tax return must be filed for each accounting period. The tax returns for both accounting periods must be filed within 12 months of the end of the **period of account**.

> **Illustration 2: Long period of account**
>
> Octo Ltd prepares accounts for the 18 months to 30 June 2016.
>
> The two accounting periods relating to this period of account are **year ended 31 December 2015 and six months to 30 June 2016**.
>
> The date by which Octo Ltd must file its Company Tax Returns based on this period of account, assuming a notice requiring the returns was issued shortly after the end of the period of account, is **30 June 2017**.

3.2 Penalties

Companies are subject to the following late filing penalties:

Return outstanding	Penalty
<3 months late	£100
>3 months late	£200
>6 months late	10% of tax due per return
>12 months late	20% of tax due per return

3.3 Record keeping

Companies must keep records until the latest of:

(a) **Six years from the end of the accounting period**
(b) The date any enquiries (compliance checks) are completed
(c) The date after which enquiries may not be commenced

All business records and accounts, including contracts and receipts, must be kept.

Failure to keep records can lead to a penalty of up to £3,000 for each accounting period affected.

3.4 Penalties for errors

The rules that apply to individuals also apply to companies.

3.5 Compliance checks and enquiries

As with an individual, HMRC may conduct a compliance check into a company's tax return.

An enquiry is a compliance check into a return that has already been filed.

HMRC must give written notice of an enquiry within:

- 12 months of actual filing date (if not late); or
- 12 months from quarter-end that the return was filed in (31 January, 30 April, 31 July, 31 October) (if the return is filed after the due filing date).

Only one enquiry may be made in respect of any one return.

HMRC may request documents.

- There is a £300 penalty if the company does not provide them.
- HMRC may then charge £60 a day until these are produced.

An enquiry ends when HMRC gives notice that it has been completed.

- HMRC will amend the return.
- The company may appeal the amendments to the Tax Tribunal within 30 days.

> **Illustration 3: Enquiries**
>
> Green Ltd prepares accounts for the 12 months to 30 April 2016. The Company Tax Return for the year was filed on 31 March 2017.
>
> The date by which HMRC may commence an enquiry into the return based on these accounts is:
>
> **31 March 2018** (12 months from the actual filing date)

4 Payment of tax and interest

All tax must be paid electronically.

4.1 Non-large companies

Corporation tax is due for payment nine months and one day after the end of the accounting period for a company with augmented profits (taxable total profits plus gross dividends) **of less than £1,500,000** for a 12-month accounting period, where there are no related 51%-group companies.

If a company owns more than 50% of another company then the £1,500,000 limit is divided by the number of related 51%-group companies; eg if Co A owns 100% of both Co B and Co C, the £1,500,000 limit is divided by 3.

> **Illustration 4: Corporation tax due date**
>
> K Ltd makes up accounts to 31 March 2017. Its profits do not exceed £1,500,000. The corporation tax for the year to 31 March 2017 is £30,000.
>
> The corporation tax is due on 1 January 2018.

4.2 Large companies

Large companies, which have augmented profits of £1,500,000 or above (adjusted by the length of the period and the number of 51%-related group companies), are required to pay their estimated tax liability in four quarterly instalments, due on the 14th day of months 7, 10, 13 and 16 following the start of the accounting period.

Assessment focus point

You will not be expected to deal with periods other than 12-month periods in your assessment.

Illustration 5: Payment in instalments

A company which draws up accounts to 31 December 2016 will pay instalments as follows:

Instalment	Due date
1	14 July 2016
2	14 October 2016
3	14 January 2017
4	14 April 2017

Activity 1: Payment of corporation tax

A plc has a 31 March 2017 year end, taxable total profits (TTP) of £2.1m per year and no 51%-related group companies.

Required

Show how the corporation tax will be paid.

	£

You will note that tax must be paid before the end of the accounting period on profits that have not yet been earned.

(a) At each quarter end the directors will have to estimate how much the total tax bill will be for the year.

(b) They then calculate the proportion of this tax due to date (eg by the time of the second instalment $^2/_4$ ie $^1/_2$, of the tax is due).

(c) They will then pay over the difference compared to what they have paid to date.

4.3 Interest to HMRC

Interest arises on late-paid instalments (from the due date to the actual payment date).

4.4 Interest from HMRC

Interest on overpaid instalments will run from the date that the tax was originally paid to the repayment date (note that interest on overpaid tax cannot run any earlier than from the due date of the first instalment).

Interest on tax paid late is a deductible expense and interest on overpaid tax is taxable. This will be added to, or subtracted from, interest income.

4.5 Exceptions

If a 'small' company is treated as large as a result of the related 51%-group companies rule, it will not have to pay corporation tax by instalments if its own liability is less than £10,000.

If a company is a large company for an accounting period it will not have to pay corporation tax by instalments for that period if:

(a) **Its augmented profits do not exceed £10 million** (reduced to reflect any related 51%-group companies at the end of the previous period); and

(b) **It was not a large company in the previous year**.

4.6 Incorrect instalments

Penalties will be applied if the company deliberately underpays its instalments.

HMRC may require the company to justify why it paid the instalments it did. HMRC may request working papers. A fixed penalty, followed by a daily penalty, may be imposed until the information is supplied.

4.7 Long period of account

A long period of account gives rise to two accounting periods. Each accounting period will have its own due date(s).

> ### Illustration 6: Long period of account
>
> Z Ltd, which is not a large company, has a 15-month period to 30 September 2016.
>
> Z ltd will have two chargeable accounting periods:
>
> - 12 months to 30 June 2016
> - 3 months to 30 September 2016
>
> Z Ltd will therefore have two payment dates:
>
> - 1 April 2017
> - 1 July 2017

5 Current tax reliefs available to businesses

5.1 Research and development

Tax reliefs are available to small and medium enterprises (SME) which incur expenditure on research and development (R&D).

An SME is a company with less than 500 employees with either:

- An annual turnover under €100 million; or
- A balance sheet under €86 million.

5.1.1 Qualifying R&D

To qualify as R&D, any activity must contribute directly to seeking an advance in science or technology or must be a qualifying indirect activity.

Examples of qualifying R&D expenditure includes revenue expenditure on:

- Staff directly or indirectly engaged on R&D;
- Consumables or transformable material;
- Computer software; and
- Power, water and fuel.

5.1.2 The relief

An SME is allowed to deduct 230% of its research and development expenditure from its taxable profits, giving it lower profits and therefore a lower corporation tax liability.

If the deduction of this amount turns the profit into a loss, or if the company is already loss making, the company can choose not to carry forward the loss to offset against future trade profit but to surrender this loss for an R&D tax credit

This tax credit is 14.5% of the surrenderable loss figure, limited to the total of PAYE and National Insurance contribution liabilities of the company.

6 Current tax issues

6.1 Employment vs self-employment

It is important to distinguish between employment and self-employment for tax purposes. Self-employment usually results in a lower tax burden than employment and as such, some individuals claim self-employment when they actually meet the criteria of employee. This is an issue which is often challenged by HMRC.

An employed person usually has a contract **of** service, where as a self-employed person will have a contract **for** services.

Factors to consider when deciding if an individual is employed rather than self-employed are such things as:

- Provision of own equipment – you are usually provided with equipment if you are an employee
- Sick and holiday pay – you are not entitled to this if you are self-employed
- Financial risk – as an employee you have little financial risk as you will receive your salary regardless of how well the company is performing
- Control – as an employee you will have little control over how/when and what work you do
- Exclusivity – as an employee you usually only work for one employer

6.2 Tax differences

As an employee there is Income Tax on salary, bonus and benefits plus NIC on salary and bonus. As a sole trader there is also Income Tax but NIC is at a lower rate. As the owner of a company, an individual can extract cash via dividends, on which there is Income Tax (at a lower rate than salary/profits) but no NIC.

6.3 Personal service companies (PSC) (IR35)

This anti-avoidance legislation was developed in order to stop individuals selling their services to clients through an intermediary (a company). IR35 applies if an individual would be an employee of the client if the intermediary was not there. For example, I set myself up as the 100% shareholder of a company and my company sends me to work for my old employer doing the same job. Instead of receiving a salary, I take dividends from my company and consequently end up paying less tax.

6.4 Consequences of IR35

If IR35 applies then the individual is taxed on deemed employment income. This is the amount received from the client less any allowable employment expenses such as business travel costs. This amount is then subject to Income Tax and NIC.

> **Assessment focus point**
>
> Much of this information is included in the reference material which is available to you as a pop up window in the live assessment.

Chapter summary

- A company must usually file its CT600 online return within 12 months of the end of the period of account concerned.

- Fixed penalties arise if the return is up to six months late. If the return is over six months late there may be a tax-geared penalty.

- Companies must normally keep records until six years after the end of the accounting period concerned.

- HMRC can enquire into a return. Notice of an enquiry must usually be given within 12 months of the actual filing date.

- Large companies must pay their CT liability in four instalments, starting in the seventh month of the accounting period. The final instalment is due in the fourth month following the end of the accounting period.

- Other companies must pay their corporation tax liability nine months and one day after the end of an accounting period.

- An SME can deduct 230% of its R&D expenditure from its trading profits.

- If the company is loss making it can claim an R&D tax credit instead of the expense deduction.

- Employment – a contract of service, vs self-employment – a contract for service.

- Personal service company (PSC) (IR35) anti-avoidance legislation is applied if the relationship between the worker and the client would be considered employment if the existence of the PSC was ignored.

- If IR35 applies – the worker is taxed on deemed employment income.

Keywords

- **Filing due date:** The date by which a tax return must be filed
- **Large companies:** Companies with augmented profits that exceed £1,500,000 for a 12-month accounting period, where there are no related 51%-group companies
- **Personal service company:** An intermediary set up to disguise permanent employment

Test your learning

1 A company has been preparing accounts to 30 June for many years. It submitted its CT600 return for the year to 30 June 2016 on 1 June 2017.

   By what date must HMRC give notice that it is going to commence an enquiry into the return?

2 A company filed its CT600 return for the year to 31 December 2016 on 28 February 2018.

   What is the maximum penalty in respect of the late filing of the return for the year to 31 December 2016?

   £

3 Girton Ltd has no related 51%-group companies. **When will the first payment of corporation tax be due on its taxable profits of £150,000 arising in the year ended 31 December 2016?**

	✓
14 July 2016	
1 October 2017	
31 December 2017	
1 January 2018	

4 Eaton Ltd has taxable total profits of £2,400,000 for its year ended 31 December 2017.

   The first instalment of the corporation tax liability for this year will be due on:

	✓
14 April 2017	
14 April 2018	
14 July 2017	
1 October 2018	

5 M Ltd, a large company, has an estimated corporation tax liability of £240,000 in respect of its accounting year 31 March 2017.

   What will be the amount of each of the company's quarterly instalments?

   £

6   S Ltd, an SME, spend £125,000 on qualifying R&D in the year ended
     31 March 2017.

   How much of this would be deductible from profits?

£	

7   Gavin works for Gavin Ltd. 90% of Gavin Ltd's income comes from one client who
     Gavin works for 3 days a week, on their premises for a fixed daily fee.

   Identify whether the following statement is true or false.

   Gavin Ltd is a Personal Service Company.

	✓
True	
False	

Chargeable gains – the basics

11

Learning outcomes

5.1	Calculate the capital gains tax payable by self-employed taxpayers
	• Apply the rules relating to chargeable persons, disposals and assets • Calculate chargeable gains and allowable losses • Apply current reliefs and allowances • Apply the capital gains tax rates
5.2	Calculate chargeable gains and allowable losses for limited companies
	• Apply the rules relating to disposal and assets • Calculate the computation of chargeable gains and allowable losses • Apply current reliefs and allowances

Assessment context

The assessment will test the basics of capital gains tax as well as other matters such as exemptions, losses and tax payable, all of which are covered in this chapter.

Qualification context

You will not see the information in this chapter outside of this unit unless you are also studying *Personal Tax*.

Business context

People and companies sell assets for a variety of reasons. It is important to realise when a charge to capital gains tax arises and when capital gains tax needs to be paid if a taxpayer is to avoid paying interest and penalties.

Chapter overview

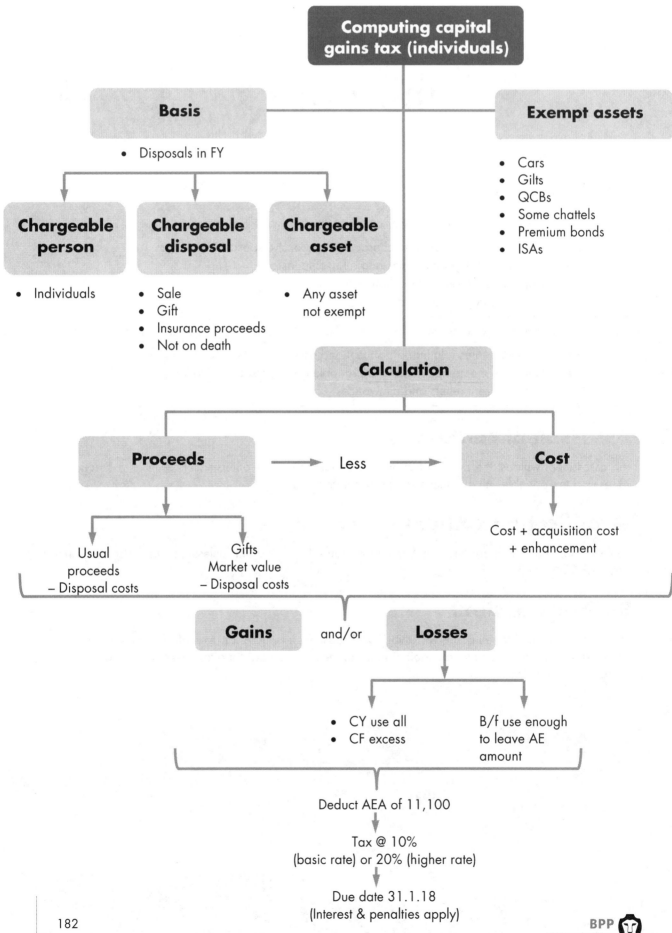

Computing capital gains tax (individuals)

Basis
- Disposals in FY

Exempt assets
- Cars
- Gilts
- QCBs
- Some chattels
- Premium bonds
- ISAs

Chargeable person
- Individuals

Chargeable disposal
- Sale
- Gift
- Insurance proceeds
- Not on death

Chargeable asset
- Any asset not exempt

Calculation

Proceeds → Less → **Cost**

Usual proceeds
– Disposal costs

Gifts
Market value
– Disposal costs

Cost + acquisition cost
+ enhancement

Gains and/or **Losses**

- CY use all
- CF excess

B/f use enough
to leave AE
amount

Deduct AEA of 11,100

Tax @ 10%
(basic rate) or 20% (higher rate)

Due date 31.1.18
(Interest & penalties apply)

BPP
LEARNING MEDIA

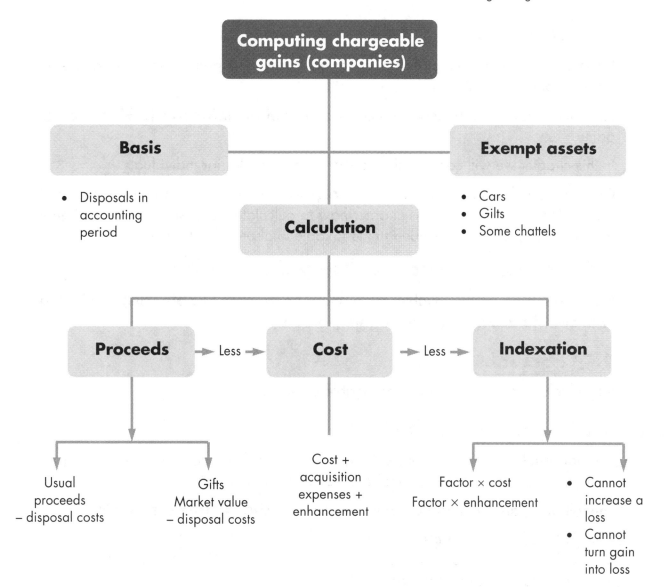

1 Introduction

Income is a regular receipt that is expected to recur. A gain arises from a one-off disposal of a capital item.

Individuals pay **income tax** on income and **capital gains tax** (CGT) on capital gains.

In this chapter we will consider the capital gains tax rules for individuals.

Companies only pay one type of tax, **corporation tax**, on all their income and gains. We will also see in this chapter how to calculate the chargeable gains figure that we have previously included in the taxable total profits calculation.

2 When does a chargeable gain arise?

For a disposal to be taxable there must be a **chargeable disposal** of a **chargeable asset** by a **chargeable person**.

2.1 Chargeable person

Individuals and companies are chargeable persons.

2.2 Chargeable disposal

An individual is taxed on gains arising from disposals in the current fiscal year. A company is taxed on disposals made in its accounting period.

The following are the most frequently encountered **chargeable disposals**:

- Sales of assets or parts of assets
- Gifts of assets or parts of assets
- The loss or destruction of an asset

A chargeable disposal occurs on the date of the contract (where there is one, whether written or oral), or the date of a conditional contract becoming unconditional.

Exempt Disposals include:

- Transfers on death
- Gifts to charities

On death the heirs inherit assets as if they bought them at death for their then market values. There is no capital gain or allowable loss on death.

2.3 Chargeable assets

All assets are chargeable unless they are classified as exempt. The following are exempt:

- Motor vehicles suitable for private use
- UK government stocks (gilt-edged securities) (individuals only)
- Qualifying corporate bonds (individuals only)

- Wasting chattels (greyhounds, racehorses) (see later)
- Premium bonds (individuals only)
- Investments held in an ISA (individuals only)

Remember that sales of assets as part of the trade of a business (ie sales of inventory) give rise to trading profits and not chargeable gains.

Assessment focus point

Make sure you identify an exempt asset, state that it is exempt and do not tax it.

3 Calculation of chargeable gains and allowable losses for individuals

Illustration 1: Basic capital gains computation

Disposal consideration (or market value)	X
Less incidental costs of disposal	(X)
Net proceeds	X
Less allowable cost (including acquisition cost)	(X)
Less enhancement expenditure	(X)
Capital gain/(capital loss)	X/(X)

We now look at each of the items in the above proforma in turn.

3.1 Disposal consideration

Usually this is proceeds received. Note though, that a disposal is deemed to take place at market value (MV) when the disposal is:

- A gift
- A sale at undervalue (for example, a sale to a friend for less than MV)
- Made for a consideration that cannot be valued
- Made to a connected person (see later)

3.2 Costs

The following costs are deducted in the above proforma:

(a) **Incidental costs of disposal**

These are the costs of selling an asset. They may include advertising costs, estate agents' fees, legal costs and valuation fees. These costs should be deducted separately from any other allowable costs.

(b) **Allowable costs**

These include:

(i) The original purchase price of the asset
(ii) Costs incurred in purchasing the asset (estate agents' fees, legal fees, etc)

(c) **Enhancement expenditure**

Enhancement expenditure is capital expenditure which enhances the value of the asset and is reflected in the state or nature of the asset at the time of disposal.

Illustration 2: Calculation of capital gain

Jack bought a holiday cottage for £25,000. He paid legal costs of £600 on the purchase.

Jack spent £8,000 building an extension to the cottage.

Jack sold the cottage for £60,000. He paid estate agents' fees of £1,200 and legal costs of £750.

Jack's gain on sale is:

£	24,450

	£
Disposal consideration	60,000
Less: incidental costs of disposal (1,200 + 750)	(1,950)
Net proceeds	58,050
Less: allowable costs (25,000 + 600)	(25,600)
Less: enhancement expenditure	(8,000)
Chargeable gain	24,450

Activity 1: Capital gain calculation (Individuals)

Mr Dunstable bought an asset for £15,000 in February 1986. He incurred legal fees of £500. He sold the asset for £38,500 incurring expenses of £1,500. While he owned the asset he improved it at a cost of £3,000.

Required

Complete the table showing Mr Dunstable's gain.

Solution

	£
Proceeds	
Less selling expenses	
Net proceeds	
Less cost	
Less legal fees on purchase	
Less enhancement	
Capital gain	

4 Computing taxable gains in a tax year

An individual pays capital gains tax on any **Taxable Gains** arising in a **tax year** (6 April to 5 April).

All the chargeable gains made in the tax year are added together, and any capital losses made in the same tax year are deducted to give net gains (or losses) for the year. Trading losses that can be offset against gains (which we saw in Chapter 8) are deducted next, and then any unrelieved capital losses brought forward from previous years. Finally, the annual exempt amount is deducted to arrive at taxable gains, on which CGT will be applied.

Illustration 3: Year-end computation

	£
Current gains	X
Current losses (all)	(X)
Net gains	X
Losses b/fwd from earlier years (restricted)	(X)
Net capital gains	X
Annual exempt amount	(11,100)
Taxable gains	X

Unused annual exempt amounts cannot be carried forward.

4.1 Annual exempt amount

Annual exempt amount (AEA)/annual exemption is the amount of gain that will be tax free. For 2016/17 this is £11,100.

This may also be referred to as an **annual exemption** in your assessment. As you can see above in Illustration 3, it is the last deduction to be made in computing taxable gains, and effectively means that for 2016/17 the first £11,100 of chargeable gains are tax free for an individual.

4.2 Losses

If losses have been made in the current year they must be offset against the gains of that year, even if this means that some or all of the annual exempt amount is wasted.

If the losses in a year are greater than the gains, then the excess losses are carried forward. When a capital loss is carried forward it is set against net gains in the next tax year – but only to reduce the net gains in the next tax year down to the level of the annual exempt amount. This means the taxpayer does not lose the benefit of the annual exempt amount. Any further loss remaining is carried forward.

Illustration 4: Capital losses

(a) Tim has chargeable gains for 2016/17 of £25,000 and allowable losses of £16,000. As the losses are current year losses they must be fully relieved against the gains to produce net gains of £9,000, despite the fact that net gains are below the annual exempt amount.

	£
Chargeable gains in tax year	25,000
Less losses in tax year	(16,000)
Net chargeable gains	9,000
Less annual exempt amount	(11,100)
Taxable gain	0

(b) Hattie has gains of £11,600 for 2016/17 and allowable losses brought forward of £6,000. Hattie restricts her loss relief to £500 so as to leave net gains of (£11,600 – £500) = £11,100, which will be exactly covered by the annual exempt amount for 2016/17.

	£
Net chargeable gains	11,600
Less losses brought forward	(500)
Less annual exempt amount	(11,100)
Taxable gain	0

The remaining £5,500 of losses will be carried forward to 2017/18.

Activity 2: Current year losses

In 2016/17, Ted makes gains of £45,000 and £10,000. He also makes a loss of £48,000. Ted has no losses to bring forward from earlier years.

Required

Ted's net capital gain for 2016/17 before the annual exempt amount is:

£ [   ]

Ted has a loss to carry forward of £ [   ].

Workings (not provided in the CBT)

	£

Activity 3: Prior year losses

Tara makes a gain on a property in 2016/17 of £12,000 (proceeds of £25,000 less costs of £13,000). She makes no other disposals in the tax year. Tara has losses brought forward from the previous year of £10,000.

Required

Tara's net capital gain for 2016/17 before the annual exempt amount is:

£ [   ]

Tara has a loss to carry forward of £ [   ].

Workings (not provided in the CBT)

	£

5 Computing capital gains tax payable

An individual's taxable gains are chargeable to CGT at the rate of 10% or 20% (18/28% for residential properties, excluding your main home) depending on the individual's taxable income for 2016/17.

If the individual is a basic rate taxpayer, then CGT is payable at 10% on an amount of taxable gains up to the amount of the taxpayer's **unused** basic rate band and at 20% on the excess.

If the individual is a higher or additional rate taxpayer, then CGT is payable at 20% on all their taxable gains. Note the basic rate band covers taxable income and gains up to £32,000 (for 2016/17).

Illustration 5: Calculating capital gains tax

(a) Sally has taxable income (ie the amount after the deduction of the personal allowance) of £10,000 in 2016/17 and made taxable gains (ie gains after deduction of the annual exempt amount) of £20,000 in 2016/17.

Sally's CGT liability is:

£20,000 × 10%	£2,000

The taxable income uses £10,000 of the basic rate band, leaving £22,000 of the basic rate band unused, therefore all of the taxable gain is taxed at 10%.

(b) Hector has taxable income of £50,000 in 2016/17 (ie he is a higher rate taxpayer). He made taxable gains of £10,000 in 2016/17.

Hector's CGT liability is:

£10,000 × 20%	£2,000

All of Hector's basic rate band has been taken up by the taxable income, therefore the taxable gain is taxed at 20%.

(c) Isabel has taxable income of £30,000 in 2016/17 and made taxable gains of £25,000 in 2016/17.

Isabel has (£32,000 – £30,000) = £2,000 of her basic rate band unused. Isabel's CGT liability is:

	£
2,000 × 10%	200
£23,000 × 20%	4,600
£25,000	4,800

Activity 4: Computing capital gains tax payable

Mr Dunstable (see above) had a chargeable gain of £18,500 in 2016/17. He has taxable income of £31,000.

Required

What is Mr Dunstable's capital gains tax payable?

£ [   ] .

Workings (not provided in the CBT)

	£

6 Self-assessment for capital gains tax

CGT is payable on 31 January following the end of the tax year.

There are no payments on account.

An individual taxpayer who makes chargeable gains in a tax year is usually required to file details of the gains in a tax return. In many cases, the taxpayer will be filing a tax return for income tax purposes and will include the capital gains supplementary pages. If, however, the taxpayer only has chargeable gains to report, **he must notify his chargeability to HMRC by 5 October following the end of the tax year**.

The consequences of late notification, late filing, late payment of CGT and errors are the same as for income tax, so penalties and interest may be charged where applicable. Repayment interest may be paid on overpayments of CGT.

7 Computing chargeable gains and allowable losses for companies

The calculation of a chargeable gain or allowable loss for a company is very similar to the calculations we have already seen for individuals, with just a few significant differences:

- Companies claim an allowance for inflation called 'indexation'.

- Companies do not get an annual exempt amount.

- Loss relief is more straightforward. Current year gains and losses net off against each other. We then deduct capital losses brought forward.

7.1 Calculation of chargeable gains for companies

Illustration 6: Basic capital gains computation

	£
Disposal consideration (or market value)	X
Less incidental costs of disposal	(X)
Net proceeds	X
Less allowable costs (including acquisition costs)	(X)
Less enhancement expenditure	(X)
Unindexed gain	X
Less indexation on cost	(X)
Less indexation on enhancement expenditure	(X)
Indexed gain	X

7.2 Indexation allowance

Indexation allowance (IA) is given as a deduction to remove the effects of inflation from a gain.

It is calculated with reference to the movement of the retail price index (RPI) over the period of ownership.

The allowance is applied to the cost.

If the asset has been enhanced, IA must be applied separately to the enhancement.

You will be given the IA factor to use in your assessment.

Illustration 7: Indexation allowance

K Ltd bought an asset on 19 August 2000 for £10,000. Enhancement expenditure of £1,000 was incurred on 12 June 2007. The asset was sold for £41,500 on 20 February 2017. The disposal costs were £1,500.

Calculate the chargeable gain arising on the sale of the asset. Indexation factors: August 2000 to February 2017 = 0.524; June 2007 to February 2017 = 0.254.

	£
Disposal consideration	41,500
Less incidental costs of disposal	(1,500)
Net proceeds	40,000
Less purchase price	(10,000)
Less enhancement expenditure	(1,000)
	29,000
Less indexation on purchase price	
£10,000 × 0.524	(5,240)
Less indexation on enhancement expenditure	
£1,000 × 0.254	(254)
Chargeable gain	23,506

Activity 5: Capital gain calculation (companies)

Dunstable Ltd

	£
Asset purchased February 1986	15,000
Legal fees on purchase	500
Sale July 2016	38,500
Selling expenses July 2016	1,500
Enhancement expenditure October 1995	3,000
IA February 1986 – July 2016	0.781
IA October 1995 – July 2016	0.478

Required

Complete the table showing Dunstable Ltd's gain.

Solution

	£
Proceeds	
Less selling expenses	
Net proceeds	
Less cost	
Less legal fees on purchase	
Less enhancement	
Unindexed gain	
Less indexation on cost	
Less indexation on enhancement expenditure	
Capital gain	

The indexation allowance cannot create or increase an allowable loss. If there is a gain before the indexation allowance, the allowance can reduce that gain to zero, but no further. If there is a loss before the indexation allowance, there is no indexation allowance.

Activity 6: Indexation

Jek Ltd bought an asset for £50,000. Indexation is 0.761.

Required

What is the capital gain/(loss) if it was sold for:

(a) **£20,000?**   £

(b) **£70,000?**   £

(c) **£150,000?**   £

Workings (not provided in the CBT)

Assessment focus point

In the live assessment you will be provided with 'Taxation Data' that can be accessed through pop-up windows. The content of these taxation data tables has been reproduced at the back of this Course Book.

In addition, please refer to the reference material at the end of this Course Book to see which elements of this chapter will also be available to you as a window pop-up in the live assessment.

Chapter summary

- A chargeable gain arises when there is a chargeable disposal of a chargeable asset by a chargeable person.

- Enhancement expenditure can be deducted in computing a chargeable gain if it is reflected in the state and nature of the asset at the time of disposal.

- Chargeable gains are computed for individuals and companies in a similar way but for companies there is an indexation allowance.

- Taxable gains for an individual are net chargeable gains for a tax year (ie minus allowable losses of the current tax year and any unrelieved capital losses brought forward) minus the annual exempt amount.

- Losses brought forward by an individual can only reduce net chargeable gains down to the amount of the annual exempt amount.

- The rates of CGT are 10% and 20%, but the lower rate of 10% only applies if and to the extent that the individual has any unused basic rate band.

- CGT is payable by 31 January following the end of the tax year.

- CGT is self-assessed and has the same rules about notification of chargeability, penalties and interest as income tax.

- The indexation allowance gives relief for the inflation element of a gain for a company.

- **Annual exempt amount (AEA):** The amount of gains an individual can make before they have to pay CGT (£11,100 for 2016/17)

- **Chargeable asset:** Any asset that is not an exempt asset

- **Chargeable disposal:** A sale or gift of an asset

- **Chargeable person:** An individual or company

- **Exempt disposal:** A disposal on which no chargeable gain or allowable loss arises

- **Enhancement expenditure:** Capital expenditure that enhances the value of the asset and is reflected in the state or nature of the asset at the time of disposal

- **Taxable gains:** The chargeable gains of an individual for a tax year, after deducting allowable losses of the same tax year, any unrelieved capital losses brought forward and the annual exempt amount

Test your learning

1 **Tick to show if the following disposals would be chargeable or exempt for CGT.**

	Chargeable ✓	Exempt ✓
A gift of an antique necklace		
The sale of a building		

2 Yvette buys an investment property for £325,000. She sells the property on 12 December 2016 for £560,000.

Her chargeable gain on sale is:

£ [   ]

3 Philip has chargeable gains of £171,000 and allowable losses of £5,300 in 2015/16. Losses brought forward at 6 April 2016 amount to £10,000.

The amount liable to CGT in 2016/17 is:

£ [   ]

The losses carried forward are:

£ [   ]

4 Martha is a higher rate taxpayer who made chargeable gains (before the annual exempt amount) of £23,900 in October 2016.

Martha's CGT liability for 2016/17 is:

£ [   ]

5 **The payment date for capital gains tax for 2016/17 is (insert date as XX/XX/XX):**

[   ]

6 **Fill in the blanks with words of explanation.**

Indexation allowance runs from the date [   ] **to** [   ].

7 J plc bought a plot of land in July 2006 for £80,000. It spent £10,000 on drainage in April 2009, and sold the land for £200,000 in August 2016. The indexation factors from July 2006 – August 2016 = 0.302 and from April 2009 – August 2016 = 0.222.

Using the proforma layout provided, compute the gain on sale.

	£
Proceeds of sale	
Less cost	
Less enhancement expenditure	
Less indexation allowance on cost	
Less indexation allowance on enhancement	
Chargeable gain	

Further aspects of chargeable gains

12

Learning outcomes

5.1	Calculate the capital gains tax payable by self-employed taxpayers
	• Apply the rules relating to chargeable persons, disposals and assets
	• Calculate chargeable gain and allowable losses
	• Apply the rules relating to the disposal of chattels and wasting assets
	• Apply current reliefs and allowances

Assessment context

There are lots of rules regarding different assets so be sure you watch out for them in the assessment. It is crucial that you also notice if you are calculating a gain for an individual or a company as the tax treatment is different.

Qualification context

You will not see the information in this chapter outside of this unit unless you are also studying *Personal Tax*.

Business context

There are a number of very specific rules that apply in particular circumstances. It is vital to spot when these apply and use them correctly to ensure a business pays the right amount of tax on time and avoids penalties.

Chapter overview

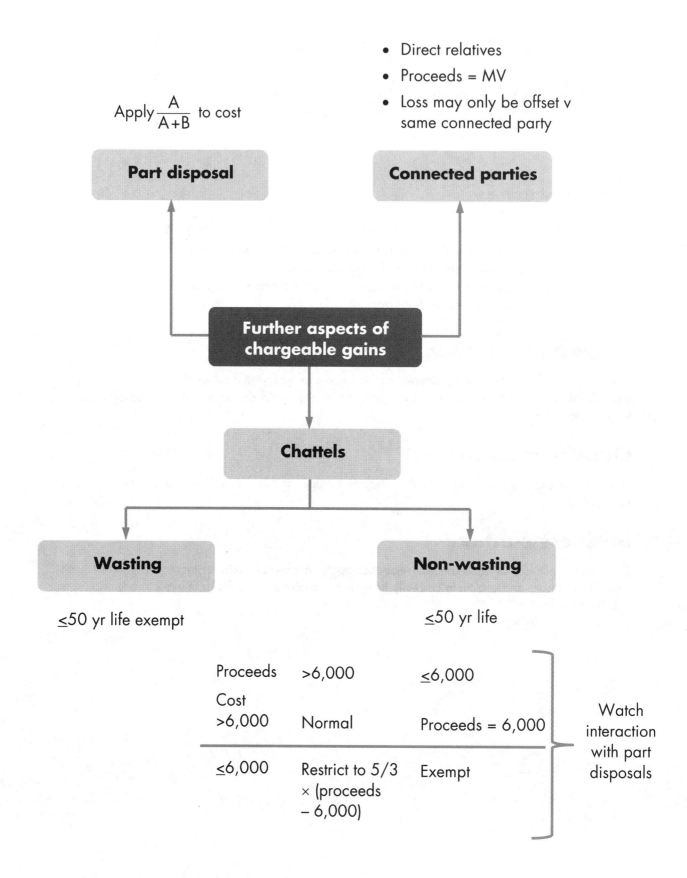

1 Introduction

This chapter looks in more detail at specific aspects of capital gains.

We will consider how to deal with part disposals of assets, and the calculation for disposals of a particular type of asset – a chattel.

There are special capital gains rules applying to disposals to certain individuals such as a spouse and other family members so we will consider how these calculations are different.

2 Part disposals and chattels for individuals

2.1 Part disposals

A **part disposal** occurs when only part, rather than the whole, of an asset is disposed of. For instance, one-third of a piece of land may be sold. In this case, we need to be able to compute the chargeable gain or allowable loss arising on the part of the asset disposed of.

The problem is that although we know what the disposal proceeds are for the part of the asset disposed of, we do not usually know what proportion of the 'cost' of the whole asset relates to that part. The solution to this is to **use the following fraction to determine the cost of the part disposed of**.

Formula to learn

The fraction is:

$$\frac{A}{A+B} = \frac{\text{Value of the part disposed of}}{\text{Value of the part disposed of} + \text{Market value of the remainder}}$$

A is the 'gross' proceeds (or market value) before deducting incidental costs of disposal.

B is the market value of the part of the asset that was not sold.

Illustration 1: Part disposal calculation

	£
Gross proceeds	X
Less selling costs	(X)
	X
Less:	
Original cost of the whole asset $\times \dfrac{A}{A+B}$	(C)
Gain	X

Illustration 2: Part disposal

Mr Jones bought four acres of land for £270,000. He sold one acre of the land at auction for £200,000, before auction expenses of 15%. The market value of the three remaining acres is £460,000.

The cost of the land being sold is:

$$\frac{200,000}{200,000+460,000} \times £270,000 = £81,818$$

	£
Disposal proceeds	200,000
Less incidental costs of sale (15% × £200,000)	(30,000)
Net proceeds	170,000
Less cost (see above)	(81,818)
Chargeable gain	88,182

Activity 1: Part disposal

Tom bought ten acres of land for £20,000.

He sold three acres of land for £10,000, incurring disposal costs of £950, when the remaining seven acres were worth £36,000.

Required

The gain on the disposal of the land is £ [   ].

The cost of the remaining land carried forward is £ [   ].

Workings (not provided in the CBT)

	£

2.2 Chattels

Chattels are tangible movable properties.

Wasting chattel is a chattel with an estimated remaining useful life of 50 years or less, eg a racehorse or greyhound.

Wasting chattels are exempt from capital gains tax (CGT) so there are no chargeable gains and no allowable losses.

Non-wasting chattels are chargeable to CGT in the normal way, subject to the following exceptions/restrictions.

Illustration 3: Rule for computing gains/losses on non-wasting chattels

Cost	Proceeds		
≤ 6,000	≤ 6,000	Wholly exempt	No need to calculate any gain.
≤ 6,000	> 6,000	Any gain restricted to max of: $\frac{5}{3}$ (Gross proceeds – £6,000)	Calculate gain, compare to the maximum, take the lower figure.
>6,000	≤ 6,000	Gross proceeds deemed to be £6,000	Do normal calculation but always use £6,000 as proceeds figure.
>6,000	>6,000	Wholly Taxable	Calculate a gain using the normal rules

Illustration 4: Proceeds > £6,000 cost < £6,000

John purchased a painting for £3,000. On 1 January 2017 he sold the painting at auction.

If the gross sale proceeds are £4,000, the gain on sale will be exempt.

If the gross sale proceeds are £8,000 with costs of sale of 10%, the gain arising on the disposal of the painting will be calculated as follows:

	£
Gross proceeds	8,000
Less incidental costs of sale (10% × £8,000)	(800)
Net proceeds	7,200
Less cost	(3,000)
Chargeable gain	4,200
Gain cannot exceed $\frac{5}{3}$ × £(8,000 – 6,000)	£3,333
Therefore chargeable gain is £3,333.	

Illustration 5: Proceeds < £6,000 cost > £6,000

Magee purchased an antique desk for £8,000. She sold the desk in an auction for £4,750 net of auctioneer's fees of 5% in November 2016.

Magee obviously has a loss and therefore the allowable loss is calculated on deemed proceeds of £6,000. The costs of disposal can be deducted from the deemed proceeds of £6,000.

	£
Deemed disposal proceeds	6,000
Less incidental costs of disposal (£4,750 × 5/95)	(250)
	5,750
Less cost	(8,000)
Allowable loss	(2,250)

Activity 2: Chattels

(a) Orlando Gibbons purchased a rare manuscript for £500. He sold it several years later for £9,000, before deducting the auctioneer's commission of £1,000.

(b) Antique bought for £7,000 and sold two years later for £3,000.

Required

(a) The chargeable gain on the disposal is £ [   ].

(b) The loss on the disposal is £ [   ].

3 Further rules for individuals

3.1 Transfers to connected persons

If a disposal by an individual is made to a connected person, **the disposal is deemed to take place at the market value (MV) of the asset**.

If an **allowable loss arises** on the disposal, it can **only be set against gains** arising in the same or future tax years from disposals **to the same connected person**, and the loss can only be set off if he or she is still connected with the person making the loss.

For this purpose an individual is connected with:

Direct relatives

Parents + spouses (+ grandparents + spouses)

↑

Brothers/sisters ←-------- Taxpayer --------→ Brothers/sisters
+   +   +
Spouses   Spouse   Spouses

↓

Children + spouses (+ grandchildren + spouses)

3.2 Transfers between spouses/civil partners

Spouses/civil partners are taxed as two separate people. Each individual has an annual exempt amount, and allowable losses of one individual cannot be set against gains of the other.

Disposals between spouses/civil partners do not give rise to chargeable gains or allowable losses. The disposal is said to be on a '**no gain/no loss**' basis. The acquiring spouse/civil partner takes the base cost of the disposing spouse/civil partner.

Activity 3: Transfers between spouses/civil partners

William sold an asset to his wife Kate in May 2015 for £32,000 when its market value was £45,000. William acquired the asset for £14,000 in June 2005.

Calculate the chargeable gain on this transfer. Tick ONE box.

	✓
Nil	
£18,000	
£31,000	
£13,000	

Assessment focus point

Please refer to the reference material at the end of this Course Book to see which elements of this chapter will be available to you as a pop-up window in the live assessment.

Chapter summary

- On the part disposal of an asset the formula A/(A + B) must be applied to work out the cost attributable to the part disposed of.

- Wasting chattels are exempt assets (eg racehorses and greyhounds).

- If a non-wasting chattel is sold for gross proceeds of £6,000 or less, any gain arising is exempt.

- If gross proceeds exceed £6,000 on the sale of a non-wasting chattel, but the cost is less than £6,000, any gain arising on the disposal of the asset is limited to $\frac{5}{3}$ × (Gross proceeds − £6,000).

- If the gross proceeds are less than £6,000 on the sale of a non-wasting chattel, any loss otherwise arising is restricted by deeming the gross proceeds to be £6,000.

- A disposal to a connected person takes place at market value.

- For individuals, connected people are, broadly, brothers, sisters, lineal ancestors and descendants and their spouses/civil partners plus similar relations of a spouse/civil partner.

- Losses on disposals to connected people can only be set against gains on disposals to the same connected person.

- Disposals between spouses/civil partners take place on a no gain/no loss basis.

Keywords

- **Chattel:** Tangible moveable property
- **Part disposal:** When part of an asset, rather than a whole asset, is disposed of
- **Wasting chattel:** A chattel with an estimated remaining useful life of 50 years or less

Test your learning

1 **Tick to show the correct answer.**

Richard sells four acres of land (out of a plot of ten acres) for £38,000 in July 2016. Costs of disposal amount to £3,000. The ten-acre plot cost £41,500. The market value of the six acres remaining is £48,000.

The chargeable gain/allowable loss arising is:

	✓
£16,663	
£17,500	
£19,663	
£18,337	

2 Mustafa bought a non-wasting chattel for £3,500.

The gain arising if he sells it for:

(a) **£5,800 after deducting selling expenses of £180 is:**

£ [ ]

(b) **£8,200 after deducting selling expenses of £220 is:**

£ [ ]

3 Simon bought a racehorse for £4,500. He sold the racehorse for £9,000 in December 2016.

The gain arising is:

£ [ ]

4 Santa bought a painting for £7,000. He sold the painting in June 2016 for £5,000.

The loss arising is (both minus signs and brackets can be used to indicate negative numbers):

£ [ ]

5 X Ltd bought four acres of land for £50,000 in December 2010. In February 2017, it sold one acre of the land for £80,000. At the time of the sale, the value of the three remaining acres was £120,000. The indexation factor between December 2010 and February 2017 is 0.138.

(a) The cost of the part of the land sold is:

£ [   ]

(b) The chargeable gain arising on the disposal is:

£ [   ]

6 M plc purchased a non-wasting chattel for £3,500 in August 2013. In October 2016 it sold the chattel at auction for £8,000. The indexation factor between August 2013 and October 2016 is 0.031.

The gain arising is:

£ [   ]

7 S Ltd bought a non-wasting chattel for £8,700 in October 2009. It sold the chattel for £4,300 in May 2016. The indexation factor between October 2009 and May 2016 is 0.194.

Calculate the allowable loss on sale. Tick ONE box.

	✓
£(6,088)	
£(4,400)	
£(2,700)	
£(4,388)	

8 **Decide whether the following statement is true or false.**

A loss arising on a disposal to a connected person can be set against any gains arising in the same tax year or in subsequent tax years.

	✓
True	
False	

9 **Decide whether the following statement is true or false.**

No gain or loss arises on a disposal to a spouse/civil partner.

	✓
True	
False	

10 **Complete the table by ticking the appropriate box for each scenario.**

	Actual proceeds used ✓	Deemed proceeds (market value) used ✓	No gain or loss basis ✓
Paul sells an asset to his civil partner Joe for £3,600			
Grandmother gives an asset to her grandchild worth £1,000			
Sarah knowingly sells an asset worth £20,000 to her best friend Cathy for just £12,000			

Share disposals

13

Learning outcomes

5.1	Calculate the capital gains tax payable by self-employed taxpayers
	• Apply the rules relating to the disposal of shares
5.2	Calculate chargeable gains and allowable losses for limited companies
	• Apply the rules relating to the disposal of shares

Assessment context

This task is likely to be assessed by free data entry of all workings and will be human marked.

Qualification context

Share disposals by individuals also feature in *Personal Tax*. You will not see these rules anywhere else in your qualification.

Business context

A tax practitioner needs to be able to calculate capital gains tax payable on the disposal of shares for their clients.

Chapter overview

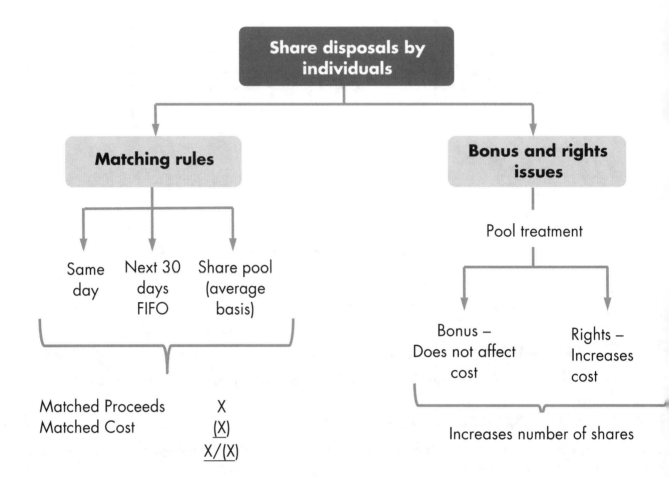

Share disposals by individuals

Matching rules

Same day

Next 30 days FIFO

Share pool (average basis)

Matched Proceeds   X
Matched Cost   (X)
                   X/(X)

Bonus and rights issues

Pool treatment

Bonus – Does not affect cost

Rights – Increases cost

Increases number of shares

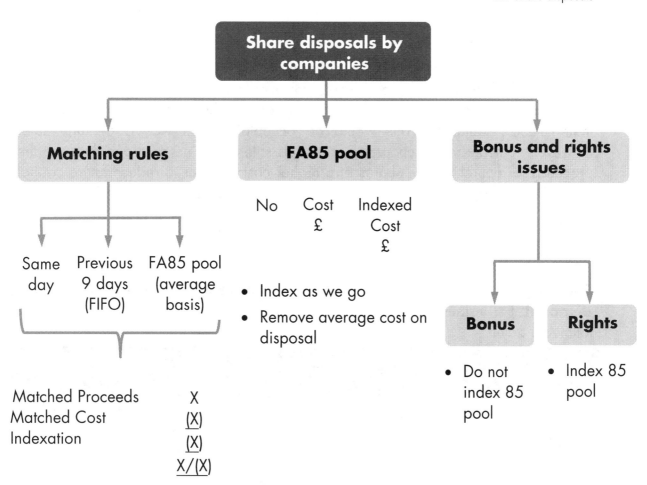

Matched Proceeds   X
Matched Cost   (X)
Indexation   (X)
    X/(X)

1 Introduction

When a sale of shares takes place the gain or loss could be manipulated by choosing which shares to sell and when. For example, an individual could have lots of shares in one company and choose to sell some in the tax year in order to utilise their annual exemption. This would be acceptable if it was a genuine sale. However, someone could choose to make this sale, make no gain and then use the proceeds to repurchase the shares at a higher cost in order to reduce future capital gains. In this chapter we look at the rules created to stop this behaviour.

2 Rules for individuals

2.1 Matching rules for individuals

Shares present special problems when computing gains or losses on disposal. For instance, suppose that a taxpayer buys some shares in X plc on the following dates:

	No of shares	Cost £
5 July 1992	150	195
17 January 1997	100	375
2 July 2016	100	1,000

On 15 June 2016, he sells 220 of his shares for £3,300. **To work out his chargeable gain, we need to be able to identify which shares** out of his three holdings **were actually sold**. Since one share is identical to any other, it is not possible to work this out by reference to factual evidence.

As a result, it has been necessary to devise 'matching rules'. These allow us to identify, on a disposal, which shares have been sold and so **work out what the allowable cost** (and therefore the gain) **on disposal should be**. These matching rules are considered in detail below.

Assessment focus point

It is very important that you understand the matching rules. These rules are very regularly assessed and if you do not understand them you will not be able to get any of this part of a task right.

Matching rules

Shares sold should be matched with purchases in the following order:

1   Acquisitions on the same day as disposal.

2   Acquisitions within the following 30 days, on a first in, first out (FIFO) basis.

3   Shares from the share pool. The share pool includes all other shares not acquired on the dates above, and is explained below.

Illustration 1: Matching rules

Noah acquired shares in Ark Ltd as follows.

2 August 2012   10,000 shares
25 April 2014   10,000 shares
17 June 2016   1,000 shares
19 June 2016   2,000 shares

Noah sold 15,000 shares on 17 June 2016.

Which shares is he selling for capital gains tax purposes?

Noah will match his disposal of 15,000 shares on 17 June 2016 as follows:

1   1,000 shares bought on 17 June 2016 (same day)
2   2,000 shares bought on 19 June 2016 (next 30 days, FIFO basis)
3   12,000 shares from the 20,000 shares in the share pool

Illustration 2: Basic computation

	£	£
For each batch of matched shares:		
Proportion of proceeds	X	
Less cost (if from share pool W1)	(X)	
		X

(W1)   Share pool

	No of shares	Cost £
Shares bought/sold	X	X

2.2 Share pool

The share pool includes shares acquired up to the day before the disposal on which we are calculating the gain or loss. It grows when an acquisition is made and shrinks when a disposal is made.

2.2.1 The calculation of the share pool value

To compute the value of the share pool, set up two columns of figures:

(a)   The number of shares
(b)   The cost of the shares

Each time shares are acquired, both the number and the cost of the acquired shares are added to those already in the pool.

When there is a disposal from the pool, both the number of shares being disposed of, and a cost relating to those shares, are deducted from the pool. The cost of the disposal is calculated as a proportion of total cost in the pool, based on the number of shares being sold.

Illustration 3: The share pool

Jackie bought 10,000 shares in X plc for £6,000 in August 1996 and another 10,000 shares for £9,000 in December 2008.

She sold 12,000 shares for £24,000 in August 2016.

The gain is:

	£
Proceeds of sale	24,000
Less allowable cost (W1)	(9,000)
Chargeable gain	15,000

(W1) The share pool is:

	No of shares	Cost £
August 1996 acquisition	10,000	6,000
December 2008 acquisition	10,000	9,000
	20,000	15,000
August 2016 disposal ($£15,000 \times {}^{12,000}\!/_{20,000} = £9,000$)	(12,000)	(9,000)
c/f	8,000	6,000

Activity 1: Matching rules for individuals

Mr L made the following purchases of ordinary shares in H plc:

Date	Number	Cost
15.5.02	2,200	8,800
1.5.16	400	3,000
17.5.16	500	4,500

On 1.5.16 Mr L sold 1,600 shares for £14,000.

Required

What is the chargeable gain or loss for 2016/17 on the disposal of these shares? Clearly show the balance of shares to be carried forward.

Solution

	£	£

Activity 2: Share pool for individuals

Mr Lambert purchased the following holdings in Grande plc:

Date	Number	Cost £
January 1985	3,000	5,000
February 1987	1,000	4,000

In May 2016 he sold 2,000 shares for £14,000.

Required

What is the chargeable gain or loss for 2016/17 on the disposal of these shares? Clearly show the balance of shares to be carried forward.

Solution

	£	£

2.3 Bonus and rights issues for individuals

2.3.1 Bonus issues

Bonus issues are free shares given to existing shareholders in proportion to their existing shareholding. For example, a shareholder may own 2,000 shares. The company makes a 1 share for every 2 shares held bonus issue (called a 1 for 2 bonus issue). The shareholder will then have an extra 1,000 shares, giving him 3,000 shares overall.

Bonus shares are treated as being acquired at the date of the original acquisition of the underlying shares giving rise to the bonus issue.

Since bonus shares are issued at no cost there is **no need to adjust the original cost**.

2.3.2 Rights issues

In a **rights issue**, a **shareholder is offered the right to buy additional shares by the company in proportion to the shares already held**.

The difference between a bonus issue and a rights issue is that, in a rights issue, the new shares are paid for. This results in an **adjustment to the original cost**.

For matching purposes, bonus and rights shares are treated as if they were acquired on the same day as the shareholder's original holdings.

Illustration 4: Bonus and rights issues

Jonah acquired 20,000 shares for £34,200 in T plc in April 2005. There was a 1 for 2 bonus issue in May 2010 and a 1 for 5 rights issue in August 2015 at £1.20 per share.

Jonah sold 30,000 shares for £45,000 in December 2016.

The gain on sale is:

	£
Proceeds of sale	45,000
Less allowable cost (W1)	(34,500)
Chargeable gain	10,500

(W1) The share pool is constructed as follows:

	No of shares	Cost £
April 2005 acquisition	20,000	34,200
May 2010 bonus 1 for 2 ($\frac{1}{2} \times 20{,}000 = 10{,}000$)	10,000	–
	30,000	34,200
August 2015 rights 1 for 5 @ £1.20 ($\frac{1}{5} \times 30{,}000 = 6{,}000$ shares $\times$ £1.20 = £7,200)	6,000	7,200
	36,000	41,400
December 2016 disposal (£41,400 $\times \frac{30{,}000}{36{,}000}$ = £34,500)	(30,000)	(34,500)
c/f	6,000	6,900

Activity 3: Bonus and rights issues for individuals

Richard had the following transactions in S plc.

1.10.95	Bought 10,000 shares for £15,000
11.9.99	Bought 2,000 shares for £5,000
1.2.00	Took up rights issue 1 for 2 at £2.75 per share
5.9.05	2 for 1 bonus issue
14.10.16	Sold 15,000 shares for £15,000

Required

Calculate the gain or loss made on these shares. All workings must be shown in your calculations.

Solution

	£	£

	£	£

3 Rules for companies

3.1 Matching rules for companies

There are different matching rules for companies.

Illustration 5: Matching rules for companies

Shares sold should be matched with purchases in the following order:

1   Acquisitions on the same day
2   Acquisitions in the previous nine days – FIFO basis
3   Shares from the FA 1985 pool

There is no indexation allowance on shares acquired in the previous nine days, even if the acquisition is in the previous month to the disposal.

Illustration 6: The application of the matching rules for companies

Z Ltd acquired the following shares in L plc:

9 November 2007   10,000 shares

15 December 2009 20,000 shares

11 July 2016   5,000 shares

15 July 2016   5,000 shares

Z Ltd disposed of 20,000 of the shares on 15 July 2016.

We match the 20,000 shares sold to acquisitions as follows.

(a)   Acquisition on same day: 5,000 shares acquired 15 July 2016.

(b)   Acquisitions in previous 9 days: 5,000 shares acquired 11 July 2016.

(c)   FA 1985 share pool: 10,000 shares out of 30,000 shares in FA 1985 share pool (9 November 2007 and 15 December 2009).

A disposal computation is produced for each matching rule.

3.2 The FA 1985 pool

The FA 1985 pool comprises the following shares:

Shares acquired by that company on or after 1 April 1985

We must keep track of:

(a)   The number of shares
(b)   The cost of the shares ignoring indexation
(c)   The indexed cost of the shares

Illustration 7: Basic computation

	£	£
For each batch of matched shares:		
Proportion of proceeds	X	
Less cost (if from share pool W1)	(X)	
		X

(W1) Share pool

Contains 3 columns

	No of shares	Cost £	Indexed cost £
Shares bought/sold	X	X	X

You must reflect each operative event in the FA 1985 pool. However, prior to reflecting an operative event within the FA 1985 share pool, a further indexation allowance (sometimes described as an indexed rise) must be computed up to the date of the operative event you are looking at. You must look at each operative event in chronological order.

Illustration 8: FA85 pool (from 1 April 1985)

J Ltd has a share pool at 1 April 1985 containing 20,000 shares with a cost of £15,000 and an indexed cost of £16,329. Now assume that J Ltd acquired 4,000 more shares on 1 January 1990 at a cost of £6,000.

Show the value of the FA 1985 pool on 1 January 1990 following the acquisition. The indexation factor April 1985 – January 1990 = 0.261.

	No of shares	Cost £	Indexed cost £
1 April 1985	20,000	15,000	16,329
Index to January 1990			
0.261 × £16,329			4,262
			20,591
January 1990 acquisition	4,000	6,000	6,000
	24,000	21,000	26,591

If there are several operative events, the procedure described must be performed several times over. In the case of a disposal, following the calculation of the indexed rise, the cost and the indexed cost attributable to the shares disposed of are deducted from the cost and the indexed cost columns within the FA 1985 pool. This is computed on a pro-rata basis if only part of the holding is being sold.

Illustration 9: FA85 pool – a disposal from the pool

Following on from the above example, suppose that J Ltd now disposes of 12,000 shares on 9 January 2017 for £26,000.

Show the value of the FA 1985 pool on 10 January 2017 following the disposal. Compute the gain on the disposal. The indexation factor January 1990 – January 2017 = 1.172.

(W1)

	No of shares	Cost £	Indexed cost £
Value at January 1990	24,000	21,000	26,591
Indexed rise to January 2017			
(1.172 × £26,591)			31,165
	24,000	21,000	57,756
Disposal			
(cost or indexed cost × $\frac{12,000}{24,000}$)	(12,000)	(10,500)	(28,878)
Pool c/f	12,000	10,500	28,878

The gain on the disposal is calculated as follows:

	£
Sale proceeds	26,000
Less cost (W1)	(10,500)
	15,500
Less indexation (£28,878 – £10,500)	(18,378)
Gain	Nil

Note that the indexation for the shares sold is the difference between the indexed cost and the cost, and that the indexation cannot create or increase a loss.

Activity 4: Matching rules for companies

ABC Ltd bought 1,000 shares in XYZ Ltd for £2,750 in August 1996 and another 1,000 for £3,250 in December 1998. On 4 July 2016 it bought 500 shares for £2,511 and on 10 July 2016 it bought 1,000 shares for £4,822.

ABC Ltd sold 2,500 shares on 10 July 2016 for £12,500.

Indexed rises: August 96 to December 98 = 0.008

December 98 to July 16   = 0.157

Required

Compute the gain on the disposal of these shares. Clearly show the balance to be carried forward.

Solution

		£	£

		£	£

3.3 Bonus and rights issues for companies

Indexation is not required when bonus shares are received as there is no additional cost.

Indexation will be required if there is a rights issue, as the shares are acquired at a cost. The FA 1985 pool will need to be indexed to the date of the rights issue as this is classed as an 'operative event'.

Activity 5: Bonus and rights issues for companies

Wotan Ltd sold 800 shares in Krimpton Ltd on 5 September 2016 for £10,000. The holding had been built up as follows:

500 acquired for £1,000 on 1 May 1985

1 for 2 rights issue for £5 per share on 5 August 1987

1 for 1 bonus issue on 15 September 1989

Indexation factors are as follows:

May 85 → August 87	0.347
August 87 → August 89	0.135
August 89 → September 16	0.543
August 87 → September 16	0.917

Required

Calculate the chargeable gain in September 2016.

Solution

		£	£

	£	£

Assessment focus point

Please refer to the reference material at the end of this Course Book to see which elements of this chapter will be available to you as a pop-up window in the live assessment.

Chapter summary

- The matching rules for individuals are:
  - Same-day acquisitions
  - Next 30 days' acquisitions, on a FIFO basis
  - Shares in the share pool
- The share pool runs up to the day before disposal.
- Bonus issue and rights issue shares are acquired in proportion to the shareholder's existing holding.
- The difference between a bonus and a rights issue is that in a rights issue shares are paid for.
- The matching rules for companies are:
  - Same-day acquisitions
  - Previous 9 days' acquisitions on a FIFO basis
  - Shares in the FA 1985 share pool
- In the FA 1985 share pool, we must keep track of the number of shares, the cost of the shares and the indexed cost.
- Operative events increase or decrease the amount of expenditure within the FA 1985 pool.
- For a company, a rights issue is treated as an operative event, whereas a bonus issue is not.

Keywords

- **Bonus shares:** Shares that are issued free to shareholders, based on original holdings

- **Operative events:** Disposals/acquisitions of shares that decrease/increase the amount of expenditure within the FA 1985 pool

- **Rights issues:** Similar to bonus issues except that in a rights issue shares must be paid for

Test your learning

1   Tasha bought 10,000 shares in V plc in August 1994 for £5,000 and a further 10,000 shares for £16,000 in April 2009. She sold 15,000 shares for £30,000 in November 2016.

    Tick to show what her chargeable gain is.

	✓
£15,750	
£11,500	
£17,000	
£14,250	

2   **Tick to show whether the following statement is true or false.**

    In both a bonus issue and a rights issue, there is an adjustment to the original cost of the shares.

	✓
True	
False	

3   Marcus bought 2,000 shares in X plc in May 2003 for £12,000. There was a 1 for 2 rights issue at £7.50 per share in December 2004. Marcus sold 2,500 shares for £20,000 in March 2017.

    His chargeable gain is:

    £ _____

4   Mildred bought 6,000 shares in George plc in June 2011 for £15,000. There was a 1 for 3 bonus issue in August 2012. Mildred sold 8,000 shares for £22,000 in December 2016.

    Her chargeable gain is:

    £ _____

5   **What are the share matching rules for company shareholders?**

6   Q Ltd bought 10,000 shares in R plc in May 2003 at a cost of £90,000. There was a 1 for 4 rights issue in June 2009 at the cost of £12 per share and Q Ltd took up all of its rights entitlement.

    Q Ltd sold 10,000 shares in R plc for £150,000 in January 2017.

The indexed rise between May 2003 and June 2009 is 0.176 and between June 2009 and January 2017 is 0.216.

(a) Using the proforma layout provided, show the share pool.

		No of shares	Cost £	Indexed cost £

(b) Using the proforma layout provided, compute the gain on sale.

	£

Reliefs for chargeable gains 14

Learning outcomes

4.2	Demonstrate an understanding of current tax reliefs and other tax issues
	• Current tax reliefs available to businesses
5.1	Calculate capital gains tax payable by self-employed taxpayers
	• Calculate chargeable gains and allowable losses
	• Apply current reliefs and allowances
	• Apply the capital gains tax rates
5.2	Calculate chargeable gains and allowable losses for limited companies
	• Calculate the computation of chargeable gains and allowable losses
	• Apply current reliefs and allowances

Assessment context

In the assessment you could be tested on capital gains tax exemptions, losses, reliefs and tax payable.

Qualification context

You will not see these rules outside of this unit.

Business context

Nobody likes to pay tax! These reliefs are extremely useful in the real world to postpone, reduce or eliminate a tax liability.

Chapter overview

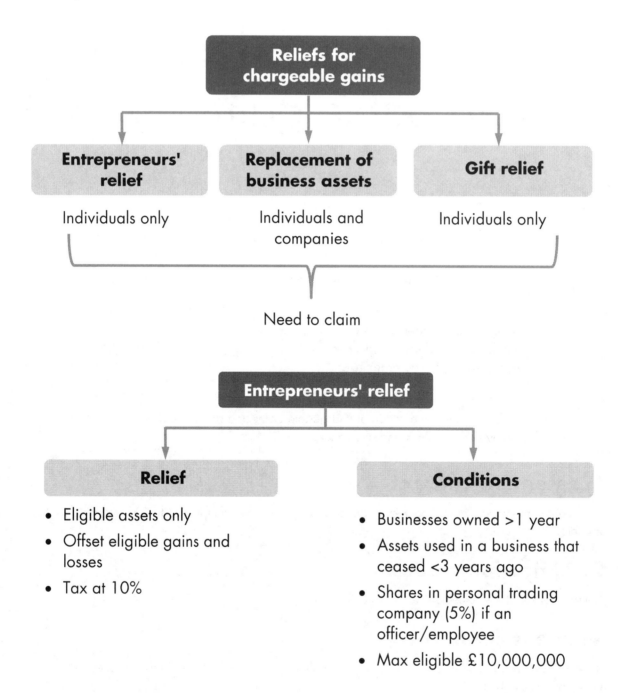

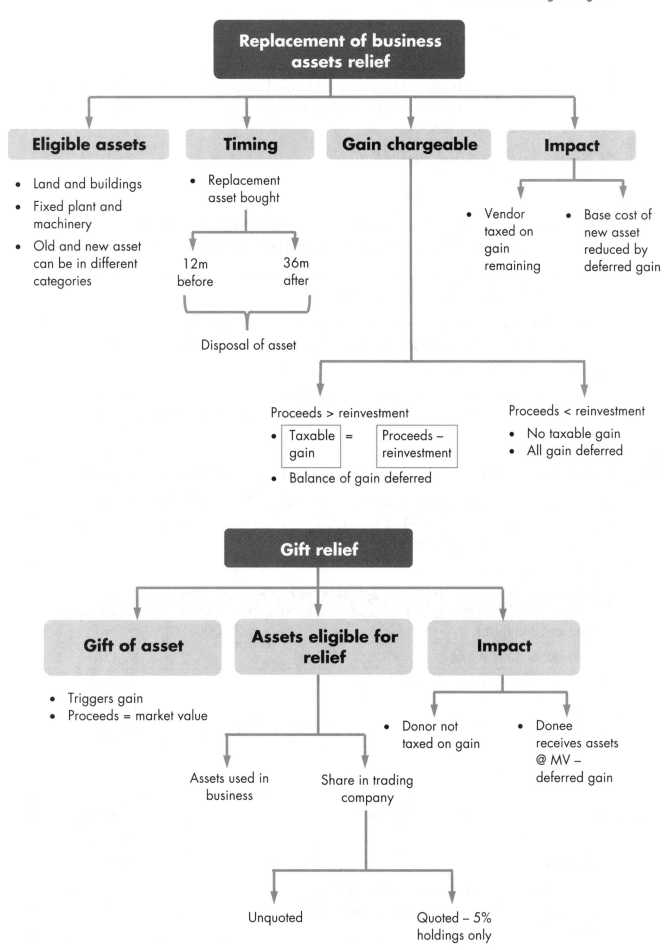

1 Introduction

This chapter looks at the reliefs available to individuals and companies to reduce their capital gains liabilities. Entrepreneurs' relief and gift relief are available to individuals only. Replacement of business assets relief is available to both individuals and companies.

2 Entrepreneurs' relief

2.1 The relief

Individuals can claim entrepreneurs' relief (ER) to reduce the rate of capital gains tax (CGT) on a material disposal of business assets.

Gains on assets qualifying for entrepreneurs' relief are **taxed at 10%** regardless of the level of a person's taxable income.

If a taxpayer has both gains that are eligible for entrepreneurs' relief and gains that are ineligible they should offset the annual exempt amount and any ineligible losses against the ineligible gains first.

Although gains eligible for the relief are taxed at 10%, they are deemed to be taxed before ineligible gains when deciding whether any of the basic rate band remains available.

Illustration 1: Losses, annual exempt amount and basic rate band

Steve makes gains eligible for entrepreneurs' relief (ER) of £15,000, and gains not eligible for entrepreneurs' relief of £40,000. He has taxable income of £25,000 and capital losses brought forward of £4,000.

The CGT payable is:

Equity	£	£
Gains eligible for ER	15,000	
Gains not eligible for ER		40,000
Loss capital loss brought forward		(4,000)
Annual exemption		(11,100)
Taxable gains	15,000	24,900
Tax:		
£15,000 × 10% (gains eligible for ER)		1,500
£24,900 × 20%		4,980
CGT due:		6,480
Note. There is no basic rate band remaining after taxing income and the gain eligible for ER (£25,000 + £15,000)		

Activity 1: Entrepreneurs' relief – calculation of capital gains tax

Poins disposes of his business on 21 August 2016, realising a gain of £10,000 which qualifies for entrepreneurs' relief. He has other gains in the year of £50,000 which do not qualify for entrepreneurs' relief.

Poins has taxable income of £19,370.

Required

Capital gains tax payable at 10% due to ER is £ [   ] .

Capital gains tax payable at 10% to utilise the remaining basic rate

band is £ [   ] .

Capital gains tax payable at 20% is £ [   ] .

Workings (not provided in the CBT)

	Other gains £	Eligible gains £

2.2 Conditions

Entrepreneurs' relief applies when there has been a material disposal of business assets, such as:

2.2.1 Disposal of an unincorporated business

The disposal of the whole or part of a business (as a going concern) which has been owned by the individual throughout the period of one year ending with the date of the disposal.

A business includes one carried on as a partnership of which the individual is a partner.

The business must be a trade, profession or vocation conducted on a commercial basis with a view to the realisation of profits.

Relief is only available on relevant business assets. These are assets used for the purposes of the business and cannot include shares and securities or assets held by the business as investments. Gains and losses on relevant business assets are netted off.

2.2.2 Disposal of assets used in an unincorporated business that has ceased trading

The disposal of assets used in the business prior to the cessation of the business, provided that:

- The business was owned for one year prior to the cessation
- The assets were sold within three years of the date of cessation

2.2.3 Disposal of shares

The disposal of shares or securities where:

- The company is the individual's personal company (ie owns at least 5% of the shares and can exercise 5% of the votes);

- The company is a trading company; and

- The individual is an officer or employee of the company.

These conditions must be met:

- For one year before the date of disposal; or

- For one year up to the date at which the company ceases to trade. The shares must then be sold within three years of this date.

Activity 2: Disposals eligible for entrepreneurs' relief

The following assets are disposed of in 2016/17 by various individuals.

Identify which, if any, are qualifying disposals for entrepreneurs' relief. Tick the relevant box.

	✓
Part of a business in which the individual has been a partner since August 2014	
A freehold factory which the individual uses in his business and has owned for ten years	
Unquoted shares held by the individual in a personal trading company in which he is employed and which he has owned for the previous two years	
Quoted shares held by the individual in a personal trading company in which he is employed and which he has owned for the previous two years	

2.3 Lifetime limit

There is a lifetime limit of £10 million of gains on which entrepreneurs' relief can be claimed.

> **Illustration 2: Lifetime limit**
>
> Carrie has made several disposals qualifying for entrepreneurs' relief. The gains on these disposals are as follows:
>
> 1 May 2016   £7,750,000
> 1 June 2016   £2,300,000
> 1 February 2017 £2,200,000
>
> Entrepreneurs' relief will be given on the following amounts:
>
> 1 May 2016 £7,750,000 (less than the lifetime limit of £10,000,000).
>
> 1 June 2016 £2,250,000 (lifetime limit £10,000,000 less relief already used of £7,750,000). £50,000 is not eligible for relief.
>
> 1 February 2017 None of the lifetime limit is left, therefore £2,200,000 is not eligible for entrepreneurs' relief.

Activity 3: Entrepreneurs' relief – calculating gains eligible for relief

Hal has run his business for many years. In January 2017 he sells it, realising the following gains and (losses).

Equity	£
Goodwill	500,000
Factory	300,000
Office block	(100,000)
Shares	80,000

All the assets were used in his business except the shares.

He has never previously claimed entrepreneurs' relief.

Required

The total net taxable gain eligible for entrepreneurs' relief is

£ [   ] .

The total net taxable gain not eligible for entrepreneurs' relief is

£ [   ] .

Workings (not provided in the CBT)

	£	£

If the gain on the factory was £9,800,000, then the total net taxable gain eligible for entrepreneurs' relief is

£ [   ] .

The total net taxable gain not eligible for entrepreneurs' relief is

£ [   ] .

Workings (not provided in the CBT)

	£	£

2.4 Claim

The relief must be claimed within one year following the 31 January after the tax year of disposal. Relief for 2016/17 must, therefore, be claimed by 31 January 2019.

3 Replacement of business assets (rollover) relief

3.1 The relief

Rollover relief is available to **both individuals and companies**.

A gain may be 'rolled over' where it arises **on the disposal of a business asset** (the 'old' asset) **if another business asset** (the 'new' asset) **is acquired**.

The following conditions must be met:

(a)   The old asset and the new asset must **both be used in a trade**.

(b)   The old asset and the new asset must **both be qualifying assets**.

The 'new' asset can be one asset or more than one asset and the new asset can be for use in a different trade from the old asset.

Deferral is usually obtained by deducting the gain on the old asset from the cost of the new asset.

3.2 Qualifying assets

Both the old and new assets must fall into one of the following categories:

- Land and buildings used for the purpose of the trade
- Fixed plant and machinery
- Goodwill (for individuals only)

3.3 Timing

Reinvestment of the proceeds of the old asset must take place in a period beginning **one year before** and ending **three years after** the date of the disposal.

Illustration 3: Rollover relief – all proceeds reinvested

A freehold factory was purchased by a sole trader on 13 May 2002 for £60,000 and sold for £90,000 on 18 September 2016. A replacement factory was purchased on 6 December 2016 for £100,000. Rollover relief was claimed on the sale of the first factory.

(a)   Gain on sale September 2016

	£
Disposal proceeds	90,000
Less cost	(60,000)
Gain (all proceeds reinvested therefore defer full gain)	30,000

(b)   Revised base cost of asset purchased in December 2016

Original cost	100,000
Less rolled over gain	(30,000)
Revised base cost (this will be used to calculate gain on subsequent sale of new asset)	70,000

3.4 Taxed now

For all the gain to be deferred, all the proceeds of the old asset must be reinvested in the new asset. Any proceeds not reinvested in a qualifying asset are deducted from the gain to be rolled over.

If the amount of proceeds not reinvested exceeds the gain, no amount of the gain can therefore be rolled over. This is the same as saying the amount chargeable is the lower of the gain and the amount not reinvested.

Illustration 4: Rollover relief – not all proceeds reinvested

Susannah realised a gain of £300,000 on the disposal of an office block used in her business. The office block was sold for £700,000. A new office block was bought for £600,000 in the following month.

The proceeds not reinvested are £100,000 so this amount of the gain is immediately chargeable. The remaining gain of £200,000 can be rolled over and set against the base cost of the new office block. This means the base cost of the new office block is £(600,000 – 200,000) = £400,000.

Activity 4: Rollover relief

Henry Ltd sells fixed plant for £200,000. It cost £150,000, indexation allowance is 10%. Six months later Henry Ltd buys a building for £190,000.

Both assets are used in the trade.

Required

The gain taxed on Henry Ltd now is

£ [   ] .

The base cost of the building is

£ [   ] .

Workings (not provided in the CBT)

4 Gift relief

4.1 The relief

Individuals can claim **gift relief** to defer a gain arising **on the gift of a business asset**.

The gift is deemed to be made at market value (MV).

The transferee is deemed to acquire the asset for its market value less the deferred gain.

Illustration 5: Gift relief

John bought a business asset in 2010 for £20,000. On 1 May 2016 John gave the asset to Marie Louise. The market value of the asset on the date of the gift was £90,000.

John is deemed to dispose of the asset for its market value of £90,000 so the gain arising on the gift is:

	£
Deemed disposal proceeds	90,000
Less cost	(20,000)
Gain	70,000

The gain of £70,000 is deferred by setting it against the value of £90,000 at which Marie Louise is deemed to acquire the gift. Therefore Marie Louise is deemed to acquire the gift for £20,000 (£90,000 – £70,000) and this will be used as the base cost for future disposals.

4.2 Conditions

The disposal must be made to a UK individual.

Qualifying assets for gift relief purposes include:

(a)   Assets used in a trade carried on:

    (i)   By the donor
    (ii)   By the donor's personal company

(b)   Shares in:

    (i)   An unquoted trading company
    (ii)   The donor's personal trading company

A 'personal company' is one in which not less than 5% of the voting rights are controlled by the donor.

4.3 Impact of claim

The donor does not have to pay CGT.

The gain is rolled over into (deducted from) the base cost of the asset now owned by the recipient.

The gift relief claim to defer the gain must be made jointly by the donor and the recipient.

Activity 5: Gift relief

Bill gave a workshop used in his trade to his son, Ludovic. Its market value was £25,000.

Bill had purchased the workshop for £7,000.

A valid gift relief claim is made.

Required

The gift relief claim must be signed by ☐ .

Picklist:

Bill and Ludovic
Bill only
Ludovic only

Bill's chargeable gain on disposal is

£ ☐ .

Ludovic's base cost is

£ ☐ .

Workings (not provided in the CBT)

Activity 6: With and without gift relief

Julie bought 10,000 shares in an unquoted trading company for £50,000 in July 2007. Julie gave her shares to Jack in May 2015, when they were worth £85,000. Jack sold the shares for £95,000 in December 2015.

Required

(a) **If gift relief is not claimed, Julie's chargeable gain is**

£ [   ]

and Jack's chargeable gain is

£ [   ] .

(b) **If gift relief is claimed, Julie's chargeable gain is**

£ [   ]

and Jack's chargeable gain is

£ [   ] .

Workings (not provided in the CBT)

Assessment focus point

In the live assessment you will be provided with 'Taxation Data' that can be accessed through pop-up windows. The content of these taxation data tables has been reproduced at the end of this Course Book.

In addition you are also provided with reference material which has been reproduced at the end of this Course Book. Please review this material to see which elements of this chapter will be available to you as a pop-up window in the live assessment.

Chapter summary

- Entrepreneurs' relief reduces the rate of CGT on gains made by an individual, on certain business disposals, to 10%.

- There is a lifetime limit of £10 million for entrepreneurs' relief.

- Entrepreneurs' relief applies to disposals of an unincorporated business (or part of a business), disposals of business assets on cessation, and shares in a trading company that is the individual's personal company and of which he is an officer or employee.

- Rollover relief can be used by individuals and companies to defer a gain when a qualifying business asset is replaced with another qualifying business asset.

- Qualifying business assets for rollover relief include land and buildings, fixed plant and machinery and, for individuals, goodwill. Both the old and the new assets must be used for the purposes of a trade.

- If sale proceeds are not fully reinvested, an amount of the gain equal to the proceeds not reinvested is immediately chargeable. The remainder of the gain may be rolled over.

- The rolled-over gain reduces the cost of the new asset.

- The new asset must be acquired in the period commencing one year before and ending three years after the disposal.

- Gift relief can be used by an individual to defer a gain on the gift of business assets.

- The recipient acquires the gift at its market value less the amount of the deferred gain.

- Qualifying assets for gift relief include assets used in a trade by the donor or his personal company, unquoted shares in a trading company and shares in a personal trading company.

Keywords

- **Entrepreneurs' relief:** Reduces the effective rate of tax on the disposal of certain business assets from 20% (if they would be taxed at the higher rate) to 10%

- **Gift relief:** Can defer a gain on a gift of business assets by an individual

- **Rollover relief:** Can defer a gain when business assets are replaced

1 Ian sold his business as a going concern to John in May 2016. The gains on sale were £10,400,000. Ian had not previously made any claims for entrepreneurs' relief, and made no other disposals in 2016/17. Ian is a higher rate taxpayer.

Ian's CGT liability for 2016/17 is:

£	

2 Jemma sold her shareholding in J Ltd in January 2017. She had acquired the shares in August 2006 for £10,000. The proceeds of sale were £80,000. The disposal qualified for entrepreneurs' relief.

Jemma's CGT on the disposal, assuming she has already used the annual exempt amount for 2016/17, is:

£	

3 K Ltd sold a factory on 10 November 2016. It purchased the following assets:

Date of purchase	Asset
21 September 2015	Office block
15 February 2017	Freehold factory
4 June 2018	Fork lift truck
8 December 2019	Freehold warehouse

All of the above assets are used for the purpose of the trade of K Ltd.

Against which purchase may K Ltd claim rollover relief in respect of the gain arising on disposal of the factory?

	✓
Office block	
Freehold factory	
Fork lift truck	
Freehold warehouse	

4 Trevor bought land for £100,000 in March 2007. In March 2016, this land was sold for £400,000 and replacement land was bought for £380,000. The replacement land was sold in May 2017 for £500,000. Both pieces of land were used in Trevor's trade, which is still continuing.

What is the chargeable gain arising in May 2016? Assume all available reliefs were claimed.

	✓
£120,000	
£200,000	
£400,000	
£420,000	

5 **Decide whether the following statement is true or false.**

Provided both assets are used in Mr Astro's trade, a gain arising on the sale of freehold land and buildings can be rolled over against the cost of goodwill.

	✓
True	
False	

6 **Fill in the blank boxes.**

A company sells freehold land and buildings in 2016.

If relief for replacement of business assets is to be claimed, reinvestment of the proceeds must take place in a period beginning

[   ] **months before and ending**

[   ] **months after the date of disposal.**

7 H Ltd sells a warehouse for £400,000. The warehouse cost £220,000 and the indexation allowance available is £40,000. The company acquires another warehouse 10 months later for £375,000 and claims rollover relief.

The chargeable gain after rollover relief is:

£ [   ]

8 **Decide whether the following statement is true or false.**

If Sara gives some jewellery to her daughter Emily, gift relief can be claimed.

	✓
True	
False	

9   Tommy gave Sinbad a factory in June 2016 that had been used in his trade. The factory cost £50,000 in October 2006 and was worth £200,000 at the date of the gift. Sinbad sold the factory for £350,000 in May 2017.

If gift relief is claimed, the gain on the gift by Tommy is:

£

and the gain on the sale by Sinbad is:

£

Activity answers

CHAPTER 1 Tax framework

Activity 1: Taxable income

£	19,750

	Non-savings income £	Savings income £	Dividend income £	Total £
Trading income	16,000			
Building society interest		6,000		
Dividends			8,750	
Net income	16,000	6,000	8,750	30,750
Less personal allowance	(11,000)			(11,000)
Taxable income	5,000	6,000	8,750	19,750

Activity 2: Calculation of income tax liability

	Non-savings income £	Savings income (excluding dividends) £	Dividend income £
Employment income	17,000		
Savings income		10,000	
Dividends			20,000
Total income	17,000	10,000	20,000
PA	(11,000)		
Taxable income	6,000	10,000	20,000
Non-savings income			
6,000 × 20%			1,200
Savings income			
500 × 0% (Higher rate savings allowance)			0
9,500 × 20%			1,900
Dividends			
5,000 × 0% (dividend allowance)			0
$\frac{11,000}{32,000} \times 7.5\%$			825
4,000 × 32.5% (20,000 − 16,000)			1,300
Tax liability			5,225

CHAPTER 2 Computing trading income

Activity 1: Adjustment of profits (i)

	£
Profit for the year in accounts	38,000
Add **entertaining expenses**	2,000
Add **depreciation**	4,000
	44,000
Less **capital allowances**	(3,500)
Taxable trading profit	40,500

Activity 2: Capital versus revenue

	Revenue ✓	Capital ✓
Paying employee wages	✓	
Paying rent for premises	✓	
Buying machinery		✓
Buying a van		✓
Building an extension to shop		✓
Paying for repairs to car	✓	

Activity 3: Calculation of add back

Amount to add back	✓
£17,450	
£16,000	
£18,450	✓
£11,450	

The redundancy payments are allowable. The payment of a salary to the proprietor of a business is not deductible because it is just a method of extracting a profit from the business and that profit is taxable in the normal way as part of the taxable trading profits. 15% of leasing costs of car with CO_2 emissions exceeding 130g/km are disallowable.

Activity 4: Entertainment and gifts

Expenditure	£	Add back ✓
Staff tennis outing for 30 employees	1,800	
2,000 tee shirts with firm's logo given to race runners	4,500	
Advertising and sponsorship of an athletic event	2,000	
Entertaining customers	7,300	✓
Staff Christmas party (30 employees)	2,400	

Activity 5: Adjustment of profits (ii)

Adjustment to profit	£	£
Net profit per the accounts		30,900
Add back		
Depreciation	5,000	
Entertaining	100	
Staff wages	5,000	
Council tax	1,000	
Total added back		11,100
Deduct		
Bank interest		(4,000)
Adjusted profits before capital allowances		38,000

CHAPTER 3 Capital allowances

Activity 1: Annual investment allowance

Delson can claim annual investment allowance of | £ | 150,000 | .

Workings (on-screen free text area provided in the CBT as part of larger question)

Nine-month period.

Max entitlement is therefore $\frac{9}{12} \times 200,000 = 150,000$

Assets eligible are:

		£
6 April 2016	Computer equipment	120,000
7 May 2016	Office furniture	75,000
13 May 2016	Delivery vans	60,000
		255,000

As the eligible assets are greater than the limit, Delson may only claim £150,000.

Note. The balance of expenditure will be eligible for other allowances.

Activity 2: Annual investment allowance – accounting period straddles 1 January 2016

Delia can claim annual investment allowance of | £ | 420,000 | .

Workings (on-screen free text area provided in the CBT as part of larger question)

Max entitlement for year ended 31 March 2016

		£
Pre 1.1.16	$\frac{9}{12} \times 500,000$	375,000
Post 31.12.15	$\frac{3}{12} \times 200,000$	50,000
		425,000

Assets eligible are:

		£
5 April 2015	Machinery	320,000
8 April 2015	Computers	80,000
10 June 2015	Vans	20,000
		420,000

As the eligible assets are lower than the limit, Delia may claim the full AIA of £420,000.

Activity 3: Writing-down allowances in the main pool

Jamie can claim annual investment allowance of **£** 9,000 .

Jamie can claim writing-down allowances of **£** 2,880 .

Workings (on-screen free text area provided in the CBT as part of larger question)

	AIA £	Main pool £	Total £
TWDV b/f		10,000	
Additions (no AIA on car)	9,000	8,000	
Disposals		(2,000)	
		16,000	
AIA @ 100%	(9,000)		9,000
WDA @ 18%		(2,880)	2,880
			11,880
TWDV c/f		13,120	

Note. The AIA limit is £200,000.

Activity 4: Short period of account

Edward Ltd can claim capital allowances of £ | 192,356 | .

Workings (on-screen free text area provided in the CBT as part of larger question)

	AIA £	Main pool £	Allowances £
TWDV b/f		12,000	
P/e 31.12.16			
Disposal			
7.7.16 van		(2,000)	
AIA additions			
15.4.16	446,750		
AIA 200,000 × $\frac{9}{12}$	(150,000)		150,000
	296,750		
Transfer to main pool	(296,750)	296,750	
Non-AIA addition			
13.4.16 car		7,000	
		313,750	
WDA @ 18% × $\frac{9}{12}$		(42,356)	42,356
TWDV c/f		271,394	
			192,356

Activity 5: Cessation of a business

(a) If Baxter sells his plant for £15,500 then he will have a | balancing charge | of

£ [   ] .

Workings (on-screen free text area provided in the CBT as part of larger question)

	Main pool £	Allowances £
TWDV b/f	12,000	
Additions	2,000	
Disposals	(15,500)	
	(1,500)	
Balancing charge	1,500	(1,500)
TWDV c/f	–	

(b) If Baxter sells his plant for £11,500 then he will have a | balancing allowance |

of £ | 2,500 | .

Workings (on-screen free text area provided in the CBT as part of larger question)

	Main pool £	Allowances £
TWDV b/f	12,000	
Additions	2,000	
Disposals	(11,500)	
	2,500	
Balancing allowance	(2,500)	2,500
TWDV c/f	–	

Activity 6: Special rate pool

Myles Ltd can claim capital allowances of $\boxed{\text{£} \quad 9,000}$.

Workings (on-screen free text area provided in the CBT as part of larger question)

	Main pool £	Special rate £	Allowances £
Y/e 31.3.17			
TWDV b/f	25,000	10,000	
Additions	17,000	8,000	
	42,000	18,000	
WDA 18%/8%	(7,560)	(1,440)	9,000
TWDV c/f	34,440	16,560	

Activity 7: Private-use assets

(a)   Sweeney can claim capital allowances of $\boxed{\text{£} \quad 4,160}$.

Workings (on-screen free text area provided in the CBT as part of larger question)

	Main pool £	Sweeney's car 80% business use £	Restriction £	Total £
TWDV b/f	16,000	20,000		
WDA @ 18%	(2,880)			2,880
WDA @ 8%		(1,600)	× 80%	1,280
				4,160
TWDV c/f	13,120	18,400		

Note. As there is no restriction for the private use of an employee, Doris's car would be in the main pool.

(b) What capital allowances would Sweeney claim if the business ceased in this period and both cars were sold for £15,000 each?

£ | 5,000

Workings (on-screen free text area provided in the CBT as part of larger question)

	£
Sweeney's car	
Balancing allowance (20,000 – 15,000) × 80% =	4,000
Main pool (Doris's car)	
Balancing allowance (16,000 – 15,000) =	1,000
	5,000

Note. There is no restriction for the private use of an employee.

Activity 8: Short life asset election

Workings (on-screen free text area provided in the CBT as part of larger question)

By making the election the asset is depooled for eight years until 31 December 2024.
The asset has been sold before the election expires. It is therefore treated separately to the assets in the main pool, so a balancing allowance or charge will arise on disposal.
If the asset is sold for £5,000 there will be a balancing allowance of £20,000 – £5,000 = £15,000.
If the asset is sold for £50,000 there will be a balancing charge of £50,000 – £20,000 = £30,000.

Activity 9: Calculation of capital allowances

The capital allowances claim that Oscar can make for the period ended 30 June 2017 is calculated as follows:

	AIA £	Main pool £	Allowances £
18 m/e 30 June 2017			
B/f		81,000	
Disposal 1.6.17		(30,000)	
AIA acquisition			
10.7.16 Plant	210,000		
12.9.16 Plant	550,000		
AIA £200,000 × 18/12	(300,000)		300,000
	460,000		
Transfer balance to pool	(460,000)	460,000	
FYA acquisition			
10.8.16 Car	11,000		
FYA @ 100%	(11,000)		11,000
		511,000	
WDA @ 18% × 18/12		(137,970)	137,970
C/f		373,030	
Allowances			448,970

Notes

1   The AIA limit and WDA are scaled up for the 18 month period, whereas the FYA is never scaled up or down.

2   This working would not be the same had it related to a company, as the 18-month period would be split into two accounting periods (a 12-month period and a 6-month period). We look at accounting periods for companies later in the Course Book.

Activity 1: Calculating taxable total profits

Corporation tax computation y/e 31 December 2016

	£
Trading profits	2,440,000
Rental income	150,000
Interest income (40,000 + 10,000)	50,000
Capital gains (350,000 + 70,000 – 80,000)	340,000
Less qualifying charitable payment	(70,000)
Taxable total profits	2,910,000

Note. The dividends received are not taxable.

Activity 2: Calculating taxable total profits – long period of account

Long period of account

	12 months to 31.8.16 £	4 months to 31.12.16 £
Adjusted trading profits (12:4)	2,700,000	900,000
Less capital allowances (W1)	(6,750)	(8,720)
Trading profits	2,693,250	891,280
Interest income (12:4)	24,000	8,000
Gain	–	40,000
Less qualifying charitable payment	(20,000)	–
TTP	2,697,250	939,280

Workings (not provided in CBT)

	AIA £	Main pool £	Allowances £
1.9.15 to 31.8.16 (12m)			
TWDV @ 1.9.15		37,500	
WDA (18%)		(6,750)	6,750
		30,750	
1.9.16 to 31.12.16 (4m)			
Addition	6,875		
AIA*	(6,875)		6,875
WDA (18%) × $^4/_{12}$		(1,845)	1,845
		28,905	
			8,720

*AIA available = 200,000 × $^4/_{12}$ = 66,667

Activity 3: Corporation tax payable

£	304,000

Workings (not provided in CBT)

	£
Trading profits	1,500,000
Gain	50,000
Qualifying charitable payments	(30,000)
Taxable total profits	1,520,000
Corporation tax dues £1,520,000 × 20%	£304,000

Activity 1: Current year basis (i)

Correct option is year ended 31 December 2016.

Workings (not provided in the CBT)

Tax accounting period ending in fiscal year 2016/17 ie between 6 April 2016 and 5 April 2017.

Activity 2: Current year basis (ii)

(a)   Correct option is fiscal year 2016/17

Workings (not provided in the CBT)

Period ended 30 June 2016 ends between 6 April 2016 and 5 April 2017, ie fiscal year 2016/17.

(b)   Correct option is fiscal year 2016/17

Workings (not provided in the CBT)

Period ended 31 January 2017 ends between 6 April 2016 and 5 April 2017, ie fiscal year 2016/17.

Activity 3: The first fiscal year

What is the first fiscal year of the trade? (XXXX/XX format) | 2014/15 |

What profits will be assessed in the first fiscal year?

| £ | 6,000 |

Workings (not provided in the CBT)

2014/15
Actual basis 01/01/15 to 05/04/15
$\frac{3}{12} \times 24,000 = £6,000$

Activity 4: The second fiscal year (trader has 12 month accounting period)

What is the second fiscal year of the trade? (XXXX/XX format) | 2015/16

What profits will be assessed in the second fiscal year?

£ | 24,000

Workings (not provided in the CBT)

Trade begins in fiscal year 2014/15 so this is the first year.
The second year is therefore 2015/16
12m period ending in 2015/16 ⇒ Current year basis
CYB y/e 31.12.15 = £24,000

Activity 5: Overlap profits

His overlap period is (XX/XX/XX) | 01/01/14 | to | 05/04/15

His overlap profits are | £ | 6,000

Activity 6: Opening year rules (short first period)

		Profits taxed		
	Fiscal year (XXXX/XX)	From (XX/XX/XX)	To (XX/XX/XX)	Amount taxed £
First fiscal year	2014/15	01/01/15	05/04/15	9,000
Second fiscal year	2015/16	01/01/15	31/12/15	42,000
Third fiscal year	2016/17	01/07/15	30/06/16	48,000
Overlap periods and profits				
First overlap period		01/01/15	05/04/15	9,000
Second overlap period		01/07/15	31/12/15	24,000
Total overlap				33,000

Workings (not provided in the CBT)

	£
2014/15 **Actual** 01/01/15 to 05/04/15	
$\frac{3}{6} \times 18{,}000 = £9{,}000$	
2015/16	
6m period ending in 2015/16 $\Rightarrow$ tax first 12 months of profits	
6m to 30/06/15	18,000
6m to 31/12/15 ($\frac{6}{12} \times 48{,}000$)	24,000
	42,000
2016/17 – CYB 12m period ending 30/06/16	£48,000
Overlap 01/01/15 to 05/04/15	
$\frac{3}{6} \times 18{,}000$	9,000
Plus 01/07/15 to 31/12/15	
$\frac{6}{12} \times 48{,}000$	24,000
Total	£33,000

Activity 7: Opening year rules (long first period ending in second fiscal year)

		Profits taxed		
	Fiscal year (XXXX/XX)	From (XX/XX/XX)	To (XX/XX/XX)	Amount taxed £
First fiscal year	2014/15	01/07/14	05/04/15	9,000
Second fiscal year	2015/16	01/01/15	31/12/15	12,000
Third fiscal year	2016/17	01/01/16	31/12/16	30,000
Overlap period and profits		01/01/15	05/04/15	3,000

Workings (not provided in the CBT)

2014/15
Actual 01/07/14 to 05/04/15
$\frac{9}{18} \times 18{,}000 = £9{,}000$
2015/16
18m period ending in 2015/16 $\Rightarrow$ tax 12m to normal accounting year end $\Rightarrow$ 01/01/15 to 31/12/15
$\frac{12}{18} \times 18{,}000 = £12{,}000$
2016/17
Y/e 31/12/16   £30,000
Overlap 01/01/15 to 05/04/15
$\frac{3}{18} \times 18{,}000 = £3{,}000$

Activity 8: Opening year rules (long first period ending in third fiscal year)

		Profits taxed		
	Fiscal year (XXXX/XX)	From (XX/XX/XX)	To (XX/XX/XX)	Amount taxed £
First fiscal year	2014/15	01/12/14	05/04/15	8,000
Second fiscal year	2015/16	06/04/15	05/04/16	24,000
Third fiscal year	2016/17	01/06/15	31/05/16	24,000
Overlap period and profits		01/06/15	05/04/16	20,000

Workings (not provided in the CBT)

2014/15
Actual 01/12/14 to 05/04/15
$\frac{4}{18} \times 36{,}000 \qquad = £8{,}000$
2015/16
– no accounting period ending in 2015/16 $\Rightarrow$ **Actual** 06/04/15 to 05/04/16
$\frac{12}{18} \times 36{,}000 \qquad = £24{,}000$
2015/16
12m to y/e $\Rightarrow$ 12m to 31/05/16
$\frac{12}{18} \times 36{,}000 \qquad = £24{,}000$
Overlap 01/06/15 to 05/04/16
$\frac{10}{18} \times 36{,}000 \qquad = £20{,}000$

Activity 9: Closing year rules (one period ending in final fiscal year)

	Profits taxed			
	Fiscal year (XXXX/XX)	From (XX/XX/XX)	To (XX/XX/XX)	Amount taxed £
Penultimate fiscal year	2015/16	01/01/15	31/12/15	22,000
Final fiscal year	2016/17	01/01/16	30/04/16	8,000

Workings (not provided in the CBT)

Business finishes 30/04/16 so final year is 2016/17	
2015/16 CYB (y/e 31/12/15)	£22,000
2016/17 4 months: 01/01/16 – 30/04/16	12,000
Less overlap profits	(4,000)
	£8,000

Activity 10: Closing year rules (two periods ending in final fiscal year)

	Fiscal year (XXXX/XX)	From (XX/XX/XX)	To (XX/XX/XX)	Amount taxed £
	Profits taxed			
Penultimate fiscal year	2015/16	01/01/2015	31/12/2015	30,000
Final fiscal year	2016/17	01/01/2016	31/03/2017	17,000

Workings (not provided in the CBT)

Business finishes on 31 March 2017 ie in fiscal year 2016/17. This is his final year.

2015/16 y/e 31 December 2015	£30,000
2016/17 y/e 31 December 2016	25,000
p/e 31 March 2017	4,000
	29,000
Less overlap profits	(12,000)
	£17,000

Activity 11: Short accounting period

Year of change 2016/17

	£
2015/16 y/e 31 August 2015	20,000
2016/17 gap 9 months to 31 May 2016	
Tax 12 months to 31 May 2016	
$\frac{3}{12}$ × 20,000 + 15,000	20,000
2017/18 y/e 31.5.17	30,000

Creates overlap profits

1.6.15 – 31.8.15 3/12 x 20,000 = £5,000

Activity 12: Two accounting periods ending in the year

Year of change 2016/17

	£
2015/16 y/e 30.6.15	25,000
2016/17 Gap 18 months to 31.12.16	45,000
Less $6/9 \times 21,000$	(14,000)
	31,000
2017/18 y/e 31.12.17	35,000

CHAPTER 6 Partnerships

Activity 1: Partnership profit allocation

	Ron £	Steve £
Profit share	38,000	22,000

Workings (not provided in the CBT)

	Ron £	Steve £	Total £
Year ended 30 June			
Salary	5,000	–	5,000
Balance (3:2)	33,000	22,000	55,000 (bal)
Assessments	38,000	22,000	60,000

Activity 2: Change in profit-sharing arrangements

	Ron £	Steve £
Profit share	50,500	39,500

Workings (not provided in the CBT)

	Ron £	Steve £	Total £
Year ended 30 June			
1 July – 31 December			
Salary $\frac{6}{12} \times 5,000$	2,500		2,500
Balance (3:2)	25,500	17,000	42,500
$\frac{6}{12} \times 90,000$			45,000
1 January – 30 June			
$\frac{6}{12} \times 90,000$			
Split 1:1	22,500	22,500	45,000
	50,500	39,500	90,000

Activity 3: Change in partnership personnel

	M £	G £	B £
2014/15	16,500	24,250	5,667
2015/16	29,750	0	20,500
2016/17	48,000	0	24,000
Overlap			17,667

Workings (not provided in the CBT)

Sharing of profits

	Total £	M £	G £	B £
Y/e 31.5.14, ie £33,000				
(1:1)	33,000	16,500	16,500	–
Y/e 31.5.15, ie £51,000				
Up to 1.12.14 (1:1) $51,000 \times \frac{6}{12}$	25,500	12,750	12,750	–
From 1.12.14 (2:1 each) $51,000 \times \frac{6}{12}$	25,500	17,000		8,500
	51,000	29,750	12,750	8,500
Y/e 31.5.16, ie £72,000				
(2:1)	72,000	48,000		24,000

New partner (B): Trading profits

	£
Started trading 1.12.14	
6 months to 31.5.15	8,500
Year ended 31.5.16	24,000

New partner (B): Trading assessments

	£
2014/15 actual 1.12.14 – 5.4.15	
$8,500 \times \frac{4}{6}$	5,667
2015/16 (first 12 months), ie 1.12.14 – 30.11.15	
$8,500 + \frac{6}{12} \times 24,000$	20,500
2016/17 (y/e 31.5.16)	24,000

New partner (B): Overlap

	£
1.12.14 – 5.4.15	5,667
1.6.15 – 30.11.15 ($^6/_{12}$ × 24,000)	12,000
	17,667

Retiring partner (G): Trading assessments

	£
Retires on 1.12.14, ie 2014/15	
2014/15 (y/e 31.5.14)	16,500
2014/15 (p/e 1.12.14)	12,750
Less overlap	(5,000)
Total 2014/15	24,250

Continuing partner (M): Trading assessments

	£
2014/15 (y/e 31.5.14)	£16,500
2015/16 (y/e 31.5.15)	£29,750
2016/17 (y/e 31.5.16)	£48,000

CHAPTER 7 National insurance

Activity 1: National insurance contributions

(a) Mr Bull

His Class 2 NI contributions for the year are:

£	145.60

His Class 4 NI contributions at 9% are:

£	534.60

Workings (not provided in the CBT)

Class 2	52 × 2.80	145.60
Class 4	(14,000 – 8,060) × 9%	534.60

(b)   Mr Seye

His Class 4 NI contributions at 9% are:

£	3,144.60

His Class 4 NI contributions at 2% are:

£	100.00

Workings (not provided in the CBT)

Class 4 at 9%	$(43,000 - 8,060) \times 9\%$	3,144.60
Class 4 at 2%	$(48,000 - 43,000) \times 2\%$	100.00

CHAPTER 8 Losses

Activity 1: Income tax trading loss options

Show if the following statements are true or false by ticking the correct box for each.

	True ✓	False ✓
Edward may offset the loss against total income in 2014/15 and then in 2013/14.		✓
Edward may offset the loss against total income in 2016/17.		✓
Edward may offset the loss against trading income only in 2014/15.		✓
Edward may offset the loss against the rental income in 2015/16.	✓	

Workings (not provided in CBT)

Notes

1   The loss has been made in fiscal year 2015/16. It can, therefore, be used in 2015/16 and/or 2014/15, so the first option is false.

2   If Edward lets the loss carry forward to 2016/17 then it offsets automatically against trading income only, so the second option is false.

3   If Edward chooses to carry the loss back to 2014/15 it will offset against total income, not just trading income, so the third option is false.

4   If Edward makes a claim for 2015/16 it will offset against his total income. The only income he has is rental income so the fourth option is true.

Activity 2: Utilisation of income tax losses

(a)

	2013/14 £	2014/15 £	2015/16 £	2016/17 £
Trading income	2,000	0	8,000	4,000
Loss carried forward	0	0	(8,000)	(3,600)
	0	0	0	400
Property income	400	1,000	1,000	1,000
	2,400	1,000	1,000	1,400
CY loss relief	0	(1,000)	0	0
PY loss relief	(2,400)	0	0	0
Net income	0	0	1,000	1,400

Workings (not provided in the CBT)

	Trading loss
Loss made in 2014/15	15,000
Carry back against total income in 2013/14	(2,400)
Use against total income in current year 2014/15	(1,000)
Carry forward against trading income in year 2015/16	(8,000)
Carry forward against trading income in year 2016/17 (balancing figure)	(3,600)
	0

(b)   Show if the following statement is true or false by ticking the correct box.

	True ✓	False ✓
Pike has used his loss in the most tax-efficient way possible		✓

Workings (not provided in the CBT)

Pike's income is below the personal allowance in all years so it is a waste to carry back the loss or use it in the year of the loss.

It is wasteful to use it in the future years as well but Pike has no control over this. The carry forward is automatic.

Note. The question told you to use the loss as soon as possible so prior year relief should be claimed before current year.

Activity 3: Carry forward loss relief

The loss carried forward at 31 December 2016 is

£	9,000

Workings (not provided in the CBT)

	Year ended 31 December		
	2014 £	2015 £	2016 £
Trading profit	–	5,000	6,000
Carry forward loss relief	–	(5,000)	(6,000)
Trading profit	–	–	
Property income	–	2,000	2,000
TTP	–	2,000	2,000

Loss memorandum			£
Y/e 31 December 2014			20,000
Loss relief y/e 31 December 2015			(5,000)
			15,000
Loss relief y/e 31 December 2016			(6,000)
c/f			9,000

Activity 4: Current year and carry back relief

	True ✓	False ✓
Kay Ltd may choose to offset the loss against total profits in 2015 only.		✓
If Kay Ltd makes the maximum permissible claims it will have £90,000 loss to carry forward at 2016.		✓
Kay Ltd may offset the loss against total profits in 2015 and then against total profits in 2016.		✓
Kay Ltd may choose to offset the loss against total profits in 2016 only.	✓	

Workings (not provided in CBT)

The loss arises in year ended 31 December 2016, so this is the current year.

We cannot carry back to the prior year of 31 December 2015 unless we have used the loss in 2016 first, so the first statement is false.

If the company makes the maximum permissible claims it will offset in the current year of 2016 then carry back to 2015 setting losses against total profits including gains (see below). It will have insufficient losses to reduce the 2015 income to nil so there will be no losses to carry forward. The second statement is, therefore, false.

If we wish to offset in 2015 and 2016 we must offset 2016 before 2015, so the third statement is false.

We can choose to offset the loss in 2016 only, so the fourth statement is true. Once we have offset in 2016 we could choose to make a further claim to offset in 2015.

| | Year ended 31 December | | |
	2014 £	2015 £	2016 £
Trading income	20,000	10,000	–
Capital gains	50,000	50,000	50,000
Total profits	70,000	60,000	50,000
Loss relief		(ii) (50,000)	(i) (50,000)
TTP	70,000	10,000	–

Workings (not provided in CBT)

Loss memorandum

	£
Y/e 31.12.16	100,000
Less relief y/e 31.12.16 (optional claim)	(50,000)(i)
Less relief y/e 31.12.15 (additional optional claim after 2016 claim)	(50,000)(ii)
	Nil

Activity 5: Comprehensive example

	Y/e 30.6.14 £	P/e 31.12.14 £	Y/e 31.12.15 £	Y/e 31.12.16 £
Trading profits	20,000	30,000	0	15,000
Losses carried forward	0	0	0	(15,000)(iv)
	20,000	30,000	0	0
Investment income	10,000	10,000	10,000	10,000
	30,000	40,000	0	10,000
Current year relief	0	0	(10,000)(i)	0
Prior year relief	(15,000)(iii)	(40,000)(ii)	0	0
	15,000	0	0	10,000
Qualifying charitable donations	(5,000)	(5,000)	(5,000)	(5,000)
Taxable total profits	10,000	0	0	5,000

Workings (not provided in CBT)

Loss memo £

Y/e 31.12.15		155,000
Current – y/e 31.12.15	(i)	(10,000)
Carry back – 6m P/E 31.12.14	(ii)	(40,000)
– Y/e 30.6.14 – max claim 6/12 × 30,000	(iii)	(15,000)
		90,000
C/fwd y/e 31.12.16	(iv)	(15,000)
C/fwd		75,000

CHAPTER 9 Self-assessment for individuals

Activity 1: Penalties

Kelly's penalty can be reduced from | 70 | % of the potential lost revenue (for a

deliberate, but not concealed error) to | 20 | %, with the unprompted disclosure
of her error.

Activity 2: Payments on account and balancing payments

In 2015/16 the following income tax was subject to self-assessment:

	£
Income tax payable 7,000 – 4,000 =	3,000
The instalments for 2016/17 are therefore	
31.1.17 ½ × 3,000	1,500
31.7.17 ½ × 3,000	1,500
The final payment is therefore	
Income tax liability	8,000
Less PAYE	(2,500)
Less payments on account	(3,000)
	2,500
Capital gains tax liability	1,000
31.1.18 Final payment	3,500

CHAPTER 10 Self-assessment for companies

Activity 1: Payment of corporation tax

A plc has a 31 March year end and has TTP of £2.1m per year.

	£
Corporation tax due	
FY16, 2,100,000 × 20%	420,000
Due by instalments on the 14th day of month 7, 10, 13 and 16, counting from the start of the period – ie 1 April 2016.	
£105,000 on 14 October 2016	
£105,000 on 14 January 2017	
£105,000 on 14 April 2017	
£105,000 on 14 July 2017	

CHAPTER 11 Chargeable gains – the basics

Activity 1: Capital gain calculation (individuals)

	£
Proceeds	38,500
Less selling expenses	(1,500)
Net proceeds	37,000
Less cost	(15,000)
Less legal fees on purchase	(500)
Less enhancement	(3,000)
Capital gain	18,500

Activity 2: Current year losses

Ted's net capital gain for 2016/17 before the annual exempt amount is:

£ | 7,000

Ted has a loss to carry forward of £ nil .

Workings (not provided in the CBT)

	£
Gains 45,000 + 10,000	55,000
Less loss	(48,000)
Net capital gains	7,000
Less annual exempt amount	(11,100)
Taxable gains	Nil
The balance of the annual exempt amount is wasted.	

Activity 3: Prior year losses

Tara's net capital gain for 2016/17 before the annual exempt amount is:

£ | 11,100

Tara has a loss to carry forward of £ 9,100 .

Workings (not provided in the CBT)

	£
Gain of 2016/17	12,000
Less losses b/f (bal)	(900)
Net gain	11,100
Less annual exempt amount	(11,100)
Taxable gains	Nil
Losses to c/f £(10,000 – 900)	9,100

Activity 4: Computing capital gains tax payable

What is Mr Dunstable's capital gains tax payable? £ 1,380 .

Workings (not provided in the CBT)

	£
Capital gain	18,500
Less annual exempt amount	(11,100)
Taxable gain	7,400
Basic rate band	32,000
Taxable income	(31,000)
Basic rate band remaining	1,000

	£
Capital gains tax payable	
1,000 × 10%	100
6,400 × 20%	1,280
7,400	1,380

Activity 5: Capital gain calculation (companies)

	£
Proceeds	38,500
Less selling expenses	(1,500)
Net proceeds	37,000
Less cost	(15,000)
Less legal fees on purchase	(500)
Less enhancement	(3,000)
Unindexed gain	18,500
Less indexation on cost ((15,000 + 500) × 0.781)	(12,106)
Less indexation on enhancement expenditure (3,000 × 0.478)	(1,434)
Capital gain	4,960

Activity 6: Indexation

Jek Ltd bought an asset for £50,000.

What is the capital gain/(loss) if it was sold for:

(a)   £20,000?

| £ | (30,000) |

(b)   £70,000?

| £ | nil |

(c)   £150,000?

| £ | 61,950 |

Workings (not provided in the CBT)

			£	£	£
Proceeds			20,000	70,000	150,000
Less cost			(50,000)	(50,000)	(50,000)
			(30,000)	20,000	100,000
IA	(a)	N/A	–		
	(b)	50,000 × 0.761 = 38,050			
		restrict to 20,000		(20,000)	
	(c)	50,000 × 0.761			(38,050)
Indexed gain/(loss)			(30,000)	–	61,950

Activity 1: Part disposal

The gain on the disposal of the land is £ | 4,702 |.

The cost of the remaining land carried forward is £ | 15,652 |.

Workings (not provided in the CBT)

	£
Gross proceeds	10,000
Less disposal costs	(950)
Net proceeds	9,050
Cost $\dfrac{10}{10+36} \times 20,000$	(4,348)
	4,702
Cost of remaining land for future CGT calculations: = 20,000 – 4,348	15,652

Activity 2: Chattels

(a)   The chargeable gain on the disposal is £ | 5,000 |.

Workings (not provided in the CBT)

Non-wasting chattel: cost ≤ £6,000, proceeds > £6,000	£
Proceeds	9,000
Less commission	(1,000)
	8,000
Less cost	(500)
	7,500
$\dfrac{5}{3}$ (Gross proceeds – 6,000)	
= $\dfrac{5}{3}$ (9,000 – 6,000)	
= 5,000	
∴ take lower gain 5,000	5,000

(b)   The loss on the disposal is £ | 1,000 .

Workings (not provided in the CBT)

Non-wasting chattel: cost > £6,000, proceeds ≤ £6,000	£
Proceeds (deemed)	6,000
Less cost	(7,000)
Allowable loss	(1,000)

Activity 3: Transfers between spouses/civil partners

The chargeable gain on transfer is:

	✓
Nil	✓
£18,000	
£31,000	
£13,000	

The transfer takes place at no gain/no loss and Kate assumes the base cost of £14,000 as her cost.

CHAPTER 13 Share disposals

Activity 1: Matching rules for individuals

	Shares
Same day	400
Next 30 days	500
Share pool	700 ß
Disposal	1,600

ß is a balancing figure

(1) Match with same day

	£	£
Proceeds $400/1,600 \times 14,000$	3,500	
Cost	(3,000)	
		500

(2) Match with next 30 days

	£	£
Proceeds $500/1,600 \times 14,000$	4,375	
Cost	(4,500)	
		(125)

(3) Match with share pool

	£	£
Proceeds $700/1,600 \times 14,000$	6,125	
Cost (W)	(2,800)	
		3,325
Net gain		£3,700

(W) Share pool

	Number	Cost
15.5.02	2,200	8,800
Disposal $700/2,200 \times 8,800$	(700)	(2,800)
	1,500	£6,000

Activity 2: Share pool for individuals

Matching rules: The shares were all acquired prior to the date of disposal so they are all in the share pool.

	£
Proceeds	14,000
Cost (W1)	(4,500)
Gain	9,500

Share pool (W1)

	Number	Cost £
January 1985		
Purchase	3,000	5,000
February 1987		
Purchase	1,000	4,000
	4,000	9,000
May 2016		
Disposal $\frac{2,000}{4,000} \times 9,000$	(2,000)	(4,500)
	2,000	4,500

Activity 3: Bonus and rights issues for individuals

Matching rules: All bought prior to date of disposal so all from share pool.

Gain

	£
Proceeds	15,000
Less cost (W1)	(10,139)
Gain	4,861

(W1) Share pool

	Number	Cost £
1.10.95	10,000	15,000
11.9.99 acquisition	2,000	5,000
	12,000	20,000
1.2.00 1:2 rights @ £2.75	6,000	16,500
	18,000	36,500
5.9.05 2:1 bonus	36,000	–
	54,000	36,500
14.10.16 sale $\frac{15,000}{54,600} \times 36,500$	(15,000)	(10,139)
	39,000	26,361

Activity 4: Matching rules for companies

	£
Match same day	1,000
Last 9 days	500
FA85 pool	1,000
	2,500

Same-day sale	£
Proceeds $\frac{1,000}{2,500} \times 12,500$	5,000
Cost	(4,822)
	178

Last 9 days	£
Proceeds $\frac{500}{2,500} \times 12,500$	2,500
Cost	(2,511)
	(11)

FA85 pool	Number	Cost £	Indexed cost £
Aug 1996	1,000	2,750	2,750
Index up to December 1998			
0.008 × 2,750 =			22
	1,000	2,750	2,772
Addition December 1998	1,000	3,250	3,250
	2,000	6,000	6,022
Index up to July 2016			
0.157 × 6,022 =			945
	2,000	6,000	6,967
Disposal 1,000/2,000 × 6,000 1,000/2,000 × 6,967	(1,000)	(3,000)	(3,484)
C/f	1,000	3,000	3,483

	£
Proceeds 1,000/2,500 × 12,500	5,000
Cost	(3,000)
Unindexed gain	2,000
IA (3,484 – 3,000)	(484)
Indexed gain	1,516

Total gains	£
Same day	178
Last 9 days	(11)
FA85 pool	1,516
	1,683

Activity 5: Bonus and rights issues for companies

Matching rules: The shares were all acquired prior to the date of disposal so they are all in the share pool.

Total gains	£
Proceeds	10,000
Less cost (W)	(1,200)
Less indexation (2,655 – 1,200)	(1,455)
Chargeable gain	7,345

1985 pool working	Number	Cost £	Indexed cost £
1.5.85	500	1,000	1,000
5.8.87 rights			
Index up to August 87			
1,000 × 0.347			347
	500	1,000	1,347
Rights 1:2 @ £5	250	1,250	1,250
	750	2,250	2,597
15.9.89 bonus	750	–	–
	1,500	2,250	2,597
5.9.16 disposal			
Index up to September 16			
2,597 × 0.917			2,381
	1,500	2,250	4,978
Disposal 800/1,500 × 2,250 800/1,500 × 4,978	(800)	(1,200)	(2,655)
	700	1,050	2,323

CHAPTER 14 Reliefs for chargeable gains

Activity 1: Entrepreneurs' relief – calculation of capital gains tax

Capital gains tax payable at 10% due to ER is

£ | 1,000 | .

Capital gains tax payable at 10% to utilise the remaining basic rate band is

£ | 263 | .

Capital gains tax on other gains payable at 20% is

£ | 7,254 | .

Workings (not provided in the CBT)

	Other gains £	Eligible gains £
Chargeable gains	50,000	10,000
Less annual exempt amount	(11,100)	
	38,900	10,000
		£
Basic rate band		32,000
Taxable income		(19,370)
Basic rate band remaining		12,630
Eligible gains		£
10,000 × 10%		1,000
Other gains		
2,630 × 10% (12,630 – 10,000)		263
36,270 × 20%		7254
38,900		
		8,517

Activity 2: Disposals eligible for entrepreneurs' relief

	✓
Part of a business in which the individual has been a partner since August 2014	✓
A freehold factory which the individual uses in his business and has owned for ten years	
Unquoted shares held by the individual in a personal trading company in which he is employed and which he has owned for the previous two years	✓
Quoted shares held by the individual in a personal trading company in which he is employed and which he has owned for the previous two years	✓

Activity 3: Entrepreneurs' relief – calculating gains eligible for relief

The total net taxable gain eligible for entrepreneurs' relief is

£ | 700,000 | .

The total net taxable gain not eligible for entrepreneurs' relief is

£ | 68,900 | .

Workings (not provided in the CBT)

	£
Eligible gains	
Goodwill	500,000
Factory	300,000
Office block	(100,000)
	700,000
Other gains	
Shares	80,000

	Other gains £	Eligible gains £
Chargeable gains	80,000	700,000
Less annual exempt amount	(11,100)	
Taxable gains	68,900	700,000

If the gain on the factory was £9,800,000 then the total net taxable gain eligible for entrepreneurs' relief is

| £ | 10,000,000 | .

The total net taxable gain not eligible for entrepreneurs' relief is

| £ | 268,900 | .

Workings (not provided in the CBT)

Eligible gains

	£	£
Goodwill	500,000	
Factory	9,800,000	
Office block	(100,000)	
	10,200,000	
Less entrepreneurs' relief		
Max	(10,000,000)	
Gain not eligible		200,000
Shares		80,000
Other gains		280,000

	Other gains £	Eligible gains £
Chargeable gains	280,000	10,000,000
Less annual exempt amount	(11,100)	
Taxable gains	268,900	10,000,000

Activity 4: Rollover relief

The gain taxed on Henry Ltd now is:

| £ | 10,000 | .

The base cost of the new building is:

| £ | 165,000 | .

Workings (not provided in the CBT)

Disposal of fixed plant

	£
Proceeds	200,000
Less cost	(150,000)
IA 150,000 × 10%	(15,000)
Indexed gain	35,000
Rollover relief β (balancing figure)	(25,000)
Proceeds not reinvested taxed now (200 – 190)	10,000
Base cost of building = £190,000 – £25,000	165,000

Activity 5: Gift relief

The gift relief claim must be signed by: | Bill and Ludovic | .

Bill's chargeable gain on disposal is £ | Nil | .

Ludovic's base cost is £ | 7,000 | .

Workings (not provided in the CBT)

	£
Proceeds (deemed)	25,000
Less cost	(7,000)
	18,000
Gain rolled over	(18,000)
Chargeable gain	Nil
Base cost for Ludovic:	
MV (deemed consideration)	25,000
Less gain held over	(18,000)
Adjusted base cost	7,000

Activity 6: With and without gift relief

(a)   If gift relief is not claimed, Julie's chargeable gain is:

£ | 35,000

	£
Deemed sale proceeds (MV)	85,000
Less cost	(50,000)
Gain	35,000

and Jack's chargeable gain is:

£ | 10,000

	£
Proceeds	95,000
Less cost (MV)	(85,000)
Gain	10,000

(b)   If gift relief is claimed, Julie's chargeable gain is:

£ | 0

	£
Deemed sale proceeds	85,000
Less cost	(50,000)
	35,000
Less gift relief	(35,000)
Gain	0

and Jack's chargeable gain is:

£ | 45,000

	£	£
Proceeds		95,000
Less cost	85,000	
Less gift relief	(35,000)	
		(50,000)
Gain		45,000

Test your learning: answers

CHAPTER 1   Tax framework

1

	✓
Integrity	✓
Objectivity	✓
Professional competence and due care	
Confidentiality	
Professional behaviour	✓

Integrity: It would not be honest to knowingly reduce profits by including expenditure that was not incurred in the year.

Objectivity: If you agreed to her request because of your job prospects, you are allowing bias to affect your judgement.

Professional behaviour: Submitting a tax return that does not follow tax law is illegal.

2

	✓
True	
False	✓

Tax evasion can lead to fines/imprisonment.

3

	✓
True	
False	✓

A company pays **corporation tax** on its total profits.

4   Each tax year all of an individual's components of income are added together, then a personal allowance is deducted to arrive at | taxable income | .

5

£	6,475

Non-savings income £	Savings income £	Dividend income £	Total £
25,000			
	12,000		
		10,000	
25,000	12,000	10,000	47,000
(11,000)			(11,000)
14,000	12,000	10,000	36,000

Tax	£
Non-savings income	
£14,000 × 20%	2,800
Savings income	
£500 × 0% (Higher rate taxpayer allowance)	0
£11,500 × 20%	2,300
£12,000	
Dividend income	
£5,000 × 0% (allowance)	0
£1,000 × 7.5% (remainder of BR band)	75
£4,000 × 32.5%	1,300
£10,000	**6,475**

CHAPTER 2 Computing trading income

1

	Allowable ✓
Legal fees incurred on the acquisition of a factory to be used for trade purposes	
Heating for factory	✓
Legal fees incurred on pursuing trade receivables	✓
Acquiring a machine to be used in the factory	

Legal fees on the acquisition of factory are capital expenditure and so not allowable. Heating is a revenue expense and so allowable. Legal fees incurred on pursuing trade receivables are allowable as they relate to a revenue source. Acquiring a machine is a capital expense and so not allowable (although capital allowances will be available for this expenditure).

2

£	700

The cost of staff entertaining is allowable. Gifts of food to customers are never allowable. The entertaining of customers is never allowable.

3

	Allowable ✓	Disallowable ✓
Parking fines incurred by business owner		✓
Parking fines incurred by an employee while on the employer's business	✓	
Parking fines incurred by the director of a company while on company business		✓
Legal costs incurred in relation to acquiring a 10-year lease of property for the first time		✓
Legal costs incurred in relation to the renewal of a lease for 20 years	✓	
Gifts of calendars to customers, costing £4 each and displaying an advertisement for the company	✓	
Gifts of bottles of whisky to customers, costing £12 each		✓

4

	✓
£80 must be deducted from the accounts profit	
£80 must be added back to the accounts profit	
£96 must be deducted from the accounts profit	
£96 must be added back to the accounts profit	✓

The normal selling price of £80 + (20% × £80) = £96 must be added to the accounts profit.

5

£	700

Added back	Deducted
✓	✓
	✓

The movement on the general provision is disallowable (if an increase)/not taxable (if a decrease). This means that the decrease in the general provision of **£700** (£2,500 – £1,800) must be deducted from the accounts profit.

6

£	360

80% × £450 is disallowable for tax purposes.

CHAPTER 3 Capital allowances

1

£	2,000

A maximum of the original cost is deducted from the pool.

2

£	173,896

Workings

Year ended 30 September 2017

	AIA £	Main pool £	Allowances £
B/f		22,500	
Addition qualifying for AIA			
Addition 1.12.16	171,250		
AIA (£200,000 available)	(171,250)		171,250
Disposal 1.8.17			
Proceeds		(7,800)	
		14,700	
WDA @ 18%		(2,646)	2,646
C/f		12,054	
Allowances			173,896

3

£	6,620

6 months ended 31 December 2016

	FYA @ 100% £	Main pool £	Allowances £
Addition (no AIA)		18,000	
WDA @ 18% × 6/12		(1,620)	1,620
		16,380	
Addition	5,000		
FYA @ 100%	(5,000)		5,000
C/f		16,380	
			6,620

Note. The AIA and WDAs are time apportioned in a short period. FYAs are not. AIAs and FYAs are not available on a car with CO_2 emissions of 115g/km.

4

	✓
True	
False	✓

There is no AIA or WDA in the final period so a **balancing allowance** arises as follows:

	£
B/f	12,500
Addition	20,000
Proceeds	(18,300)
	14,200
Balancing allowance	**(14,200)**

5

£	1,440

Year ended 30 April 2017

	Private use asset @ 60% £	Allowances £
Addition	30,000	
WDA @ 8%	(2,400) × 60%	**1,440**
C/f	27,600	

CHAPTER 4 Computing corporation tax

1

	True	False
A company with a nine-month period of account will calculate capital allowances for nine months and deduct them from adjusted trading profits.	✓	
A company with an 18-month period of account will calculate capital allowances for 18 months and deduct them from adjusted trading profits, and then pro-rate the answer between the appropriate accounting periods.		✓
A company with an 18-month period of account will calculate capital allowances for the first 12 months, then capital allowances for the remaining 6 months, and deduct them from the relevant pro-rated trading profits allocated to each accounting period.	✓	
Dividends are not included in the taxable total profits. They are taxed separately.		✓

Capital allowances are calculated separately for each accounting period and then deducted from the pro-rated adjusted profits.

Dividends are not taxable for the company (for the purpose of the *Business Tax* assessment).

2

	✓
Added to trading income	
Added to net non-trading interest	
Deducted from trading income	✓
Deducted from net non-trading interest	

The loan is for trading purposes and is interest **paid**, not received, so it is included as an expense.

3

£	385

Companies make donations gross.

4

	✓
1 June 2015 – 31 March 2016 and 1 April 2016 – 31 August 2016	
1 June 2015 – 31 May 2016 and 1 June 2016 – 31 August 2016	✓
1 June 2015 – 31 December 2015 and 1 January 2016 – 31 August 2016	
1 June 2015 – 31 August 2015 and 1 September 2015 – 31 August 2016	

The first accounting period is always 12 months in length in a long period of account.

5

	Year ended 31.12.16 £	4 months ended 30.4.17 £
Trading profits ($^{12}/_{16}$: $^{4}/_{16}$)	240,000	80,000
Interest (accrued for each period)	1,200	400
Chargeable gain (allocate to period made)	0	20,000
Qualifying charitable donation (allocate to period paid)	(15,000)	0
Taxable total profits	226,200	100,400

6

£	51,000

FY16 £255,000 × 20% = **£51,000**

7

£	98,000

FY15 and FY16 £490,000 × 20% = **98,000**

8

	✓
True	✓
False	

Financial Year 2016 (FY16) begins on 1 April 2016 and ends on 31 March 2017.

CHAPTER 5 Taxing unincorporated businesses

1

Tax year	Basis period
2016/17	1 May 2016 – 5 April 2017
2017/18	Year ended 31 December 2017
2018/19	Year ended 31 December 2018
Overlap profits	1 January 2017 – 5 April 2017

2

	✓
True	✓
False	

When the trade ceases, overlap profits are deducted from the final tax year's taxable profits.

3

Tax year	Basis period	Taxable profits £
2014/15	1 June 2013 to 31 May 2014	18,000
2015/16	1 June 2014 to 31 May 2015	32,000
2016/17	1 June 2015 to 31 December 2016	30,000

In 2016/17, taxable profits are (£25,000 + £15,000 – £10,000) = £30,000

4

Tax year	Basis period	Taxable profits £
2015/16	1 February 2016 – 5 April 2016	34,000 × 2/17 = 4,000
2016/17	6 April 2016 – 5 April 2017	34,000 × 12/17 = 24,000
2017/18	12 months ended 30 June 2017	34,000 × 12/17 = 24,000

His overlap profits are:

£	18,000

(1 July 2016 to 5 April 2017)

9/17 × £34,000

5 (a) Her taxable profits for 2015/16 are:

$£$ | 40,000

(1 December 2015 – 5 April 2016)   4/7 × £70,000

(b) Her taxable profits for 2016/17 are:

$£$ | 95,000

(1 December 2015 – 30 November 2016) £70,000 + 5/12 × £60,000

(c) Her taxable profits for 2017/18 are:

$£$ | 60,000

(1 July 2016 to 30 June 2017)

(d) Her overlap profits are:

$£$ | 65,000

	$£$
1 December 2015 – 5 April 2016	40,000
1 July 2016 – 30 November 2016	25,000
	65,000

6 (a) Her taxable profits for 2015/16 are:

$£$ | 80,000

(Current year basis 12 months to 31 October 2015)

(b) Her taxable profits for 2016/17 are:

$£$ | 90,000

(Short period therefore tax 12 months to new date, 30 April 2016: $^{6}/_{12} \times$ £80,000 + 50,000)

(c) Her taxable profits for 2017/18 are:

$£$ | 120,000

(Current year basis 12 months to 30 April 2017)

(d) Her overlap profits are:

$£$ | 40,000

(1 May 2015 to 31 October 2015) $\dfrac{6}{12} \times$ £80,000

7 (a)

Tax year	Basis period	Taxable profits £
2015/16	1/8/14 – 31/7/15	15,000
2016/17	1/8/15 – 31/10/16 (15 months less overlap)	22,000
2017/18	1/11/16 - 31/10/17	32,000

(b)

£	5,000

2016/17: 15 months to 31/10/16 £25,000 less £3,000 $\frac{3}{8}$ × £8,000

3 months overlap can be deducted from the profits for the 15 month period to leave a 12 month period taxable. The remainder of the overlap profit is carried forward (£8,000 – £3,000).

CHAPTER 6   Partnerships

1

	✓
The calendar year	
The tax year	
The period of account concerned	✓
The period agreed by the partners	

2   Dave's taxable profits for 2016/17 are:

£	9,450

and Joe's taxable profits for 2016/17 are:

£	8,550

Working

	Total £	Dave £	Joe £
1.1.16 – 30.9.16 (9/12) 1:1	13,500	6,750	6,750
1.10.16 – 31.12.16 (3/12) 3:2	4,500	2,700	1,800
	18,000	**9,450**	**8,550**

3

	Total £	Holly £	Jasmine £
Salary	85,000	5,000	80,000
Division of profits 1:1	115,000	57,500	57,500
	200,000	62,500	137,500

4

	✓
£60,000	
£15,000	
£45,000	
£20,000	✓

2016/17 (year ended 31 March 2017)

Taxable profits on Steve for 2016/17 are £20,000 ($\frac{1}{4} \times £80,000$).

5   The profits assessable on Sase in 2016/17 are:

£	14,000

The opening year rules apply to Sase.
(1 September 2016 – 5 April 2017) $\frac{7}{12} \times £24,000$

The profits assessable on Sase in 2017/18 are:

£	24,000

(year ended 31 August 2017)

The overlap profits arising for Sase are:

£	14,000

(1/9/16 – 5/4/17)

Workings

Year ended 31 August 2017

	Total £	Abdul £	Ghita £	Sase £
Profits (2:2:1)	120,000	48,000	48,000	24,000

6 (a)

	Total £	William £	Ann £	John £
Y/e 31.10.15	21,000	7,000	7,000	7,000
Y/e 31.10.16	33,000	11,000	11,000	11,000
Y/e 31.10.17				
1.11.16 – 31.12.16 (2/12)	6,000	2,000	2,000	2,000
1.1.17 – 31.10.17 (10/12)	30,000	0	15,000	15,000
	36,000	2,000	17,000	17,000

(b)

	William £	Ann £	John £
2015/16 (y/e 31.10.15)	7,000	7,000	7,000
2016/17 (y/e 31.10.16)	8,000	11,000	11,000
2017/18 (y/e 31.10.17)	0	17,000	17,000

Ann and John will be taxed on the current year basis of assessment throughout. The cessation rules apply to William in 2016/17, the year he left the business:

1 November 2015 – 31 December 2016 (£11,000 + £2,000 – £5,000) = £8,000

CHAPTER 7 National insurance

1 Acker

£	00	.	00

No Class 2 NICs, as earnings below small earnings exemption of £5,965

No Class 4 NICs due, as profits below annual lower earnings limit of £8,060

2 Bailey

£	3430	.	20

		£
Class 2 NICs	52 × £2.80	145.60
Class 4 NICs	(£43,000 – £8,060) × 9%	3144.60
	(£50,000 – £43,000) × 2%	140.00
Total NICs		**3,430.20**

3 Cartwright

£	396	.	70

Class 2 NICs 52 × £2.80 = £145.60

Class 4 NICs (£10,850 – £8,060) × 9% = £251.10

Total NICs = **£396.70**

CHAPTER 8   Losses

1

	✓
2016/17 only	
2017/18 and/or 2016/17	
2015/16 only	
2016/17 and/or 2015/16	✓

The tax year of the loss is 2016/17. Claims against total income are for this year and/or 2015/16.

2

	✓
True	
False	✓

Trading losses can be carried forward indefinitely.

3

	✓
Against non-savings income	
Against total income	
Against trading income arising in the same trade	✓
Against trading income arising in all trades carried on by the taxpayer	

4   The loss is a loss of 2016/17.

It can be:

(a)   Deducted from total income of £9,000 in 2016/17 and/or from total income of £19,000 in 2015/16

(b)   Carried forward to be deducted from taxable trading profits of £25,000 in 2017/18 and then in later years

5

(a) The amount of trading loss remaining to be carried forward at 1 November 2016 (assuming that all possible loss relief claims against total profits are made) is:

£	(85,000)

(£320,000 – £60,000 – £175,000)

	Year ended 31 October	
	2015 £	2016 £
Trading profit	170,000	0
Interest	5,000	60,000
Capital gain £(12,000 – 20,000)	0	0
Total profits	175,000	60,000
Less: current period loss relief	0	(60,000)
Less: carry back loss relief	(175,000)	0
Less: qualifying charitable donation	0	0
	0	0
Unrelieved qualifying charitable donations	5,000	5,000

(b) The amount of capital loss remaining to be carried forward at 1 November 2016 is:

£	(8,000)

(£20,000 – £12,000)

6

	✓
£Nil	
£2,000	✓
£4,000	
£3,000	

	Year ended 31.3.15 £	Six months 30.9.15 £	Year ended 30.9.16 £
Trading profit	4,000	6,000	0
Less: current period loss relief	0	0	0
carry back loss relief	(2,000)	(6,000)	0
qualifying charitable donation	(1,000)	–	–
Taxable total profits	1,000	–	–

The maximum relief for year ended 31.3.15 is £4,000 × $\frac{6}{12}$.

CHAPTER 9   Self-assessment for individuals

1   The due filing date for an income tax return for 2016/17, assuming the taxpayer will submit the return online is

31/01/18

2   The 2017/18 payments on account will be calculated as

1 50%

of the income tax payable for

2 2016/17

and will be due on

3 31 January 2018

and

4 31 July 2018

.

3   £100 penalty for failure to deliver return on time.

Possible £10 per day penalty from 1 May 2018 until date of filing.

5% penalty on tax paid late. Interest on tax paid late.

4

	✓
31 January 2019	
31 March 2019	
6 April 2019	
28 January 2019	✓

A year after the actual filing date, because Susie filed the return before the due filing date (31 January 2018).

5   Jamie's 2016/17 payments on account will each be

£	6,000

and will be due on

31/01/17

and

31/07/17

Jamie's balancing payment will be

£	4,000

and will be due on

31/01/18

.

6

£	0

No penalties for late payment are due on late payments on account.

7 (a)

	✓
30 September 2017	
31 October 2017	✓
31 December 2017	
31 January 2018	

Paper returns must usually be submitted by 31 October following the end of the tax year.

(b)

	✓
31 January 2018 and 31 July 2018	
31 January 2017 and 31 July 2017	✓
31 October 2017 and 31 January 2018	
31 July 2017 and 31 January 2018	

Payments on account are due on 31 January in the tax year and 31 July following the end of the tax year.

8

	✓
£5,100	
£3,400	
£1,020	✓
£2,380	

30% × PLR = **£1,020**

PLR = £17,000 × 20% = £3,400

CHAPTER 10   Self-assessment for companies

1

1 June 2018

(12 months after the actual filing date)

2

£	100

(The return is less than 3 months late)

3

	✓
14 July 2016	
1 October 2017	✓
31 December 2017	
1 January 2018	

Girton Ltd is not a large company, so all CT is due nine months and one day after the end of the accounting period.

4

	✓
14 April 2017	
14 April 2018	
14 July 2017	✓
1 October 2018	

Eaton Ltd is a large company and is required to pay corporation tax by instalments. The first instalment is due in the seventh month of the accounting period.

5

£	60,000

$\frac{1}{4} \times £240,000$

6

£	287,500

230% of £125,000

7

	✓
True	✓
False	

The structure shows several indicators of an employment relationship.

CHAPTER 11   Chargeable gains – the basics

1

	Chargeable ✓	Exempt ✓
A gift of an antique necklace	✓	
The sale of a building	✓	

2   Her chargeable gain on sale is:

£ | 235,000

	£
Proceeds	560,000
Less cost	(325,000)
Chargeable gain	235,000

3   The amount liable to CGT in 2016/17 is:

£ | 144,600

The losses carried forward are:

£ | 0

	£
Gains	171,000
Less current year losses	(5,300)
	165,700
Less losses b/f	(10,000)
	155,700
Less annual exempt amount	(11,100)
Taxable gains	144,600

4   Martha's CGT liability for 2016/17 is:

£ | 2,560

	£
Chargeable gains	23,900
Less annual exempt amount	(11,100)
Taxable gains	12,800
CGT on £12,800 @ 20%	2,560

5   The payment date for capital gains tax for 2016/17 is:

31/01/18

6 Indexation allowance runs from the date ┃ the expenditure was incurred ┃ to ┃ the date of disposal ┃.

7

	£
Proceeds of sale	200,000
Less cost	(80,000)
Less enhancement expenditure	(10,000)
	110,000
Less indexation allowance on cost £80,000 × 0.302	(24,160)
Less indexation allowance on enhancement £10,000 × 0.222	(2,220)
Chargeable gain	83,620

CHAPTER 12 Further aspects of chargeable gains

1 The chargeable gain/allowable loss arising is:

	✓
£16,663	✓
£17,500	
£19,663	
£18,337	

	£
Proceeds	38,000
Less costs of disposal	(3,000)
	35,000
Less £41,500 × $\dfrac{38,000}{38,000+48,000}$	(18,337)
Chargeable gain	16,663

2 The gain arising if he sells it for:

(a) £5,800 after deducting selling expenses of £180 is:

£	Nil

There is no gain as the chattel is sold for gross proceeds of less than £6,000.

(b) £8,200 after deducting selling expenses of £220 is:

£	4,033

	£
Gross proceeds	8,420
Less selling expenses	(220)
Net proceeds	8,200
Less cost	(3,500)
	4,700

Gain cannot exceed 5/3 (8,420 – 6,000) = £4,033

Therefore, gain is £4,033

3 The gain arising is:

£	Nil

A racehorse is an exempt asset as it is a wasting chattel, so no chargeable gain or allowable loss arises.

4   The loss arising is:

£	(1,000)

	£
Deemed proceeds	6,000
Less cost	(7,000)
Allowable loss	(1,000)

5

(a)   The cost of the part of the land sold is:

£	20,000

$$\frac{80,000}{80,000+120,000} \times £50,000 = \textbf{£20,000}$$

(b)   The chargeable gain arising on the disposal is:

£	57,240

	£
Proceeds of sale	80,000
Less cost (W)	(20,000)
	60,000
Less indexation allowance £20,000 × 0.138	(2,760)
Chargeable gain	**57,240**

6   The gain arising is:

£	3,333

	£
Proceeds of sale	8,000
Less cost	(3,500)
	4,500
Less indexation allowance £3,500 × 0.031	(109)
Chargeable gain	4,391
Gain cannot exceed £(8,000 − 6,000) × $\frac{5}{3}$	**3,333**

7

	£
Deemed proceeds of sale	6,000
Less cost	(8,700)
Allowable loss	**(2,700)**

	✓
£(6,088)	
£(4,400)	
£(2,700)	✓
£(4,388)	

No indexation allowance is due as indexation cannot create or increase a loss.

8

	✓
True	
False	✓

A loss on a disposal to a connected person can be set only against gains arising on disposals to the same connected person.

9

	✓
True	✓
False	

10

	Actual proceeds used ✓	Deemed proceeds (market value) used ✓	No gain or loss basis ✓
Paul sells an asset to his civil partner Joe for £3,600			✓
Grandmother gives an asset to her grandchild worth £1,000		✓	
Sarah sells an asset worth £20,000 to her best friend Cathy for £12,000		✓	

CHAPTER 13 Share disposals

1 Her chargeable gain is:

	✓
£15,750	
£11,500	
£17,000	
£14,250	✓

	No of shares	Cost
	£	£
August 1994 acquisition	10,000	5,000
April 2009 acquisition	10,000	16,000
	20,000	21,000
November 2016 disposal	(15,000)	(15,750)
(£21,000 × 15,000/20,000 = £15,750)		
c/f	5,000	5,250

	£
Proceeds of sale	30,000
Less allowable cost	(15,750)
Chargeable gain	**14,250**

2

	✓
True	
False	✓

In a rights issue, shares are paid for and this amount is added to the original cost. In a bonus issue, shares are not paid for and so there is no adjustment to the original cost.

3   His chargeable gain is:

£ | 3,750

	No of shares	Cost
		£
May 2003 acquisition	2,000	12,000
December 2004 1 for 2 rights issue @ £7.50	1,000	7,500
($\frac{1}{2}$ × 2,000 = 1,000 shares × £7.50 = £7,500)		
	3,000	19,500
March 2017 disposal	(2,500)	(16,250)
(£19,500 × $\frac{2,500}{3,000}$)		
c/f	500	3,250

	£
Proceeds of sale	20,000
Less allowable costs	(16,250)
Chargeable gain	**3,750**

4   Her chargeable gain is:

£ | 7,000

	No of shares	Cost
		£
June 2011 acquisition	6,000	15,000
August 2012 1 for 3 bonus issue	2,000	nil
($\frac{1}{3}$ × 6,000 = 2,000 shares)		
	8,000	15,000
December 2016 disposal (ie all the shares)	(8,000)	(15,000)
c/f	nil	nil

	£
Proceeds of sale	22,000
Less allowable costs	(15,000)
Chargeable gain	**7,000**

5   The matching rules for shares disposed of by a company shareholder are:

(a)   Shares acquired on the same day

(b)   Shares acquired in the previous nine days (FIFO)

(c)   Shares from the FA 1985 pool

6 (a)

		No of shares	Cost £	Indexed cost £
5.03	Acquisition	10,000	90,000	90,000
6.09	Indexed rise			
	£90,000 × 0.176			15,840
	Rights 1:4 @ £12	2,500	30,000	30,000
		12,500	120,000	135,840
1.17	Indexed rise			
	£135,840 × 0.216			29,341
				165,181
	Disposal (× $\frac{10,000}{12,500}$)	(10,000)	(96,000)	(132,145)
		2,500	24,000	33,036

(b)

	£
Proceeds	150,000
Less cost	(96,000)
	54,000
Less indexation allowance £(132,145 – 96,000)	(36,145)
Chargeable gain	17,855

CHAPTER 14   Reliefs for chargeable gains

1   Ian's CGT liability for 2016/17 is:

£	1,077,780

	£
Gains	10,400,000
Less annual exempt amount	(11,100)
Chargeable gain	10,388,900
CGT:	
10,000,000 @ 10%	1,000,000
388,900 @ 20%	77,780
	1,077,780

2   Jemma's CGT on the disposal, assuming she has already used the annual exempt amount for 2016/17, is:

£	7,000

	£
Proceeds of sale	80,000
Less allowable cost	(10,000)
Taxable gain (no annual exempt amount available)	70,000
CGT @ 10%	**7,000**

3

	✓
Office block	
Freehold factory	✓
Fork lift truck	
Freehold warehouse	

The office block and the freehold warehouse were acquired outside the qualifying reinvestment period commencing one year before and ending three years after the disposal.

The fork lift truck is not fixed plant and machinery.

4

	✓
£120,000	
£200,000	
£400,000	✓
£420,000	

Land

	£
Sales proceeds	400,000
Less cost	(100,000)
Gain	300,000

£20,000 of the proceeds are not reinvested, so £20,000 of the gain remains chargeable; £280,000 is rolled over.

Replacement land

	£	£
Sale proceeds		500,000
Less cost	380,000	
Rolled-over gain	(280,000)	
Revised base cost		(100,000)
Chargeable gain		400,000

5

	✓
True	✓
False	

6 If relief for replacement of business assets is to be claimed, reinvestment of the proceeds must take place in a period beginning

| 12 | months before and ending

| 36 | months after the date of disposal.

7   The chargeable gain after rollover relief is:

£	25,000

The gain on the sale of first warehouse is:

	£
Proceeds	400,000
Less cost	(220,000)
	180,000
Less indexation allowance	(40,000)
	140,000
Less rollover relief (balancing figure)	(115,000)
Chargeable gain: amount not reinvested £(400,000 – 375,000)	**25,000**

8

	✓
True	
False	✓

Jewellery is not a qualifying asset for gift relief purposes.

9   If gift relief is claimed, the gain on the gift by Tommy is:

£	0

	£
Market value	200,000
Less cost	(50,000)
Gain	150,000
Less gift relief	(150,000)
Gain left in charge	**0**

and the gain on the sale by Sinbad is:

£	300,000

	£
Sale proceeds	350,000
Less cost (£200,000 – £150,000)	(50,000)
Gain	**300,000**

Tax tables and reference material

Taxation tables for *Business Tax* – 2016/17

Note that Taxation data shown below, will be available as pop-up windows throughout your live assessment.

Capital allowances	
Annual investment allowance	
From 1/6 April 2014	£500,000
From 1 January 2016	£200,000
Plant and machinery writing down allowance	
Long life assets and integral-features	8%
Other assets	18%
Motor cars	
CO_2 emissions up to 75 g/km	100%
CO_2 emissions between 76 and 130 g/km	18%
CO_2 emissions over 130 g/km	8%
Energy-efficient and water-saving plant	
First year allowance	100%
Capital gains	
Annual exempt amount	£11,100
Standard rate (residential property/other disposals)	18/10%
Higher rate (residential property/other disposals)	28/20%
Entrepreneurs' relief rate	10%
Entrepreneurs' relief limit	£10,000,000

National insurance rates	
Class 2 contributions	£2.80 per week
Small earnings exemption	£5,965 pa
Class 4 contributions:	
Main rate	9%
Additional rate	2%
Lower profits limit	£8,060
Upper profits limit	£43,000

Corporation tax		
Financial year	2016	2015
All profits and gains	20%	20%

Introduction to business tax

Administration

- Taxation administered by HM Revenue & Customs (HMRC).

- Rules covering tax are contained in statute (law). Law passed every year (Finance Act).

- Decisions reached by the courts interpreting the law are known as case law.

- HMRC also issue guidance – Extra Statutory Concessions and Statements of Practice.

Taxes

- Corporation Tax – paid by companies on both income and capital gains.
- Income Tax – paid by individuals on their income.
- Capital Gains Tax – paid by individuals on their capital gains.

Tax avoidance and tax evasion

- **Tax evasion**

  Any action taken to evade tax by illegal means; this carries a risk of criminal prosecution.

  Examples or tax evasion include failing to declare income and claiming false expenses.

- **Tax avoidance**

  Use of legitimate means to minimise taxpayer's tax liability, for example by investing in a tax-free ISA (Individual Savings Account).

Adjustment of profits – sole traders, partnerships and companies

Pro forma for adjustment of profits

	£	£
Net profit as per accounts		X
Add: Expenses charge in the accounts that are not allowable as trading expenses	X	
		X
		X
Less: Income included in the accounts which is not accessible as trading income	X	
		(X)
Adjusted profit/(loss)		X

Disallowed expenses

- Expenses that fail the remoteness test so not "wholly and exclusively" for trading purposes.

- Fines on the business or fraud by directors/owners.

- Donations to national charities – might be allowed as a charge on income if Gift Aid donations. Political donations are never allowable.

- Capital expenditure eg purchase of equipment included in profit and loss account.

- Depreciation. Capital allowances granted instead.

- Costs of bringing newly acquired second-hand assets to useable condition.

- Legal and professional expenses relating to capital items or breaking the law.

- Customer entertaining. Staff entertaining can be allowable.

- Customer gifts unless gift incorporates business advertising, cost is less than £50 per annum per customer and gift is not food, drink, tobacco or cash vouchers.

Non-assessable income

- Income taxed in any other way, eg interest or property income for individuals.

- Profits on sale of fixed assets.

Unincorporated businesses – trading income

Trading income calculated for each period of account:

	£
Adjusted accounting profit	X
Less: Capital allowances	
Plant and machinery	(X)
Plus: Balancing charges	X
Trading income for the period of account	X

Expenses charged in the accounts which are not allowable as trading expenses

- See Adjustment of profits – sole traders, partnerships and companies

- Transactions with the owner of the business. For example:

    - Add back salary paid to owner. Salaries paid to family members do not need to be added back.

    - Private expenditure included in accounts.

    - Class 2 National Insurance contributions.

    - Goods taken for own use.

Private use assets

- Private use assets have separate column in Capital Allowance computation.
- Disallow private use % of WDA/AIA/FYA.

Capital allowances – business cessation

- In the cessation period of account, no WDA/AIA/FYA.

- Include additions and disposals as normal. Any asset taken over by owner, treat as a disposal at market value. Balancing adjustment made (balancing charge or balancing allowance).

Sole traders – basis periods

Tax year – 2016/17 tax year runs from 6 April 2016 to 5 April 2017

Basis period rules

- First Year – runs from start date of trading to the next 5 April.

- Second Year and Third Year:

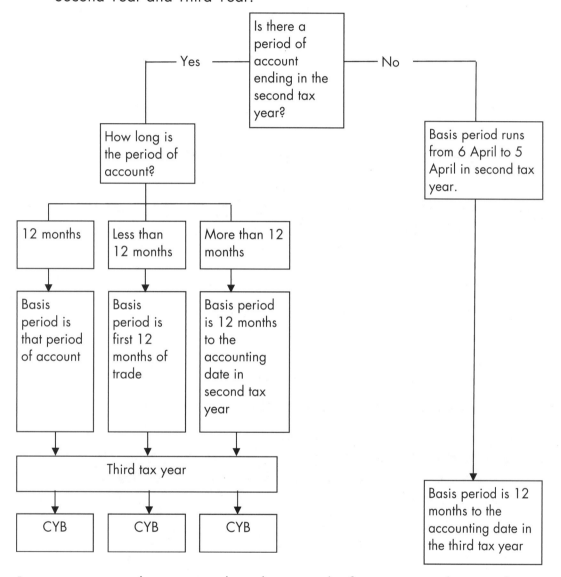

Later years – basis period is the period of account ending in the tax year = Current Year basis (CYB).

Final year – basis period is the period from the end of the basis period for the previous tax year to cessation date.

Overlap profits – opening year rules may lead to profits being taxed twice. Relief is given on cessation of the business.

Sole traders – change of accounting date

For an accounting date change to be recognised for tax purposes the following conditions must be satisfied.

- The first accounts ending on the new date must not exceed 18 months in length.

- The sole trader or partnership must give notice of the change in the tax return by the filing date of the tax return.

Year of change – is the first tax year in which accounts are made up to the new date.

Relevant period – is the time to the new accounting date from the end of the previous basis period.

Example 1 – relevant period is less than 12 months

Jasmin changes her accounting date as follows:

Accounts	Year	Basis period
Year to 31 December 2014	2014/15	11/1/14 to 31/12/14
9 months to 30 September 2015	2015/16	1/10/14 to 30/9/15
Year to 30 September 2016	2016/17	1/10/15 to 30/9/16

Year of change – 2015/16

Relevant period – 9 months to 30 September 2015

Example 2 – relevant period is greater than 12 months

Vaughan changes his accounting date as follows:

Accounts	Year	Basis period
Year to 31 December 2014	2014/15	11/1/14 to 31/12/14
15 months to 31 March 2016	2015/16	1/1/15 to 31/3/16
Year to 31 March 2017	2016/17	1/4/16 to 31/3/17

Year of change – 2015/16

Relevant period – 15 months to 31 March 2016

The rules for determining basis periods on a change of accounting date are complex. Significant examples of changes in accounting dates include:

- After the 3rd year of trading
- With accounts of 18 months or less
- Not straddling a tax year.

Capital allowances on plant and machinery

Layout of capital allowances on plant and machinery computation (see Taxation Tables for rates)

	First Year Allowance (FYA)	Annual Investment Allowance (AIA)	General pool	Special rate pool	Short Life Asset	Total Allowances
	£	£	£	£	£	£
WDV b/f			X	X	X	
Additions	X	X	X			
Disposals	X		(X)		(X)	
	X	X	X	X	X	
Balancing allowance/ balancing charge (BA/BC)					X/(X)	X/(X)
					Nil	
AIA/FYA	(X)	(X)				X
Writing down allowance @ 18% p.a.			(X)			X
Writing down allowance @ 8% p.a.				(X)		X
WDV c/f	Nil	Nil	X	X		
Total allowances						X

- Plant – defined by 'function/setting' distinction and case law.

- AIA – 100% allowance for expenditure (other than cars) in 12 month period (pro-rata). Expenditure in excess of AIA qualifies for writing down allowance (WDA).

- Full WDA for the period is given regardless of date of purchase of item. WDA is scaled for periods other than 12 months.

- FYA – 100% allowance given on purchase of environmentally friendly cars and energy saving/water efficient plant. FYA is not scaled for short accounting periods.

- If the written down value (WDV) on the general pool (= WDV b/f + additions – disposals) is £1,000 or less then pool is written off as small pools annual writing down allowance.

- Short life assets (SLA) – de-pool asset if life expected to be than 8 years. Not available for cars.

Partnerships

- Each partner is taxed like a sole trader on their share of the partnership profits.

- First step is to share accounting profits between partners:

  - Allocate the correct salaries and interest on capital for the period to each partner.

  - Divide the remaining profit for each set of accounts between the partners based upon the profit sharing arrangement.

  - You may need to split the period if there is a change such as a partner joining or leaving.

- Opening year and cessation rules apply to partners individually when they join or leave the partnership.

- Allocate the profit for each partner to the correct tax year using basis period rules.

- Basis periods for continuing partners are unaffected by joiners or leavers.

- Each partner enters their share of profits for a tax year in the partnership pages of their own tax return.

Trading losses for sole traders and partners

- A loss is computed in the same way as a profit, making the same adjustments to the net profit as per the accounts and deducting capital allowances.

Set off of trading loss against total income

- Set off loss against total income of the preceding tax year and/or the tax year of loss, eg loss in 2016/17 set off against total income in 2015/16 and/or 2016/17.

- Cannot restrict loss to preserve use of personal allowance so personal allowance may be wasted.

- For 2016/17 loss claim needed by 31 January 2019.

Carry forward of trading losses

- If any loss remains unrelieved after current year and carry back claim has been made, or no such claims are made, then carry forward the loss against first available profits of the same trade.

Choice of loss relief – consider the following:

- Utilize loss in the tax year in which income is taxed at a higher rate.

- Possible wastage of personal allowance.

- Review the projected future profits to ensure the loss can be utilised.

- If cash flow is important, a loss carry back claim may result in a tax refund being paid to the company.

Payment and administration – sole traders and partners

The return must be filed by:

- 31 October following the end of the tax year if filing a paper return.

- 31 January following the end of the tax year if filing online.

Late filing	Late payment	Penalty
Miss filing deadline		£100
	30 days late	5% of tax due, or £300 if greater
3 months late		Daily penalty if £10 per day for up to 90 days (max £900)
6 months late		5% of tax due, or £300 if greater
	6 months late	5% of tax outstanding at that date
12 months late		5%, or £300 if greater
	12 months late	5% of tax outstanding at that date
12 months and information deliberately withheld		Based on behaviour: • deliberate and concealed withholding 100% of tax due, or £300 if greater • deliberate but not concealed 70% of tax due, or £300 if greater Reductions of up to half of the above %'s apply for cooperation with investigation

Disclosure and errors

- Taxpayer must notify HMRC by 5 October following end of the tax year if a tax return is needed.

- Taxpayer can amend a tax return within 12 months of filing date or make an error or mistake claim within 3 years of the filing date.

Payments on account (POA)

- Due 31 January (in tax year) and 31 July (after tax year end). Each instalment is 50% of the previous year's tax and Class 4 NIC liability.

- Balancing payment made 31 January after tax year end.

- No POA due if last year's tax and Class 4 National Insurance contribution (NIC) liability less than £1,000 or greater than 80% if last year's liability was deducted at source.

- Can reduce POA if this year's liability expected to be less than last year's. Penalties will be charged if a deliberate incorrect claim is made.

- Capital gains tax (CGT) liability is paid 31 January following the tax year end. No POA needed for CGT.

Interest on tax paid late/overpaid tax

- Interest charged daily on late payment.

Enquiries and other penalties

- HMRC must notify individual of enquiry within 12 months of submission of return.

- Basis of enquiry – random or HMRC believe income/expenses misstated.

- Penalty for failure to produce enquiry documents = £50 + £30 per day.

- Penalty for failure to keep proper records is up to £3,000. Records must be kept for 5 years after the filing date for the relevant tax year.

Penalties for incorrect returns are:

Type of behaviour	Maximum	Unprompted (min)	Prompted (min)
Genuine mistake, despite taking reasonable care	0%	0%	0%
Careless error and inaccuracy due to failure to take reasonable care	30%	0%	15%
Deliberate error but not concealed	70%	20%	35%
Deliberate error and concealed	100%	30%	50%

National insurance contributions

- Self-employed individuals pay Class 2 and Class 4 contributions.

- Class 4 contributions are 9% on profits between the lower and upper limits, then 2% on profits above the upper limit.

- Percentage and limits are provided in the Taxation Tables.

An outline of corporate tax

- Companies pay corporation tax on their profits for each accounting period.

- There is one rate of corporation tax set each financial year.

- Profits = income + gains – charges

- Accounting periods are usually 12 months long but can be shorter.

- If a company's accounts are longer than 12 months, the first 12 months will be one accounting period and the remainder a second accounting period.

- All UK property income is pooled as a single source of income and taxed on a accruals basis.

- Borrowing or lending money by a company is a loan relationship.

- Trading loan relationships are part of trading income.

- Non-trading loan relationships (NTL-R) are pooled to give NTL-R credits or deficits.

- Gift Aid Donations are charges on income.

- Associated companies – a company is associated with another if one company controls the other or they are both controlled by the same 'person'.

The calculation of total profits and corporation tax payable

ABC Ltd

Corporation tax computation for the year period ended DD/MM/20XX

	£
Trading Income – accruals basis	X
Interest Income – accruals basis	X
Property Income – accruals basis	X
Chargeable gains	X
	X
Less charges on income – Gift Aid donations	(X)
Total profits	X
Corporation tax payable – total profits × corporation tax rate	X

Key points

- Trading income is adjusted from net profit per company accounts less capital allowances.

- All income in computation to be gross.

- Some income may need to be grossed up. Companies receive interest gross.

- Virtually all interest receivable is taxed as Interest Income.

  Dividends payable by a company are not an allowable expense.

- UK dividends receivable by a company are not taxable.

- Net-off current year capital losses against current year capital gains. If there is a net capital loss carry it forward.

- See Taxation tables for corporation tax rates.

Non 31 March year ends

- For example – year ended 31 December 2016. 3 months of period falls in financial year 2015 (FY15) and 9 months in FY16.

- Apportion Total Profits to FY. Apply correct rate for FY.

Long periods of account

- Will consist of two accounting periods = first 12 months & remainder of period.

- Split profits as follows:

    - Adjusted trading profit and property income – time apportion.
    - Capital allowances – separate computations for each CAP.
    - Interest income – accruals basis.
    - Chargeable gains – according to date of disposal.
    - Charges on income – according to date paid.

Corporate tax – losses

- Can elect to set trading losses against current accounting period total profits. Gift aid donations (charges) will remain unrelieved.

- If the above election is made, can also carry back trading loss to set against total profits within the previous 12 months.

- Trading losses are automatically carried forward to set against the first available profits of the same trade if not utilised by the above two claims.

- If there is a choice of loss relief, firstly consider the rate of loss relief then the timing of relief.

- Set out the use of the losses in a loss memorandum.

Corporation tax – payment and administration

Payment date

- Small companies (annual profits less than £1.5 million): 9 months + 1 day after end of the accounting period (CAP).

- Large companies (annual profits greater than £1.5 million) must estimate year's tax liability and pay 25% of the years liability:

    - 6 months and 14 days after start of CAP
    - 9 months and 14 days after start of CAP
    - 14 days after end of CAP
    - 3 months and 14 days after end of CAP

- Estimate must be revised for each quarter. Penalties may be charged if company deliberately fails to pay sufficient instalments.

- No instalments due for first year company is large unless profits are greater than £10 million.

- Associated companies share the annual profit limit of £1.5 million equally.

Interest on late payments

- Interest charged daily on late payment Overpayment of tax receives interest from HMRC. Interest is taxable/tax allowable as interest income.

Filing the return

- Filed on the later of 12 months after end of CAP or 3 months after the notice to deliver a tax return has been issued.

- Late filing penalties are: less than 3 months late: £100; greater than 3 months late: £200: greater than 6 months late: 10% of tax due per return: greater than 12 months late 20% of tax due per return.

- Company must notify HMRC it is within scope of corporation tax within 3 months of starting to trade.

- Company can amend return within 12 months of the filing date.

Enquiries and other penalties

- HMRC must notify company of enquiry within 12 months of submission of return.

- Basis of enquiry — random or HMRC believe income/expenses misstated.

- Penalty for failure to produce enquiry documents: £50 + £30 per day.

- Penalty for failure to keep proper records is up to £3,000. Records must be retained for six years after the end of the relevant accounting period.

- Penalties for incorrect returns are the same as for sole traders and partners — see sole traders and partners link.

Current tax reliefs and other tax issues

Research and Development (R&D) Tax Credits for Small and Medium Sized Companies

A small or medium sized enterprise (SME) is a company with less than 500 employees with either:

- An annual turnover under €100 million. or
- A balance sheet under €86 million.

The SME tax relief scheme

From 1 April 2015. the tax relief on allowable R&D costs is 230%.

R&D tax credits

If a company makes a loss, it can choose to receive R&D tax credits instead of carrying forward a loss. The amount of tax credit is limited to the total of PAYE and National Insurance contribution liabilities of the company.

Costs that qualify for R&D tax relief

To qualify as R&D, any activity must contribute directly to seeking an advance in science or technology or must be a qualifying indirect activity.

Intermediaries (IR35) legislation

IR35 legislation prevents personal service companies ('PSC') being used to disguise permanent employment.

The rules apply where the relationship between the worker and the client, would be considered to be an employment relationship if the existence of the PSC was ignored.

If the rules apply, a deemed employment income tax charge is charged on the PSC.

The deemed employment income tax charge is calculated based upon the actual payments made to the PSC by the client.

Introduction to chargeable gains

- Individual pays Capital Gains Tax (CGT) on net chargeable gains in a tax year.

- For companies, chargeable gains are included as income in calculating total profits.

- Individuals receive an annual exempt amount from CGT – for 2016/17 this is £11,100.

- Gains/losses arise when a chargeable person makes a chargeable disposal of a chargeable asset.

- Chargeable person – individual or company.

- Chargeable disposal – sale, gift or loss/destruction of the whole or part of an asset. Exempt disposals – on death and gifts to approved charities.

- Chargeable asset – all assets unless exempt. Exempt assets are motor cars and some chattels.

Calculation of capital gains tax

Net chargeable gains – total gains in the tax year after netting off any current year or brought forward losses and the annual exempt amount.

Annual exempt amount (AE)

- For individuals only.

- AE cannot be carried forward or carried back.

- Current year losses must be netted off against current year gains before AE. This means AE can be wasted.

- Brought forward capital losses are set off against current year gains after AE so AE is not wasted.

Proforma cornputation

	£	£
Consideration received		X
Less Incidental costs of sale		X
Net sale proceeds		NSP
Less Allowable expenditure		X
Acquisition costs	X	X
Incidental costs of acquisition	X	(X)
Enhancement expenditure	X	
		(Cost)
Gain/(Loss)		X/(X)

- Consideration received is usually sales proceeds, but market value will be used instead of actual consideration where the transaction is a gift or between connected persons.

- An individual is connected with their spouse, lineal relatives (and their spouses) and spouse's relatives (and their spouses).

- Husband and wife/civil partner transfers – nil gain nil loss. Tax planning opportunity.

Part disposals – the cost allocated to the disposal = Cost × (A/(A+B))

A = consideration received on part disposal
B = market value of the remainder of the asset
Chattels – tangible moveable object. Two types:

- Wasting – expected life of 50 years or less (eg racehorse or boat). CGT exempt.

- Non-wasting – expected life greater than 50 years (eg antiques or jewellery).

CGT, £6,000 rule

Buy Sell	£6,000 or less	More than £6,000
Less than £6,000	Exempt	Allowable loss but proceeds are deemed = £6,000
More than £6,000	Normal calculation of the gain, then compare with 5/3 (gross proceeds – £6,000) – Take the lower gain	Chargeable in full

Shares and securities – disposals by individuals

CGT on shares and securities

Disposal of shares and securities are subject to CGT except for listed government securities (gilt-edged securities or 'gilts'), qualifying corporate bonds (eg company loan notes/debentures) and shares held in an Individual Savings Account (ISA).

The identification rules

Used to determine which shares have been sold and what acquisition cost can be deducted from the sale proceeds (eg match the disposal and acquisition).

Disposals are matched:

- Firstly, with acquisitions on the same day as the day of disposal.

- Secondly, with acquisitions made in the 30 days following the date of disposal (FIFO basis).

- Thirdly, with shares from the share pool.

The Share Pool

- The share pool contains all shares acquired prior to the disposal date.

- Each acquisition is not kept separately, but is 'pooled' together with other acquisitions and a running total kept of the number of shares and the cost of those shares.

- When a disposal from the pool is made, the appropriate number of shares are taken from the pool along with the average cost of those shares.

- The gain on disposal is then calculated.

Bonus issues and rights issues

- Bonus issue – no adjustment to cost needed.
- Rights issue – adjustment to cost needed.

Chargeable gains – reliefs available to individuals

Replacement of business assets (Rollover) relief – when a qualifying business asset is sold at a gain, taxpayer can defer gain by reinvesting proceeds in a qualifying replacement asset.

- Deferred gain is deducted from the cost of the replacement asset so gain crystallises when the replacement asset is sold.

- Qualifying assets (original and replacement) – must be used in a trade by the vendor and be land and buildings, fixed plant and machinery or goodwill.

- Qualifying time period – replacement asset must be purchased between 1 year before and 3 years after the sale of the original asset.

- Partial reinvestment – only some of the sales proceeds reinvested then the gain taxable is the lower of the full gain and the proceeds not reinvested.

Gift relief (holdover relief) – donee takes over asset at donor's base cost ie the gain is given away along with the asset.

- Qualifying assets – trade assets of donor or shares in any unquoted trading company or personal trading company (individual owns at least 5% of company).

Entrepreneurs' relief – gain taxable at 10% capital gains tax rate.

- The £10 million limit is a lifetime limit which is reduced each time a claim for the relief is made.

- For 2016/17 claim must be made by 31 January 2019.

- Qualifying business disposals (assets must be owned for at least 12 months prior to sale)

    - The whole or part of a business carried on by the individual (alone or in partnership).

    - Assets of the individual's or partnership's trading business that has now ceased.

    - Shares in the individual's 'personal trading company'. Individual must have owned the shares and been an employee of the company for 12 months prior to sale.

- From 17 March 2016, newly issued shares in unlisted trading companies purchased on or after 17 March 2016 by external investors qualify for entrepreneurs' relief provided they are continually held for a minimum of 3 years from 6 April 2016.

Calculation of gains and losses for companies

Proforma computation

	£	£
Consideration received		X
Less Incidental costs of sale		X
Net sale proceeds		NSP
Less Allowable expenditure	X	
Acquisition costs + [indexation factor x expenditure]	X	
Incidental costs of acquisition	X	
Enhancement expenditure	X	
Indexation allowance	X	
		(Cost)
Chargeable gain		Gain

- Indexation allowance is not available where there is an unindexed loss, nor can it turn an unindexed gain into an indexed loss.

- Note that companies do not get an annual exempt amount.

- Losses relieved in order – current year first followed by losses brought forward.

Only relief available to companies is rollover relief:

- Rollover relief is a deferral relief – see [Chargeable gains – reliefs available to individuals] for main rollover relief rules.

- Key differences applying for companies:

  - Indexation is given on disposal of the original asset.

  - Goodwill is not a qualifying asset for companies.

  - Gain deferred is the indexed gain.

  - On disposal of the replacement asset, indexation is calculated on the 'base cost not actual cost.

Shares and securities — disposals by companies

The identification rules — a disposal of shares is matched:

- Firstly, with same-day transactions

- Secondly, with transactions in the previous 9 days (FIFO). No indexation allowance is available

- Thirdly, with shares from the 1985 pool (shares bought from 1 April 1982 onwards).

1985 pool — pro forma working	No. of shares	Cost £	Indexed cost £
Purchase	X	X	X
Index to next operative event			X
			X
Operative event (purchase)	X	X	X
	X	X	X
Index to next operative event	X		X
			X
Operative event (sale)	(X)	(X)	(X)A
Pool carried forward	X	X	X

Operative event = purchase, sale, rights issue. Bonus issue is not an operative event.

Computation

	£
Proceeds	X
Less indexed cost (A from pool)	(X)
Indexed gain	X

The badges of trade

Six badges of trade:

- Subject matter
- Ownership
- Frequency of transactions
- Improvement expenditure
- Reason for sale
- Motive for profit

Duties and responsibilities of a tax adviser

- Maintain client confidentiality at all times

- AAT members must adopt an ethical approach and maintain an objective outlook

- Give timely and constructive advice to clients

- Honest and professional conduct with HMRC

- A tax advisor is liable to a £3,000 penalty if they assist in making an incorrect return

Bibliography

AAT (2014) *AAT Code of Professional Ethics 2014*. [Online.] Available from: http://www.aatethics.org.uk/code/wp-content/uploads/2014/09/ AAT_Code_of_Ethics.pdf [Accessed 16 August 2016].

Contains public sector information licensed under the Open Government Licence v3.0. www.nationalarchives.gov.uk/doc/open-government-licence/version/3/.

HMRC (2015) *Company tax return*. [Online.] Available from: www.gov.uk/government/uploads/system/uploads/attachment_data/file/420684 /CT600_2015.pdf [Accessed 27 July 2016].

HMRC (2015) *Tackling tax evasion and avoidance*. [Online.] Available from: https://www.gov.uk/government/uploads/system/uploads/attachment_data/file/ 413943/Tax_evasion_FINAL_web__with_covers_and_right_sig_.pdf [accessed 18 August 2016]

HMRC (2016) *Partnership tax return*. [Online.] Available from: www.gov.uk/government/uploads/system/uploads/attachment_data/file/503361 /sa800man-2016.pdf [Accessed 27 July 2016].

HMRC (2016) *Self-employment (full)*. [Online.] Available from: www.gov.uk/government/uploads/system/uploads/attachment_data/file/501544 /sa103f-2016.pdf [Accessed 27 July 2016].

Index

REVIEW FORM

How have you used this Course Book?
(Tick one box only)

☐ Self study

☐ On a course_____

☐ Other _____

Why did you decide to purchase this Course Book? *(Tick one box only)*

☐ Have used BPP materials in the past

☐ Recommendation by friend/colleague

☐ Recommendation by a college lecturer

☐ Saw advertising

☐ Other _____

During the past six months do you recall seeing/receiving either of the following?
(Tick as many boxes as are relevant)

☐ Our advertisement in Accounting Technician

☐ Our Publishing Catalogue

Which (if any) aspects of our advertising do you think are useful?
(Tick as many boxes as are relevant)

☐ Prices and publication dates of new editions

☐ Information on Course Book content

☐ Details of our free online offering

☐ None of the above

Your ratings, comments and suggestions would be appreciated on the following areas of this Course Book.

	Very useful	Useful	Not useful
Chapter overviews	☐	☐	☐
Introductory section	☐	☐	☐
Quality of explanations	☐	☐	☐
Illustrations	☐	☐	☐
Chapter activities	☐	☐	☐
Test your learning	☐	☐	☐
Keywords	☐	☐	☐

	Excellent	Good	Adequate	Poor
Overall opinion of this Course Book	☐	☐	☐	☐

Do you intend to continue using BPP Products?   ☐ Yes ☐ No

Please note any further comments and suggestions/errors on the reverse of this page. The BPP author of this edition can be emailed at: lmfeedback@bpp.com.

Alternatively, the Head of Programme of this edition can be emailed at: nisarahmed@bpp.com

REVIEW FORM (continued)

TELL US WHAT YOU THINK

Please note any further comments and suggestions/errors below